GED Xcelerator
PREP
Writing
WORKBOOK

Chris Ramsey

PAXEN

Melbourne, Florida
www.paxen.com

Acknowledgements

For each of the selections and images listed below, grateful acknowledgement is made for permission to excerpt and/or reprint original or copyrighted material, as follows:

Images

(cover, meeting preparation background) iStockphoto. **(cover, downtown scene)** Bilderbuch, DesignPics.com. **(cover, man typing)** Darren Greenwood, DesignPics.com. **v** iStockphoto. **vi** iStockphoto.

ISBN-13: 978-1-934350-28-7
ISBN-10: 1-934350-28-1

 2 3 4 5 6 7 8 9 10 GEDXWB5   16 15 14 13 12 11 10

Printed in the U.S.A.

Table of Contents

UNIT 1 *Essay*
LESSON

UNIT 2 *Organization*
LESSON

UNIT 3 *Sentence Structure*
LESSON

UNIT 4 *Usage*
LESSON

UNIT 5 *Mechanics*
LESSON

About the GED Tests

Simply by turning to this page, you've made a decision that will change your life for the better. Each year, thousands of people just like you decide to pursue the General Education Development (GED) certificate. Like you, they left school for one reason or another. And now, just like them, you've decided to continue your education by studying for and taking the GED Tests.

However, the GED Tests are no easy task. The tests—five in all, spread across the subject areas of Language Arts/Reading, Language Arts/Writing, Mathematics, Science, and Social Studies—cover slightly more than seven hours. Preparation time takes considerably longer. The payoff, however, is significant: more and better career options, higher earnings, and the sense of achievement that comes with a GED certificate. Employers and colleges and universities accept the GED certificate as they would a high school diploma. On average, GED recipients earn more than $4,000 per year than do employees without a GED certificate.

The GED Tests have been constructed by the American Council on Education (ACE) to mirror a high-school curriculum. Although you will not need to know all of the information typically taught in high school, you will need to answer a variety of questions in specific subject areas. In Language Arts/Writing, you will need to write an essay on a topic of general knowledge.

In all cases, you will need to effectively read and follow directions, correctly interpret questions, and critically examine answer options. The table below details the five subject areas, the amount of questions within each of them, and the time that you will have to answer them. Since different states have different requirements for the amount of tests you may take in a single day, you will need to check with your local adult education center for requirements in your state or territory.

The original GED Tests were released in 1942 and since have been revised a total of three times. In each case, revisions to the tests have occurred as a result of educational findings or workplace needs. All told, more than 17 million people have received a GED certificate since the tests' inception.

SUBJECT AREA BREAKDOWN	CONTENT AREAS	ITEMS	TIME LIMIT
Language Arts/Reading	Literary texts—75% Nonfiction texts—25%	40 questions	65 minutes
Language Arts/Writing (Editing)	Organization—15% Sentence Structure—30% Usage—30% Mechanics—25%	50 questions	75 minutes
Language Arts/Writing (Essay)	Essay	Essay	45 minutes
Mathematics	Number Sense/Operations—20% to 30% Data Measurement/Analysis—20% to 30% Algebra—20% to 30% Geometry—20% to 30%	Part I: 25 questions (with calculator) Part II: 25 questions (without calculator)	90 minutes
Science	Life Science—45% Earth/Space Science—20% Physical Science—35%	50 questions	80 minutes
Social Studies	Geography—15% U.S. History—25% World History—15% U.S. Government/Civics—25% Economics—20%	50 questions	70 minutes

Three of the subject-area tests—Language Arts/Reading, Science, and Social Studies—will require you to answer questions by interpreting passages. The Science and Social Studies Tests also require you to interpret tables, charts, graphs, diagrams, timelines, political cartoons, and other visuals. In Language Arts/Reading, you also will need to answer questions based on workplace and consumer texts. The Mathematics Test will require you to use basic computation, analysis, and reasoning skills to solve a variety of word problems, many of them involving graphics. On all of the tests, questions will be multiple-choice with five answer options. An example follows.

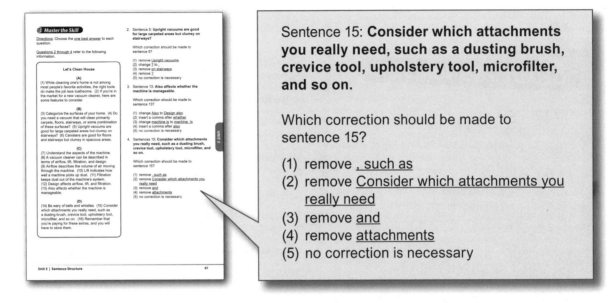

On the Mathematics Test, you will have additional ways in which to register your responses to multiple-choice questions.

As the table on p. iv indicates, the Language Arts/Writing Test contains two parts, one for editing, the other for essay. In the editing portion of Language Arts/Writing, you will be asked to identify and correct common errors in various passages and texts while also deciding on the most effective organization of a text. In the essay portion, you will write an essay that provides an explanation or an opinion on a single topic of general knowledge.

Now that you understand the task at hand—and the benefits of a GED certificate—you must prepare for the GED Tests. In the pages that follow, you will find a recipe of sorts that, if followed, will help guide you toward successful completion of your GED certificate. So turn the page. The next chapter of your life begins right now.

About *GED Prep Xcelerator*

Along with choosing to pursue your GED certificate, you've made another smart decision by selecting *GED Prep Xcelerator* as your main study and preparation tool. Simply by purchasing *GED Prep Xcelerator*, you've joined an elite club with thousands of members, all with a common goal—earning their GED certificates. In this case, membership most definitely has its privileges.

For more than 65 years, the GED Tests have offered a second chance to people who need it most. To date, 17 million Americans like you have studied for and earned GED certificates and, in so doing, jump-started their lives and careers. Benefits abound for GED holders: Recent studies have shown that people with GED certificates earn more money, enjoy better health, and exhibit greater interest in and understanding of the world around them than those without.

In addition, more than 60 percent of GED recipients plan to further their educations, which will provide them with more and better career options. As if to underscore the point, U.S. Department of Labor projections show that 90 percent of the fastest-growing jobs through 2014 will require postsecondary education.

Your pathway to the future—a brighter future—begins now, on this page, with *GED Prep Xcelerator*, an intense, accelerated approach to GED preparation. Unlike other programs, which take months to teach the GED Tests through a content-based approach, *Xcelerator* gets to the heart of the GED Tests—and quickly—by emphasizing *concepts*. That's because at their core, the majority of the GED Tests are reading-comprehension exams. You must be able to read and interpret excerpts, passages, and various visuals—tables, charts, graphs, timelines, and so on—and then answer questions based upon them.

Xcelerator shows you the way. By emphasizing key reading and thinking concepts, *Xcelerator* equips learners like you with the skills and strategies you will need to correctly interpret and answer questions on the GED Tests. Two-page micro-lessons in each student book provide focused and efficient instruction, while call-out boxes, sample exercises, and test-taking and other thinking strategies aid in understanding complex concepts. For those who require additional support, we offer the *Xcelerator* workbooks, which provide twice the support and practice exercises as the student books.

Unlike other GED materials, which were designed for the classroom, *Xcelerator* materials were designed *from* the classroom, using proven educational theory and cutting-edge classroom philosophy. The result: More than 90 percent of people who study with *Xcelerator* earn their GED certificates. For learners who have long had the deck stacked against them, the odds are finally in their favor. And yours.

GED BY THE NUMBERS

17 million
Number of GED recipients since the inception of the GED Tests

1.23 million
Amount of students who fail to graduate from high school each year

700,000
Number of GED test-takers each year

451,759
Total number of students who passed the GED Tests in 2007

$4,000
Average additional earnings per year for GED recipients

About *GED Prep Xcelerator Writing*

For those who think the GED Language Arts/Writing Test is a breeze, think again. The GED Language Arts/Writing Test is a multi-faceted exam that will assess your ability to both write and understand the basics of written text. The GED Language Arts/Writing Test consists of both an essay and an editing portion. You will have 45 minutes in which to complete an **essay,** or a short, personal piece of writing on a single subject. On the editing portion of the test, you will have 75 minutes in which to answer 50 multiple choice questions organized across four main content areas: Organization (15% of all questions), Sentence Structure (30%), Usage (30%), and (Mechanics (25%).

GED Prep Xcelerator Writing helps unlock the learning and deconstruct the different elements of the test by helping students like you build and develop key reading and thinking skills. A combination of targeted strategies, informational call-outs and sample questions, assorted tips and hints (including Test-Taking Tips and Writing Strategies), and ample assessment help to clearly focus student efforts in needed areas, all with an eye toward the end goal: Success on the GED Tests.

① *Essay:*

On the essay portion of the GED Language Arts/Writing Test, you must read a prompt, or writing topic, that will specify the topic and type of essay you are to write. The prompts will be **expository** in nature, meaning you must explain and describe your feelings about a particular topic. When doing so, ensure that you define your key point; organize your essay with a clear beginning, middle, and end; develop strong details that expertly support your main ideas; and use correct spelling, grammar, and punctuation.

Although writing is a process, it is a timed activity on the GED Language Arts/Writing Test. For that reason, you must manage your time well across all aspects of the essay. You will have 45 minutes in which to plan, write, and edit your essay. Note that Unit 1 contains a scoring rubric you may use to score your practice essays. The circle graph shown will help you visualize the amount of time you will be provided and how to use that time wisely.

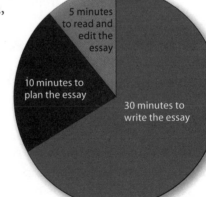

You will write your essay on a topic, or prompt, provided on the GED Language Arts/Writing Test. Many prompts will ask for your opinion on a topic of general interest. In cases such as these, use your personal observations, experiences, and knowledge to help guide your writing:

- important people you would like to meet
- an invention that has affected your life
- good advice you have been given
- the seasons of the year you like best

Other prompts will ask you to think about certain aspects of your life. In these instances, do not over-complicate things; simply write about what you know:

- family
- friends
- school
- hobbies
- sports
- pets

② **Editing:**

On the editing portion of the GED Language Arts/Writing Test, you will be asked to read and answer questions about letters, memoranda, and essays. The questions will focus on the areas of organization, sentence structure, usage, and mechanics as they relate to grammar and writing. **Grammar** is the set of rules that determines the usage of language.

The text, strategies, and tips in the *GED Prep Xcelerator Writing Workbook* are designed to provide additional practice in writing and editing. As you complete a unit in the *GED Prep Xcelerator Writing Student Book*, note the grammar rules you have learned, and then consult the corresponding lesson in this workbook for additional support.

The **Review the Skill** section redefines and provides additional information about the skill to be studied.

Callouts provide strategies and information that you may use to understand and interpret various passages or graphics.

Test-Taking Tips offer broad or specific support for answering multiple-choice questions.

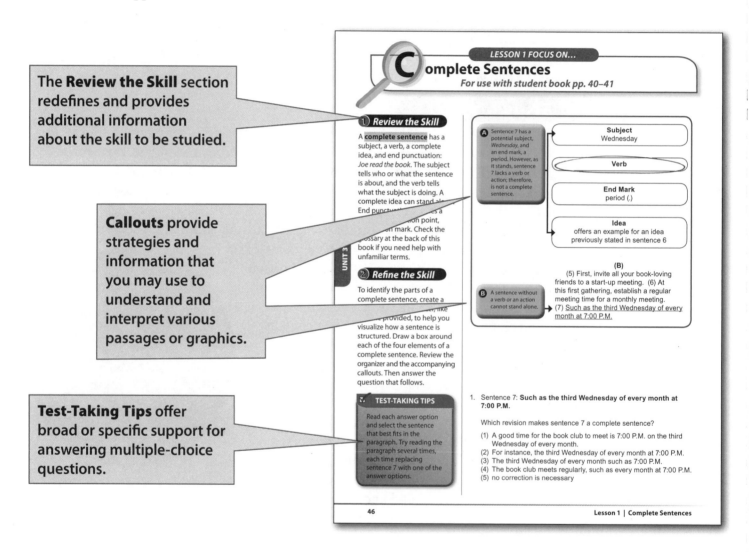

While it is important to learn grammar rules, it is also important to remember that English is an imperfect language, and there are exceptions to most rules. Remember to trust your instincts. Sometimes a sentence simply sounds wrong. If you forget a rule, read aloud the question and answers; if a sentence or series of words sounds incorrect, it probably is. Keep this in mind as you complete each lesson in this book.

Each lesson in *GED Prep Xcelerator Writing* consists of questions that relate to the lesson's content. Most questions will provide you with a sentence from the accompanying paragraph, essay, letter, or memorandum. You then will be asked to find the best spelling, punctuation, or structure correction. You also may be asked to revise the placement of the sentence within the paragraph. Other questions will ask you to identify types or parts of sentences.

---

③ *Master the Skill*

Directions: Choose the <u>one best answer</u> to each question.

<u>Questions 2 through 4</u> refer to the following information.

Let's Clean House

(A)
(1) While cleaning one's home is not among most people's favorite activities, the right tools do make the job less loathsome. (2) If you're in the market for a new vacuum cleaner, here are some features to consider.

(B)
(3) Categorize the surfaces of your home. (4) Do you need a vacuum that will clean primarily carpets, floors, stairways, or some combination of these surfaces? (5) Upright vacuums are good for large carpeted areas but clumsy on stairways? (6) Canisters are good for floors and stairways but clumsy in spacious areas.

(C)
(7) Understand the aspects of the machine. (8) A vacuum cleaner can be described in terms of airflow, lift, filtration, and design. (9) Airflow describes the volume of air moving through the machine. (10) Lift indicates how well a machine picks up dust. (11) Filtration keeps dust out of the machine's system. (12) Design affects airflow, lift, and filtration. (13) Also affects whether the machine is manageable.

(D)
(14) Be wary of bells and whistles. (15) Consider which attachments you really need, such as a dusting brush, crevice tool, upholstery tool, microfilter, and so on. (16) Remember that you're paying for these extras, and you will have to store them.

---

2. Sentence 5: **Upright vacuums are good for large carpeted areas but clumsy on stairways?**

   Which correction should be made to sentence 5?

   (1) remove <u>Upright vacuums</u>
   (2) change <u>?</u> to <u>.</u>
   (3) remove <u>on stairways</u>
   (4) remove <u>?</u>
   (5) no correction is necessary

3. Sentence 13: **Also affects whether the machine is manageable.**

   Which correction should be made to sentence 13?

   (1) change <u>Also</u> to <u>Design also</u>
   (2) insert a comma after <u>whether</u>
   (3) change <u>machine is</u> to <u>machine. Is</u>
   (4) insert a comma after <u>also</u>
   (5) no correction is necessary

4. Sentences 15: **Consider which attachments you really need, such as a dusting brush, crevice tool, upholstery tool, microfilter, and so on.**

   Which correction should be made to sentence 15?

   (1) remove <u>, such as</u>
   (2) remove <u>Consider which attachments you really need</u>
   (3) remove <u>and</u>
   (4) remove <u>attachments</u>
   (5) no correction is necessary

UNIT 3

When a sentence is provided for the question, the sentence will always appear bold.

These questions have been formatted to match those found on the GED Language Arts/Writing Test. By familiarizing yourself with this format, you will be better prepared to take the test.

The sentences will not always require corrections, so be sure to read each question and answer option carefully.

Test-Taking Tips

The GED Tests include 240 questions across the five subject-area exams of Language Arts/Reading, Language Arts/Writing, Mathematics, Science, and Social Studies. In each of the GED Tests, you will need to apply some amount of subject-area knowledge. However, because all of the questions are multiple-choice items largely based on text or visuals (such as tables, charts, or graphs), the emphasis in *GED Prep Xcelerator* is on helping learners like you to build and develop core reading and thinking skills. As part of the overall strategy, various test-taking tips are included below and throughout the book that will help you to improve your performance on the GED Tests. For example:

◆ *Always thoroughly read the directions so that you know exactly what to do.* In Mathematics, for example, one part of the test allows for the use of a calculator. The other part does not. If you are unsure of what to do, ask the test provider if the directions can be explained.

◆ *Read each question carefully so that you fully understand what it is asking.* Some questions, for example, may present extra information that is unnecessary to correctly answer them. Other questions may note emphasis through capitalized and boldfaced words (Which of the following is **NOT** an example of photosynthesis?).

◆ *Manage your time with each question.* Because the GED Tests are timed exams, you'll want to spend enough time with each question, but not *too* much time. For example, on the GED Language Arts/Writing Test, you will have 75 minutes in which to answer 50 multiple-choice questions and 45 minutes to complete an essay. That works out to a little more than 90 seconds per question. You can save time by first reading each question and its answer options before reading the passage. Once you understand what the question is asking, review the passage for the appropriate information.

◆ *Answer all questions, regardless of whether you know the answer or are guessing at it.* There is no benefit in leaving questions unanswered on the GED Tests. Keep in mind the time that you have for each test and manage it accordingly. For time purposes, you may decide to initially skip questions. However, note them with a light mark beside the question and try to return to them before the end of the test.

◆ *Note any unfamiliar words in questions.* First attempt to re-read a question by omitting any unfamiliar word(s). Next, try to substitute another word in its place.

◆ *Narrow answer options by re-reading each question and the accompanying text or graphic.* Although all five answers are possible, keep in mind that only one of them is correct. You may be able to eliminate one or two answers immediately; others may take more time and involve the use of either logic or assumptions. In some cases, you may need to make your best guess between two options. If so, keep in mind that test-makers often avoid answer patterns; that is, if you know the previous answer is (2) and are unsure of the answer to the next question but have narrowed it to options (2) and (4), you may want to choose (4).

◆ *Read all answer choices.* Even though the first or second answer choice may appear to be correct, be sure to thoroughly read all five answer choices. Then go with your instinct when answering questions. For example, if your first instinct is to mark (1) in response to a question, it's best to stick with that answer unless you later determine that answer to be incorrect. Usually, the first answer you choose is the correct one.

◆ *Correctly complete your answer sheet by marking one numbered space on the answer sheet beside the number to which it corresponds.* Mark only one answer for each item; multiple answers will be scored as incorrect. If time permits, double-check your answer sheet after completing the test to ensure that you have made as many marks— no more, no less—as there are questions.

You've already made two very smart decisions in trying to earn your GED certificate and in purchasing *GED Prep Xcelerator* to help you do so. The following are additional strategies to help you optimize success on the GED Tests.

3 weeks out ...

◆ Set a study schedule for the GED Tests. Choose times in which you are most alert and places, such as a library, that provide the best study environment.

◆ Thoroughly review all material in *GED Prep Xcelerator*, using the *GED Prep Xcelerator Writing Workbook* to extend understanding of concepts in the *GED Prep Xcelerator Writing Student Book*.

◆ Make sure you have the necessary tools for the job: sharpened pencils, pens, paper, and, for Mathematics, the Casio-fx 260 Solar calculator.

◆ Keep notebooks for each of the subject areas you are studying. Folders with pockets are useful for storing loose papers.

◆ When taking notes, restate thoughts or ideas in your own words rather than copying them directly from a book. You can phrase these notes as complete sentences, as questions (with answers), or as fragments, provided you understand them.

◆ Take the pretests, noting any troublesome subject areas. Focus your remaining study around those subject areas.

1 week out ...

◆ Prepare the items you will need for the GED Tests: admission ticket (if necessary), acceptable form of identification, some sharpened No. 2 pencils (with erasers), a watch, eyeglasses (if necessary), a sweater or jacket, and a high-protein snack to eat during breaks.

◆ Map out the course to the test center, and visit it a day or two before your scheduled exam. If you drive, find a place to park at the center.

◆ Get a good night's sleep the night before the GED Tests. Studies have shown that learners with sufficient rest perform better in testing situations.

The day of ...

◆ Eat a hearty breakfast high in protein. As with the rest of your body, your brain needs ample energy to perform well.

◆ Arrive 30 minutes early to the testing center. This will allow sufficient time in the event of a change to a different testing classroom.

◆ Pack a sizeable lunch, especially if you plan to be at the testing center most of the day.

◆ Focus and relax. You've come this far, spending weeks preparing and studying for the GED Tests. It's your time to shine.

Develop Thesis Statement
For use with student book pp. 2–3

1 Review

The **thesis statement** is the topic of the essay. Sentences in an essay that support the thesis statement provide **supporting details**. Essays generally include three supporting details that immediately follow the thesis statement. In the sample paragraph, the thesis statement is about a specific piece of advice. The advice the writer chose was "to mean what I say."

When writing an essay, carefully read the prompt to make sure you understand the topic. Use a mental map (such as the one on page 3) to organize your thoughts. Doing so will help you develop a strong thesis statement and three supporting details.

Read the prompt and examine the sample paragraph. Use the information in the callouts to make sure you understand the focus of the lesson.

Prompt: Everyone has received advice from a parent, friend, teacher, or co-worker.

Identify one piece of advice that someone has shared with you. Explain when and why the advice was given, how you applied the advice, and whether the advice was valuable. To develop your essay, use your own observations, experiences, and knowledge.

A When writing a thesis statement, first identify your topic. The topic for the prompt is *advice*.

The thesis statement is sentence 5: "This year, the best advice I have been given is to mean what I say."

B The three supporting details can be found in sentence 6. The writer lists three reasons why "mean what you say" is good advice.

(A)
(1) Many teenagers today do not heed the advice of their parents. (2) Instead, they are more likely to follow advice from a friend or an adult they trust. (3) Last year, I asked Mrs. Morgan, my former social studies teacher, advice on whether or not I should stay with my Uncle Joe and become a plumber. (4) Mrs. Morgan said to me, "Whatever you decide, just make sure you mean what you say." (5) <u>This year, the best advice I have been given is to mean what I say</u>. (6) <u>It helped me make the right decision with my dog Scout, my Uncle Joe, and my future</u>.

UNIT 1

② Refine

Directions: Below is a brainstorming method called a mental map. It is helpful in developing the thesis statement and three supporting details in your essay. Use the following blank mental map to brainstorm your own ideas for this prompt.

Prompt: Most people have a favorite food they like to eat. Think about your favorite food. Now write to explain why you like this food.

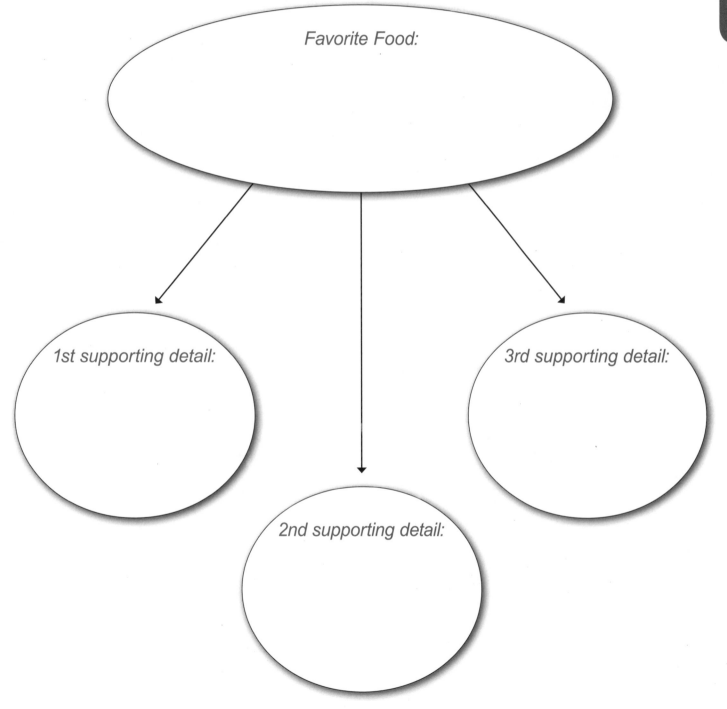

Directions: Choose the one best answer to each question.

Questions 1 and 2 refer to the following paragraph.

(1) "Ding Dong," the doorbell rang. (2) It was the delivery boy with my favorite food. (3) I ran to the door, grabbed my piping hot dinner, and paid the delivery boy. (4) Placing the box on the table, I quickly opened the top and let the delicious, spicy smell tickle my nose. (5) There it was, right in front of me, my favorite food: pizza. (6) I like pizza because it tastes great, it's easy to get, and best of all, it's cheap.

1. Which of the following sentences is the thesis statement?

   (1) It was the delivery boy with my favorite food.
   (2) I ran to the door, grabbed my piping hot dinner, and paid the delivery boy.
   (3) Placing the box on the table, I quickly opened the top and let the delicious, spicy smell tickle my nose.
   (4) There it was, right in front of me, my favorite food: pizza.
   (5) I like pizza because it tastes great, it's easy to get, and best of all, it's cheap.

2. Which of the following sentences contains the supporting details?

   (1) It was the delivery boy with my favorite food.
   (2) I ran to the door, grabbed my piping hot dinner, and paid the delivery boy.
   (3) Placing the box on the table, I quickly opened the top and let the delicious, spicy smell tickle my nose.
   (4) There it was, right in front of me, my favorite food: pizza.
   (5) I like pizza because it tastes great, it's easy to get, and best of all, it's cheap.

Directions: Choose the one best answer to each question.

Questions 3 and 4 refer to the following paragraph.

(1) In many cities, there are a lot of Chinese restaurants. (2) This is one of the reasons that many people eat Chinese food. (3) My favorite food is Chinese food, especially fried rice. (4) I like fried rice because, for the most part, it's healthy, and every Chinese restaurant makes it differently. (5) The best part is that no matter where I go in the world, I can always find a Chinese restaurant serving fried rice.

3. Which of the following sentences is the thesis statement?

   (1) In many cities, there are a lot of Chinese restaurants.
   (2) This is one of the reasons that many people eat Chinese food.
   (3) My favorite food is Chinese food, especially fried rice.
   (4) I like fried rice because, for the most part, it's healthy, and every Chinese restaurant makes it differently.
   (5) The best part is that no matter where I go in the world, I can always find a Chinese restaurant serving fried rice.

4. Which statement is a supporting detail?

   (1) Many people eat Chinese food.
   (2) There are a lot of Chinese restaurants.
   (3) My favorite food is Chinese food.
   (4) I like fried rice.
   (5) It's healthy.

Write

Directions: Read the following four writing prompts, and write a thesis statement for each. Use the boxes labeled Writing Strategies and Thesis Checklist as guides.

Prompt 1—What job would you like to have? Think about why you would like this job. Now write to explain why you would like this job.

Thesis statement: _____

_____

_____

Prompt 2—Some people think that being popular, accomplishing things, and being organized are important. Think about which one is the most important to you. Now write to explain why being popular, accomplishing things, or being organized is the most important to you.

Thesis statement: _____

_____

_____

Prompt 3—Employers want people to have good work habits. Think about a good work habit people should have. Now write to explain what good work habit you believe people should have.

Thesis statement: _____

_____

_____

Prompt 4—A true friend is loyal. Think about why it is important for a true friend to be loyal. Now write to explain why a true friend should be loyal.

Thesis statement: _____

_____

_____

WRITING STRATEGIES

Avoid using the phrase *I think* because using it may signal to the reader that you are not absolutely sure of the statement you are making. By avoiding this phrase, you are sending the message that you believe the statements in your essay.

THESIS CHECKLIST

1. Read the prompt carefully.
2. Understand exactly what is being asked.
3. Look for key terms, such as *Explain*.
4. Use the mental map to brainstorm ideas before you begin.

Plan and Write Introduction
For use with student book pp. 4–5

1 Review

Your essay should begin with an **introduction**. This introduces the reader to the essay's topic. The introduction includes the **hook**, thesis statement, and three supporting details. The hook should broadly state the topic and capture the reader's attention. A simple way to do this is by using a surprising statement, short story about a similar or historical event, or an exciting quote. The thesis statement should immediately follow the hook, and the supporting details should immediately follow the thesis statement.

- hook
- thesis statement
- three supporting details

When writing an introduction, it is important to organize your thoughts. Use a graphic organizer, like the one on page 7, to help you develop a strong introduction.

Read the prompt and examine the sample paragraph. Use the information in the callouts to make sure you understand the focus of the lesson.

Prompt: Everyone has received advice from a parent, friend, teacher, or co-worker.

Identify one piece of advice that someone has shared with you. Explain when and why the advice was given, how you applied the advice, and whether the advice was valuable. To develop your essay, use your own observations, experiences, and knowledge.

A In the paragraph, the writer has chosen to *hook* the reader using two methods: a surprising piece of information in sentence 1 and an anecdote (or short story) in sentences 3 and 4.

B The thesis statement is: "This year, the best advice I have been given is to mean what I say" and the three supporting details are: Scout, Uncle Joe, and the writer's future.

(A)

A (1) Many teenagers today do not heed the advice of their parents. (2) Instead, they are more likely to follow advice from a friend or an adult they trust. **A** (3) Last year, I asked Mrs. Morgan, my former social studies teacher, advice on whether or not I should stay with my Uncle Joe and become a plumber. **A** (4) Mrs. Morgan said to me, "Whatever you decide, just make sure you mean what you say." **B** (5) This year, the best advice I have been given is to mean what I say. **B** (6) It helped me make the right decision with my dog Scout, my Uncle Joe, and my future.

UNIT 1

<u>Directions</u>: The following graphic organizer can help you organize your thoughts. Read the prompt, and write a possible hook, thesis statement, and three supporting details. There is no need for you to write complete sentences. At this point, you are still just brainstorming your ideas and organizing your thoughts.

Prompt: Most people have a favorite food they like to eat. Think about your favorite food. Now write to explain why you like this food.

UNIT 1

Hook

_____

_____

_____

Thesis Statement

_____

_____

_____

_____

Three Supporting Details

_____

_____

_____

_____

_____

Prompt: Most teenagers have chores. Think about why it is important for teenagers to have chores. Now write to explain why it is important for teenagers to have chores.

Prewriting Exercise:

Hook: startling statements

Thesis: It's important for individuals to grow up doing daily chores.

Three Supporting Details:
1. builds responsibility
2. teaches skills
3. provides opportunity to earn spending money

Directions: Choose the one best answer to each question.

Questions 1 through 3 refer to the following paragraph.

(1) Today's paper said that one day employers may refuse to hire individuals who have not grown up performing household chores. (2) The article explains that individuals who had to do household chores may be better employees. (3) It indicates that people who do their daily chores may come to the workplace with a better work ethic. (4) The article also states that people with strong work ethics are likely to become long-term employees. (5) It's important for people to do daily chores. (6) Doing daily chores can teach people responsibility, help them develop skills, and allow them the opportunity to earn spending money.

1. Which of the following sentences is an example of a hook?

   (1) Today's paper said that one day employers may refuse to hire individuals who have not grown up performing household chores.
   (2) It's important for individuals to have grown up doing daily chores.
   (3) Doing daily chores can teach people responsibility.
   (4) Doing daily chores can help people develop skills.
   (5) Doing daily chores can allow people the opportunity to earn spending money.

2. Which of the following sentences is the thesis statement?

   (1) Today's paper said that one day employers may refuse to hire individuals who have not grown up performing household chores.
   (2) The article explains that individuals who had to do household chores may be better employees.
   (3) It indicates that people who do their daily chores may come to the workplace with a better work ethic.
   (4) The article also states that people with strong work ethics are likely to become long-term employees.
   (5) It's important for individuals to have gorwn up doing daily chores.

3. Which of the following sentences contains the three supporting details?

   (1) The article explains that teenagers who have to do household chores may be better employees.
   (2) It indicates that people who do their daily chores may come to the workplace with a better work ethic.
   (3) The article also states that people with strong work ethics are likely to become long-term employees.
   (4) It's important for individuals to have grown up doing daily chores.
   (5) Doing daily chores can teach people responsibility, help them develop skills, and allow them the opportunity to earn spending money.

Directions: Read the two following prompts, and write an introductory paragraph for each. Use the boxes labeled Writing Strategies and Introduction Checklist as guides.

Prompt 1—Most people have a favorite food they like to eat. Think about your favorite food. Now write to explain why you like this food.

_____

_____

_____

_____

_____

_____

_____

_____

Prompt 2—Some people think that being popular, accomplishing things, and being organized are important. Think about which one is the most important to you. Now write to explain why being popular, accomplishing things, or being organized is the most important to you.

_____

_____

_____

_____

_____

_____

_____

_____

_____

_____

WRITING STRATEGIES

Other good ideas for hooks include:
- **Interesting facts**—*Salmon hot dogs are a healthy alternative to traditional franks.*
- **A reference to a book, a movie, or popular culture**—*I once read a book about…*
- **A current event**—*The national news recently had a story about…*

INTRO. CHECKLIST

1. Read the prompt carefully.
2. Understand exactly what is being asked.
3. Look for key terms, such as *Explain*.
4. Use a graphic organizer to organize your thoughts before you begin.
5. Begin with a hook.
6. Introduce your thesis statement and three supporting details.

Plan and Write Body

For use with student book pp. 6–7

① Review

In a five-paragraph essay, the three paragraphs after the introduction are called the **body**. Each body paragraph includes an explanation of one of the supporting details. Each body paragraph should begin with a **transition**. Transitions are important techniques used to link the body paragraphs together because they tie what you have already written to what you are about to write.

When writing your body paragraphs, it is important to organize your thoughts by using a graphic organizer (such as the one on page 11) before you begin.

Read the prompt and examine the sample paragraph. Use the information in the callouts to make sure you understand the focus of the lesson.

Prompt: Everyone has received advice from a parent, friend, teacher, or co-worker.

Identify one piece of advice that someone has shared with you. Explain when and why the advice was given, how you applied the advice, and whether the advice was valuable. To develop your essay, use your own observations, experiences, and knowledge.

A Each body paragraph represents one of your supporting details. This paragraph is about the first supporting detail.

B Note the transitions used throughout the paragraph. Transitions are an important part of an essay because they allow the reader to move effortlessly from one paragraph or idea to the next.

(B)

(1) **B** <u>After</u> Mrs. Morgan gave me her advice, my girlfriend and I were in the mall shopping for soccer clothes when we passed Jake's Pet Store. (2) In the window was the cutest **A** <u>little beagle</u>. (3) His long, floppy ears and sad brown eyes were pleading to go home with us. (4) It must have been a weak moment for me, because thirty minutes later we were driving home with our dog Scout. (5) I had convinced my girlfriend that I would take care of this puppy. (6) Believe me, I meant what I said. (7) **B** <u>Although</u> it was hard work, I realized Scout depended on me for food and water, a place to sleep, and daily exercise. (8) **B** <u>When</u> our neighbors saw how responsible I was with Scout, they asked me to be their dog walker. (9) Soon I was taking care of half the dogs in the neighborhood.

② *Refine*

<u>Directions</u>: Before you begin to write your essay, use the lines provided to complete the following graphic organizer. This will help you organize your thoughts. Refer to your hook, thesis statement, and three supporting details from page 7. Use the prompt below to fill in the remainder of the graphic organizer.

Prompt: Most people have a favorite food they like to eat. Think about your favorite food. Now write to explain why you like this food.

UNIT 1

Hook: _____

Thesis statement: _____

Three supporting details: 1. _____

2. _____

3. _____

Transition: _____

Restate first supporting detail: _____

Transition: _____

Restate second supporting detail: _____

Transition: _____

Restate third supporting detail: _____

Prompt: Everyone has received advice from a parent, friend, teacher, or co-worker. In your essay, identify one piece of advice that someone has shared with you. Explain when and why the advice was given, how you applied the advice, and whether the advice was valuable. To develop your essay, use your own observations, experiences, and knowledge.

Directions: Choose the <u>one best answer</u> to each question.

<u>Questions 1 through 3</u> refer to the following body paragraphs.

(C)

(11) It was around this time that my Uncle Joe asked me to go to Little Rock to become a plumber. (12) A couple of summers ago I stayed with Uncle Joe and worked with him. (13) I wasn't sure what I wanted to do so I said I didn't want to go and then changed my mind. (14) I gave him mixed messages. (15) When Uncle Joe asked me this time, I knew what I wanted. (16) I told him I did not want to be a plumber, and just like my promise to my girlfriend about taking care of Scout, I meant what I said.

(D)

(17) I have found through my neighborhood dog walking job that I have a real connection with animals. (18) They seem to trust me. (19) I have been reading books about how to care for dogs. (20) One of them was written by Dr. Eugene Smith, who wrote about how important his job was, and how much he loved working with animals. (21) That's when I knew what I wanted to do with the rest of my life. (22) This summer, I am going to work for Scout's veterinarian, Dr. George. (23) In the fall, I will be going off to school to be a veterinary assistant. (24) I even found a school that will let me bring Scout. (25) When I earn my GED certificate, I am going to take classes to become a veterinary assistant, and I mean it.

1. Which of the following sentences is a transition?

   (1) I am going to work for Scout's veterinarian, Dr. George.
   (2) I wasn't sure what I wanted to do so I said I didn't want to go and then changed my mind.
   (3) I loved being with the dogs, and I loved it that my neighbors considered me dependable.
   (4) It was around this time that my Uncle Joe asked me to go to Little Rock to become a plumber.
   (5) They seem to trust me.

2. Sentence 11: **It was around this time that my Uncle Joe asked me to go to Little Rock to become a plumber.**

   Which revision should be made to the placement of sentence 11?

   (1) remove sentence 11
   (2) move sentence 11 to follow sentence 25
   (3) move sentence 11 to the beginning of paragraph D
   (4) move sentence 11 to the end of paragraph C
   (5) no correction is necessary

3. Sentence 25: **When I earn my GED certificate, I am going to take classes to become a veterinary assistant, and I mean it.**

   Which revision should be made to the placement of sentence 25?

   (1) remove sentence 25
   (2) move sentence 25 to the beginning of paragraph D
   (3) move sentence 25 to the end of paragraph C
   (4) move sentence 25 to follow sentence 11
   (5) no correction is necessary

③ Write

Directions: Read the following prompt, and fill in the key elements of the introduction. Then, write a body paragraph for the first and the second supporting details. Use the boxes labeled Writing Strategies and Body Checklist as guides.

Prompt: Most people have a favorite food they like to eat. Think about your favorite food. Now write to explain why you like this food.

Hook: _____

Thesis statement: _____

Three supporting details: 1. _____

2. _____

3. _____

Body (first supporting detail):

_____

_____

_____

_____

_____

_____

_____

_____

Body (second supporting detail):

_____

_____

_____

_____

_____

_____

_____

_____

_____

WRITING STRATEGIES

Transitions are a way to:
- **Give examples**—*For instance; To illustrate; In fact*
- **Summarize**—*In summary; In conclusion*
- **Show time**—*Next; Later; Finally*
- **Show place or direction**—*Nearby; Beyond; Below*

BODY CHECKLIST

1. Read the prompt carefully.
2. Understand exactly what is being asked.
3. Look for key terms, such as *Explain*.
4. Use the graphic organizer.
5. Begin with a transition.
6. Be sure that each body paragraph explains one supporting detail.

Elaboration of Details

For use with student book pp. 8–9

① Review

Elaboration is important because you need to provide a large amount of detailed information in your essay. You should elaborate on each supporting detail. You can achieve enough elaboration by separating your supporting detail into parts and identifying each part, clarifying the topic, or putting it into a category. This becomes the theme of the paragraph.

You can use a mental map (such as the one shown below) for brainstorming. For example, put your first supporting detail in the larger circle. Then use the smaller circles to write down the ideas or examples you wish to use within the body paragraph. Use this technique for the second and third supporting details.

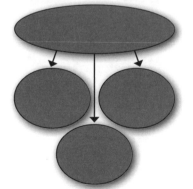

Read the prompt and examine the sample paragraph. Use the information in the callouts to make sure you understand the focus of the lesson.

Prompt: Everyone has received advice from a parent, friend, teacher, or co-worker.

Identify one piece of advice that someone has shared with you. Explain when and why the advice was given, how you applied the advice, and whether the advice was valuable. To develop your essay, use your own observations, experiences, and knowledge.

A Remember to introduce the theme of the paragraph. By reading sentence 2, you can see that the theme of this paragraph is getting the beagle.

B One way to elaborate is to use examples and illustration:

NO— In the window was a little beagle.

YES— In the window was the cutest little beagle. His long, floppy ears and sad brown eyes were pleading to go home with us.

(B)

(1) After Mrs. Morgan gave me her advice, my girlfriend and I were in the mall shopping for soccer clothes when we passed Jake's Pet Store. (2) <u>In the window was the cutest little beagle</u>. (3) <u>His long, floppy ears and sad brown eyes were pleading to go home with us</u>. (4) It must have been a weak moment for me, because thirty minutes later we were driving home with our dog Scout. (5) I had convinced my girlfriend that I would take care of this puppy. (6) Believe me, I meant what I said. (7) Although it was hard work, I realized Scout depended on me for food and water, a place to sleep, and daily exercise. (8) When our neighbors saw how responsible I was with Scout, they asked me to be their dog walker.

<u>Directions</u>: Before you begin to write your essay, use the lines provided to complete the following graphic organizer. This will help you organize your thoughts. Refer to your hook, thesis statement, and three supporting details from page 7. Use the prompt below to fill in the remainder of the graphic organizer.

Prompt: Most people have a favorite food they like to eat. Think about your favorite food. Now write to explain why you like this food.

Hook: _____

Thesis statement: _____

Three supporting details: 1. _____

2. _____

3. _____

Introduce your topic by restating the first supporting detail: _____

Support your topic: _____

Explain the details of the passage: _____

Explain why the passage supports your topic: _____

Introduce your topic by restating the second supporting detail: _____

Support your topic: _____

Explain the details of the passage: _____

Explain why the passage supports your topic: _____

Introduce your topic by restating the third supporting detail: _____

Support your topic: _____

Explain the details of the passage: _____

Explain why the passage supports your topic: _____

Directions: Choose the one best answer to each question.

Questions 1 and 2 refer to the following paragraphs.

Prompt: "Dogs are a man's best friend." This may be true, but many people think cats make better house pets. Think about which pet you like best. Now write to explain why that pet makes the best house pet.

Hook: anecdote or short story
Thesis: Dogs make the best house pets.
Three Supporting details:
- Loving
- Protective
- Companions

(B)

(1) To begin with, dogs make the best house pets because they are so loveable. (2) Every day when I come home, Riley is waiting by the door to welcome me home. (3) I put down my bag and plop on the floor to give him a kiss. (4) I hug him and kiss him and he never complains. (5) He just licks my face. (6) When I come home, there is no one to greet me and love me. (7) Riley makes me feel like he has been waiting for me to come home all day just so he can lick my face. (8) It is his way of saying he loves me.

(C)

(9) Secondly, my dog is the perfect watch dog because he is very protective of my home. (10) Just last night at midnight, Riley started barking and running around in circles. (11) It was his serious bark—much lower than his welcome home bark. (12) The hair on the back of his neck was standing straight up, not soft and silky like it is normally. (13) That night, even though it was summer, it was chilly. (14) When I went to see what all the commotion was about, he found a big, fat raccoon in the trash can. (15) Sure, the raccoon was not a big threat, but Riley showed me that no intruder is welcome in my home. (16) He alerted me to a problem, a wild animal, and would not rest until it was gone.

(D)

(17) In addition, my dog makes the perfect companion. (18) Last summer, my family went camping in the Smoky Mountains. (19) I wanted to take a friend, but there wasn't enough room. (20) I decided to take Riley because he likes to sleep on the floor, and we have a great time together. (21) The first day we took a walk through the woods to collect firewood. (22) Riley even carried a branch in his mouth to help me. (23) The next day we went swimming in the stream. (24) The second I went into the water, Riley jumped in with me. (25) He literally barked me out of bed. (26) Riley slept right in the sleeping bag with me. (27) He kept me nice and warm. (28) If I had brought a friend with me, I'm not sure he or she would have enjoyed picking up wood, swimming in the cold stream, or sharing a sleeping bag. (29) He or she might have complained or not come with me. (30) Riley did none of that; he was just happy to be with me, making him the perfect companion.

1. Which key element of an essay are paragraphs B, C, & D?

   (1) hook
   (2) introduction
   (3) conclusion
   (4) body
   (5) transition

2. Sentence 25: **He literally barked my dad out of bed.**

   Which revision should be made to sentence 25?

   (1) remove sentence 25
   (2) swap sentence 25 with sentence 13
   (3) move sentence 25 to the end of paragraph B
   (4) move sentence 25 to follow sentence 10
   (5) move sentence 25 to follow sentence 31

③ Write

Directions: Read the following prompt, and fill in the key elements of the introduction with your hook, thesis statement, and three supporting details from page 7. Then write the body paragraph for the <u>third</u> supporting detail. Use the boxes labeled Writing Strategies and Body Checklist as guides.

> **Prompt**: Most people have a favorite food they like to eat. Think about your favorite food. Now write to explain why you like this food.

Hook: _____

Thesis statement: _____

Three supporting details: 1. _____

          2. _____

          3. _____

Body (third supporting detail):

_____

_____

_____

_____

_____

_____

_____

_____

_____

_____

_____

_____

_____

_____

_____

WRITING STRATEGIES

Other ways to elaborate paragraphs:

- **Definition**—*Advice is a suggestion that someone gives you based on his or her own experience or knowledge.*
- **Analogy**—*Buying a dog is a lot like buying a car. They both come with a lot of responsibility.*
- **Comparison and contrast**—*Although my Uncle Joe thinks I should be a plumber, I think I should be a veterinary assistant.*
- **Cause and effect**—*When my neighbors saw I was responsible, they asked me to be their dog walker.*

BODY CHECKLIST

1. Read the prompt carefully.
2. Understand exactly what is being asked.
3. Look for key terms, such as *Explain*.
4. Use the graphic organizer.
5. Begin each paragraph with a transition.
6. Be sure each paragraph explains one supporting detail.
7. Use elaboration.

Plan and Write Conclusion
For use with student book pp. 10–11

① Review

A **conclusion** provides the lasting impression of your essay. A few strong sentences that restate your feelings about the essay topic will bring closure to your essay. Remember to remind the reader of the supporting details and why they support your topic. Make sure you are rephrasing, not repeating.

When writing your conclusion, be sure to spend time organizing your thoughts. By now you have developed a strong thesis statement and supporting details, so spend time deciding how to best rephrase these elements for this concluding paragraph. This is the time to wrap things up.

Read the prompt and examine the sample paragraph. Use the information in the callouts to make sure you understand the focus of the lesson.

Prompt: Everyone has received advice from a parent, friend, teacher, or co-worker.

In your essay, identify one piece of advice that someone has shared with you. Explain when and why the advice was given, how you applied the advice, and whether the advice was valuable. To develop your essay, use your own observations, experiences, and knowledge.

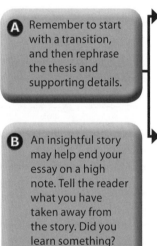

(A) Remember to start with a transition, and then rephrase the thesis and supporting details.

(B) An insightful story may help end your essay on a high note. Tell the reader what you have taken away from the story. Did you learn something? Was something gained?

(E)

(1) <u>Throughout this year</u>, I have found Mrs. Morgan's advice to be very valuable. (2) <u>I have said what I meant and followed through with it by doing what I said</u>. (3) I have taken care of <u>my dog</u> and the neighborhood dogs. (4) I told my <u>Uncle Joe</u> that I did not want to be a plumber, and I have decided to become a veterinary assistant. (5) I have learned through these experiences the importance of saying what I mean. **(B)** (6) <u>Because I have followed Mrs. Morgan's advice, I have gained the respect of my family, community, and even Scout</u>.

② Refine

Before you begin to write your essay, it is important to organize your thoughts. Use the following graphic organizer to fill in the key elements of your essay's conclusion. Prepare conclusions for the three prompts below.

> **Prompt 1**—Most people have a favorite place they like to go. Think about your favorite place. Now write to explain why you like this place.

End with an insightful thought

Transition: _____

Restate Thesis: _____

Ending: _____

> **Prompt 2**—Most people have a favorite color. Think about your favorite color. Now write to explain why you like this color.

End with a quote

Transition: _____

Restate Thesis: _____

Ending: _____

> **Prompt 3**—Most people have a favorite person they would like to meet. Think about a person you would like to meet. Now write to explain why you would like to meet this person.

End with a reference to a book, a movie, or popular culture

Transition: _____

Restate Thesis: _____

Ending: _____

Prompt: "Dogs are a man's best friend." This may be true, but many people think cats make better house pets. Think about which pet you like best. Now write to explain why that pet makes the best house pet.

Hook: anecdote or short story
Thesis: Dogs make the best house pets
Three supporting details:
- Loving
- Protective
- Companions

Transition: To begin with
1st supporting detail: Loving
Explanation:
- Greets me when I get home
- Doesn't mind hugs and kisses
- No one else greets me
- Always waiting for me

Transition: Secondly
2nd supporting detail: Protective
Explanation:
- Protects home
- Barks & runs in circles
- Gets me out of bed
- Raccoon intruder

Transition: In addition
3rd supporting detail: Companion
Explanation:
- Camping trip
- Helps gather wood
- Goes swimming
- Shares sleeping bag when it's cold

Directions: Fill in the conclusion of the graphic organizer. Then choose the one best answer to each question.

Questions 1 and 2 refer to the following conclusion paragraph.

(E)

(1) As you can see, my dog Riley is a perfect pet. (2) He's great because he is so happy to see me when I get home from work, he protects me from wild animals and intruders, and he's the perfect companion when I go camping. (3) There's a reason why the saying, "A man's best friend is his dog," is a cliché. (4) It's because it is true. (5) Just look at Riley. (6) He's the perfect example.

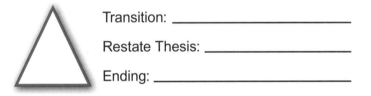

Transition: _____

Restate Thesis: _____

Ending: _____

1. Which of the following sentences restates the three supporting details?

   (1) As you can see, my dog Riley is a perfect pet.
   (2) He's the greatest because he is so happy to see me when I get home from work, he protects me from wild animals and intruders, and he's the perfect companion when I go camping.
   (3) There's a reason why the saying, "A man's best friend is his dog," is a cliché.
   (4) It's because it is true.
   (5) He's the perfect example.

2. In the conclusion, how does the writer choose to end the essay?

   (1) by using a reference to popular culture
   (2) with an insightful thought about his life
   (3) by using a quotation
   (4) by restating the most important thesis point
   (5) by telling us about his new dog

Directions: Read the following prompt, and fill in the key elements of the conclusion using the graphic organizer. Then write a conclusion for this prompt. Use the boxes labeled Writing Strategies and Conclusion Checklist as guides.

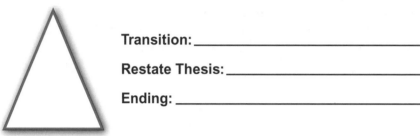

Prompt: Most people have a favorite food they like to eat. Think about your favorite food. Now write to explain why you like this food.

Transition: _____

Restate Thesis: _____

Ending: _____

Conclusion:

_____

_____

_____

_____

_____

_____

_____

_____

_____

_____

_____

_____

_____

_____

_____

_____

_____

_____

_____

WRITING STRATEGIES

Ways to end your essays:
- **Conclude by connecting the first and last paragraph**—*"I have found Mrs. Morgan's advice to be very valuable."*
- **Keep it simple**—*"I have said what I meant and followed through with it by doing what I said."*
- **Conclude with an insightful thought, something you've learned in writing this essay**—*"I have learned through these experiences the importance of saying what I mean."*

☑ CONCLUSION CHECKLIST

1. Read the prompt carefully.
2. Understand exactly what is being asked.
3. Look for key terms, such as *Explain*.
4. Use the graphic organizer.
5. Begin with a transition.
6. Restate your thesis and three supporting details.
7. Leave a lasting impression.

Review and Revise

For use with student book pp. 12–15

① Review

Now that you have written all five parts of your essay, you can start the process of **reviewing** and **revising**. Read each of your paragraphs about your favorite food from the previous lessons and be sure that you meet all the criteria for the essay portion of the GED Language Arts/Writing Test.

Remember to:
- Establish a focus
- Organize your ideas
- Show development
- Give examples
- Exhibit a wide-ranging choice of words
- Use your words wisely and accurately

Read the prompt and examine the sample paragraphs. Use the information in the callouts to make sure you understand the focus of the lesson.

Prompt: Everyone has received advice from a parent, friend, teacher, or co-worker.

In your essay, identify one piece of advice that someone has shared with you. Explain when and why the advice was given, how you applied the advice, and whether the advice was valuable. To develop your essay, use your own observations, experiences, and knowledge.

Directions: Review the two paragraphs below. Identify and circle the four mistakes within 3–5 minutes. Time yourself.

A You will have 45 minutes to write, revise, and edit your essay. Pace yourself by allowing 10 minutes to plan, 30 minutes to write, and 5 minutes to revise and edit your essay.

(D)

(1) When I earn my GED certificate, I am going to take classes to become a veterinary assistant, and I mean it. (2) I think I have a real connection with animals. (3) They seem to trust me. (4) I have been reading books about how to care for dogs. (5) One of them was written by Dr. Eugene Smith, who wrote about how important his job was and how much he loved working with animals. (6) That's when I knew what I wanted to do with the rest of my life. (7) This summer, I am going to work for Scout's veterinarian, Dr. George. (8) In the fall, I will be going to take classes to be a veterinary assistant. (9) I even found a school that will let me bring Scout.

B Mistakes: The paragraphs are not indented; the first paragraph needs a transition; the writer used *I think*; and the conclusion needs a transition.

(E)

(10) I have found Mrs. Morgan's advice to be very valuable. (11) I have said what I meant and followed through with it by doing what I said. (12) I have taken care of my dog and the neighborhood dogs. (13) I told my Uncle Joe that I did not want to be a plumber, and I have decided to become a veterinary assistant. (14) I have learned through these experiences the importance of saying what I mean. (15) Because I have followed Mrs. Morgan's advice, I have gained the respect of my family, community, and even Scout.

Directions: Read the following essay. Identify the missing key elements and mistakes. Then use the right-hand margin of this page to make the necessary corrections. Time yourself.

(A)

(1) Last year, I asked Mrs. Morgan, my former social studies teacher, advice on whether or not I should stay with my Uncle Joe and become a plumber. (2) Mrs. Morgan said to me, "Whatever you decide, just make sure you mean what you say." (3) This year, the best advice I have been given is to mean what I say. (4) It helped me make the right decision about Uncle Joe and my future.

(B)

(5) After Mrs. Morgan gave me her advice, my girlfriend and I were in the mall shopping for soccer clothes when we passed Jake's Pet Store. (6) It must have been a weak moment for me, because thirty minutes later we were driving home with my dog Scout. (7) I had convinced my girlfriend that I would take care of this puppy. (8) Believe me, I meant what I said. (9) Although it was hard work, I realized Scout depended on me for food and water, a place to sleep, and daily exercise. (10) When our neighbors saw how responsible I was with Scout, they ask me to be their dog walker.

(C)

(11) It was around this time that my Uncle Joe asked me to go to Little Rock to become a plumber. (12) A couple of summers ago I stayed with Uncle Joe and worked with him. (13) I wasn't sure what I wanted to do then, so I said I didn't want to go and then changed my mind. (14) I gave him mixed messages. (15) When Uncle Joe asked me this time, I knew what I wanted. (16) I told him I did not want to be a plumber, and just like my promise to my girlfriend about taking care of Scout, I meant what I said.

(D)

(17) When I earn my GED certificate, I am going to take classes to become a veterinary assistant. (18) I have found through my neighborhood dog walking job that I have a real connection with animals. (19) They seem to trust me. (20) This summer, I think I am going to work for Scout's veterinarian, Dr. George. (21) In the fall, I will be going to take classes to be a veterinary assistant. (22) I even found a school that will let me bring Scout.

(E)

(23) I have said what I meant and followed through with it by doing what I said. (24) I told my Uncle Joe that I did not want to be a plumber, and I have decided to become a veterinary assistant. (25) I have learned through these experiences the importance of saying what I mean. (26) Because I have followed Mrs. Morgan's advice I have gained the respect of my family, community, and even Scout.

Directions: Look back to pages 9, 13, 17, and 21 of this book to review your five-paragraph essay. Then answer **yes** or **no** to the questions below. A sample essay is provided for you to use as an example.

Prompt: Most people have a favorite food they like to eat. Think about your favorite food. Now write to explain why you like this food.

Introduction:	Yes	No
1) Do you have a hook?	❏	❏
2) Is the thesis statement clear?	❏	❏
3) Do you have three supporting details?	❏	❏
4) Do your supporting details clearly support the thesis statement?	❏	❏
5) Do you stay on topic?	❏	❏

Body Paragraphs:	Yes	No
6) Do you begin each paragraph with a transition?	❏	❏
7) Is each paragraph dedicated to a single supporting detail?	❏	❏
8) Is the supporting detail explained?	❏	❏
9) Do you elaborate?	❏	❏
10) Do you stay on topic?	❏	❏

Conclusion:	Yes	No
11) Is this your fifth paragraph?	❏	❏
12) Do you begin with a transition?	❏	❏
13) Do you restate the thesis statement?	❏	❏
14) Do you rephrase the supporting details?	❏	❏
15) Do you stay on topic?	❏	❏

(A)

(1) Raw fish makes most people squirm, but not me. (2) Sushi is my favorite food to eat. (3) Ever since I tasted sushi for the first time, anytime a friend or relative would ask what I wanted to eat for dinner, my answer was always "Sushi, please!" (4) Sushi is healthy, quick, and an edible work of art.

(B)

(5) When I was 12 years old, my father took me to lunch at a sushi restaurant. (6) It was my first time hearing the word "sushi." (7) I'm so glad he introduced me to it, because it is a healthy meal that never weighs me down. (8) Most sushi rolls are full of different vegetables, as well as raw fish. (9) Many also include avocado, which has nutrients that are good for me. (10) Sushi always gives me a burst of energy after a long day, and I can order rolls based on my hunger; instead of having a huge plate of food that makes me too full.

(C)

(11) Another thing I like about sushi is that it's quick to prepare. (12) It doesn't take long to prepare a meal that doesn't have to be cooked, so I know I will be served promptly. (13) All of the fish and vegetables that go inside a sushi roll are neatly positioned on the sushi chef's working station. (14) He or she doesn't have to go to the kitchen for food because it is all right there. (15) Sometimes I sit at the sushi bar if I'm in a hurry. (16) That way I don't have to wait for the server to bring me the food because, at the bar, I am served by the sushi chef. (17) I can even order sushi to go or place my order over the phone if I am too busy to go out, and best-of-all, I can pick up freshly packaged sushi from my local grocery store.

(D)

(18) Just because sushi is quick doesn't mean that it's thrown together. (19) In fact, it's quite the opposite. (20) Rolls are hand-crafted by the sushi chef, each served on a fancy Oriental plate. (21) Sushi is often accompanied by flowers, or vegetables cut to resemble flowers. (22) The sushi chefs take pride in their creations, and I admire the work they do. (23) When I order sushi, I take time to appreciate the edible art that is on my plate.

(E)

(24) Nowadays, with so many food options out there, it can be especially hard to make good choices. (25) Fortunately, my favorite food is sushi. (26) Sushi is healthy, quick, and nice to look at. (27) It combines nutritious vegetables with hearty fish. (28) Sushi can be ordered quickly at a sushi restaurant. (29) It's also hand-crafted by a sushi chef, who makes sure that every piece looks like edible art. (30) My friends don't have to ask me what I want for dinner anymore, because they know the answer will always be "sushi!"

If you answered **no** to any of the questions on page 24, try to rewrite those portions of your essay that need revision on separate sheets of paper. Keep the GED Essay Scoring Rubric (below) and checklist (on page 24) in mind while you rewrite portions of your essay. Use the boxes labeled Writing Strategies and Essay Checklist as guides.

> **Prompt**: Most people have a favorite food they like to eat. Think about your favorite food. Now write to explain why you like this food.

WRITING STRATEGIES

To ensure a high score on your essay, be sure to do the following:
- Write legibly in ink so that the evaluators will be able to read your writing.
- Write on the assigned topic.
- Write your essay on the pages provided.

UNIT 1

GED Essay Scoring Rubric
This tool is designed to help readers score an essay. Two scorers read the GED essay, each giving a score between 1 and 4. The average of the two is the final score for the essay portion of the test. The score must be at least 2 to pass the test. Remember that an essay that strays from the given topic receives no score.

4. Effective	**Reader understands and easily follows the writer's expression of ideas.** • presents a clearly focused main idea that addresses the prompt • establishes a clear and logical organizational plan • is coherent with specific details and examples • exhibits varied and precise word choice
3. Adequate	**Reader understands the writer's ideas.** • uses the writing prompt to establish the main idea • uses an identifiable organizational plan • has some focus, but occasionally uneven development; incorporates some specific detail • exhibits appropriate word choice
2. Marginal	**Reader occasionally has difficulty understanding or following the writer's ideas.** • addresses the prompt, though the focus may shift • shows some evidence of an organizational plan • some development, but lacks specific detail; may be limited to a listing, repetitions, or generalizations • exhibits a narrow range of word choice
1. Inadequate	**Reader has difficulty identifying or following the writer's ideas.** • little or no success in establishing a focus • fails to organize ideas • demonstrates little or no development; usually lacks details or examples, or presents irrelevant information • exhibits weak and/or inappropriate words

ESSAY CHECKLIST

1. Read the prompt carefully.
2. Look for key terms, such as *Explain*.
3. Use the graphic organizers.
4. Begin your introduction with a hook.
5. Make your thesis statement and three supporting details clear.
6. Begin each paragraph with a transition.
7. Elaborate each supporting detail in a separate body paragraph.
8. Restate the thesis statement and supporting details in the conclusion.
9. Conclude with an insightful story, reference, or quote.

Text Division

For use with student book pp. 22–23

① Review the Skill

Text must be organized into paragraphs that focus on single ideas. This is called **text division**. Writers begin new paragraphs each time there is a change in idea, scene, time, or speaker. Text division also helps writers create the introduction, body, and conclusion of an essay.

② Refine the Skill

A simple graphic organizer, like the one provided, can help you visualize how text is organized. Note that the boxes around blocks of text describe one scene or one idea, suggest a shift in time, or relay the speech of a single character. Keep in mind that not all text follows the five-paragraph format that is outlined in Unit 1. Review the graphic organizer and the accompanying callouts. Then answer the question that follows.

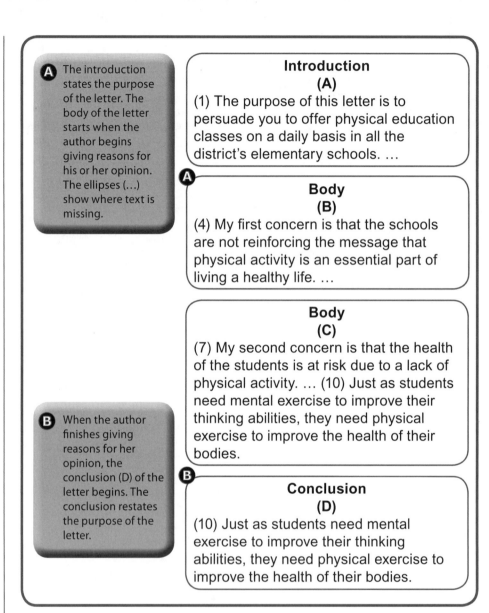

A The introduction states the purpose of the letter. The body of the letter starts when the author begins giving reasons for his or her opinion. The ellipses (…) show where text is missing.

B When the author finishes giving reasons for her opinion, the conclusion (D) of the letter begins. The conclusion restates the purpose of the letter.

Introduction (A)

(1) The purpose of this letter is to persuade you to offer physical education classes on a daily basis in all the district's elementary schools. …

A

Body (B)

(4) My first concern is that the schools are not reinforcing the message that physical activity is an essential part of living a healthy life. …

Body (C)

(7) My second concern is that the health of the students is at risk due to a lack of physical activity. … (10) Just as students need mental exercise to improve their thinking abilities, they need physical exercise to improve the health of their bodies.

B

Conclusion (D)

(10) Just as students need mental exercise to improve their thinking abilities, they need physical exercise to improve the health of their bodies.

✓ TEST-TAKING TIPS

Text is divided in the same way that a movie is divided. A movie begins by introducing the story and the characters. The body of the movie shows the characters in different scenes. Then the movie concludes with a lasting impression.

1. Sentence 1: **The purpose of this letter is to persuade you to offer physical education classes on a daily basis in all the district's elementary schools.**

   Which revision should be made to the placement of sentence 1?

   (1) move sentence 1 to the beginning of paragraph B
   (2) move sentence 1 to the end of paragraph B
   (3) move sentence 1 to the beginning of paragraph C
   (4) move sentence 1 to the end of paragraph D
   (5) no correction is necessary

UNIT 2

Directions: Choose the one best answer to each question.

Questions 2 through 4 refer to the following memorandum.

Smith Engineering Corporation
Corporate Headquarters
1212 Park Place
Brooklyn, NY 10205

MEMORANDUM

To: All Employees
From: Ken Smith, Healthcare Management
                 Coordinator
Subject: Physical requirement

(A)

(1) Beginning next month, the Healthcare Management Department requires staff to undergo yearly physicals with elected healthcare professionals. (2) In addition, the staff must set and fulfill three healthcare goals per year under the guidance of these same healthcare professionals. (3) One obvious benefit for employees of this program is that their health statuses will improve.

(B)

(4) Improved physical conditions means that staff will live longer, healthier lives. (5) Other benefits for the staff and the company are reduced healthcare costs and fewer missed work days.

(C)

(6) These benefits will increase productivity and allow everyone to save money. (7) After completion of the initial physicals, employees will submit required paperwork to this office.

(D)

(8) At the end of the calendar year, this required paperwork must be signed by the guiding healthcare professionals and re-submitted to this office. (9) Failure to fulfill this requirement will result in job-related penalties.

---

2. Sentence 3: **One obvious benefit for employees of this program is that their health statuses will improve.**

Which revision should be made to the placement of sentence 3?

(1) move sentence 3 to the beginning of paragraph A
(2) move sentence 3 to the beginning of paragraph B
(3) move sentence 3 to follow sentence 4
(4) move sentence 3 to the beginning of paragraph D
(5) remove sentence 3

3. Sentence 5: **Other benefits for the staff and the company are reduced healthcare costs and fewer missed work days.**

Which revision should be made to the placement of sentence 5?

(1) move sentence 5 to the beginning of paragraph C
(2) move sentence 5 to the beginning of paragraph A
(3) move sentence 5 to the end of paragraph A
(4) move sentence 5 to the beginning of paragraph D
(5) remove sentence 5

4. Sentence 7: **After completion of the initial physicals, employees will submit required paperwork to this office.**

Which revision should be made to the placement of sentence 7?

(1) move sentence 7 to the beginning of paragraph A
(2) move sentence 7 to the end of paragraph A
(3) move sentence 7 to the beginning of paragraph D
(4) move sentence 7 to follow sentence 2
(5) remove sentence 7

Directions: Choose the <u>one best answer</u> to each question.

<u>Questions 5 through 7</u> refer to the following information.

How to Make Barbecue Sauce

(A)

(1) How to make a mouth-watering barbecue sauce is a matter of debate at state and county fairs across the nation. (2) Fairgoers everywhere paint thick coats of red glaze on chicken and baby back ribs, hoping for the validation of a blue ribbon. (3) Here's a sauce with just the right amount of sweet, sour, and spicy for you to go head-to-head with any blue-ribbon winner.

(B)

(4) A good barbecue sauce requires time to cook so that the flavor is rich. (5) First, you need some time—about an hour or so. (6) To begin, add a little vegetable oil—about two tablespoons—to a pan at medium heat.

(C)

(7) Add a chopped Vidalia onion and three cloves of freshly pressed garlic to the oil. (8) In about five minutes, add 1 1/2 cups of ketchup; 1/2 of a cup of apple cider vinegar; 1/4 of a cup of Worcestershire sauce; 1/3 of a cup of dark brown sugar; about a tablespoon of chili powder; and Tabasco sauce to taste. (9) Stir the ingredients slowly, as you allow them to come to a low boil. (10) Finally, reduce the heat and allow the sauce to simmer for about an hour.

(D)

(11) Here's one note of warning: the neighbors will smell your sauce and your grill. (12) Meanwhile, fire up the barbecue and prepare your favorite meat or meats for grilling—the best barbecuers know that it's best to serve two or more types of meat. (13) Brush the barbecue sauce on the meat near the end of cooking.

(E)

(14) Your clean-up may be interrupted by a friendly knock (or two) at the door. (15) Don't worry, this recipe makes plenty of sauce for everyone.

---

5. Sentence 5: **First, you need some time— about an hour or so.**

   Which revision should be made to the placement of sentence 5?

   (1) move sentence 5 to the beginning of paragraph A
   (2) move sentence 5 to follow sentence 1
   (3) move sentence 5 to the end of paragraph A
   (4) move sentence 5 to the beginning of paragraph B
   (5) remove sentence 5

6. Sentence 6: **To begin, add a little vegetable oil—about two tablespoons—to a pan at medium heat.**

   Which revision should be made to the placement of sentence 6?

   (1) move sentence 6 to the beginning of paragraph C
   (2) move sentence 6 to follow sentence 15
   (3) move sentence 6 to the beginning of paragraph E
   (4) move sentence 6 to the beginning of paragraph A
   (5) remove sentence 6

7. Sentence 11: **Here's one note of warning: the neighbors will smell your sauce and your grill.**

   Which revision should be made to the placement of sentence 11?

   (1) move sentence 11 to follow sentence 9
   (2) move sentence 11 to the beginning of paragraph A
   (3) move sentence 11 to the beginning of paragraph E
   (4) move sentence 11 to the end of paragraph A
   (5) remove sentence 11

UNIT 2

Directions: Choose the one best answer to each question.

Questions 8 through 10 refer to the following information.

> **Almost Grown Up, But I Still Need My Mom**
>
> **(A)**
>
> (1) I like to think of myself as grown-up, mature, and responsible. (2) Yet every time that something goes right or wrong in my life, I call my mom. (3) I know that when I get a raise at work, my mom will cheer. (4) I also know that when a co-worker takes credit for an idea of mine, my mom will give me good advice. (5) My mom is the most important person in my life.
>
> **(B)**
>
> (6) I know that she is busy, but it feels good to have someone who is never too busy to celebrate with me. (7) I know that she shares in the happiness of my successes without any other motive than wanting to support me. (8) When I call my mom with good news, she stops what she is doing to focus on me. (9) It's wonderful to have someone whom I trust completely. (10) When I call my mom with my frustrations, angers, or failures, she never lectures me about what I should have done.
>
> **(C)**
>
> (11) She listens; she supports; and she offers advice if I ask for it. (12) However, as she listens, I often solve my own problems because she lets me talk without interrupting me. (13) My mom also has a knack for making me feel as if I'm just the person she is thinking about calling when she hears from me.
>
> **(D)**
>
> (14) I know that she has other children and plenty of friends. (15) I even suspect that she makes them feel this same way, too. (16) Her gift is that she makes everyone in her life feel special.
>
> **(E)**
>
> (17) One day, I'd like my daughter to say these same things about me. (18) I want to be someone on whom others can count and with whom others want to spend time. (19) However, for now, I still need my mom.

8. Sentence 8: **When I call my mom with good news, she stops what she is doing to focus on me.**

   Which revision should be made to the placement of sentence 8?

   (1) move sentence 8 to the beginning of paragraph A
   (2) move sentence 8 to the beginning of paragraph C
   (3) move sentence 8 to the end of paragraph A
   (4) move sentence 8 to the beginning of paragraph B
   (5) remove sentence 8

9. Sentence 10: **When I call my mom with my frustrations, angers, or failures, she never lectures me about what I should have done.**

   Which revision should be made to the placement of sentence 10?

   (1) move sentence 10 to the beginning of paragraph C
   (2) move sentence 10 to the beginning of paragraph E
   (3) move sentence 10 to the beginning of paragraph A
   (4) move sentence 10 to follow sentence 1
   (5) remove sentence 10

10. Sentence 13: **My mom also has a knack for making me feel as if I'm just the person she is thinking about calling when she hears from me.**

    Which revision should be made to the placement of sentence 13?

    (1) move sentence 13 to the end of paragraph A
    (2) move sentence 13 to the beginning of paragraph D
    (3) move sentence 13 to the beginning of paragraph E
    (4) move sentence 13 to follow sentence 19
    (5) remove sentence 13

Topic Sentence

For use with student book pp. 24–25

1 Review the Skill

The introduction of each paragraph includes a **topic sentence** that states the subject of the paragraph, offers the writer's perspective on the subject, and unifies all the sentences in the paragraph. The topic sentence is one of the first two sentences in a paragraph and connects to the thesis statement of an essay, letter, memorandum, or other piece of writing.

2 Refine the Skill

To develop an effective topic sentence, use a graphic organizer, like the one provided, to identify a common theme within the paragraph. Each paragraph should focus on one idea, scene, period of time, and/or speaker. Review the graphic organizer, paragraph, and accompanying callouts. Then answer the question that follows.

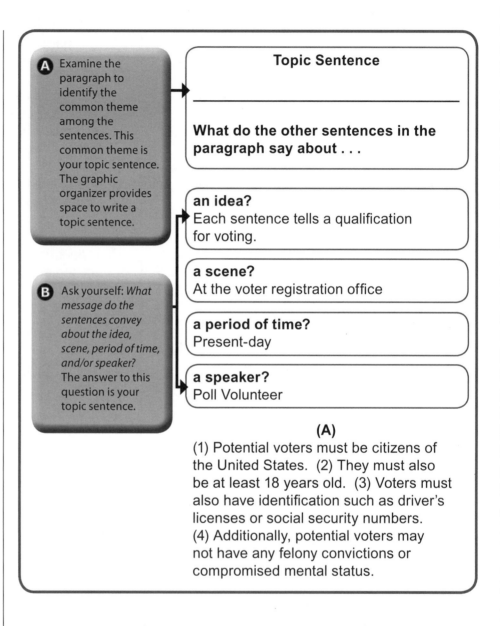

A Examine the paragraph to identify the common theme among the sentences. This common theme is your topic sentence. The graphic organizer provides space to write a topic sentence.

B Ask yourself: *What message do the sentences convey about the idea, scene, period of time, and/or speaker?* The answer to this question is your topic sentence.

Topic Sentence

_____

What do the other sentences in the paragraph say about . . .

an idea?
Each sentence tells a qualification for voting.

a scene?
At the voter registration office

a period of time?
Present-day

a speaker?
Poll Volunteer

(A)
(1) Potential voters must be citizens of the United States. (2) They must also be at least 18 years old. (3) Voters must also have identification such as driver's licenses or social security numbers. (4) Additionally, potential voters may not have any felony convictions or compromised mental status.

TEST-TAKING TIPS

A topic sentence must state what all the sentences in a paragraph have in common. Read the question carefully. Then, read the passage with each answer option to see which sentence works best.

---

1. Which sentence would be most effective if inserted at the beginning of paragraph A?

   (1) There are five simple qualifications that one must meet to vote in the United States.
   (2) Voter qualifications in the United States are strict and difficult to meet.
   (3) There should be more voting qualifications in the United States.
   (4) There should be fewer voting qualifications in the United States.
   (5) There are numerous, complex qualifications for voting in the United States.

Directions: Choose the <u>one best answer</u> to each question.

Questions 2 through 4 refer to the following information.

Answer the Telephone

(A)

(1) An important aspect of any business is the ability to communicate effectively with associates and clients. (2) _____ _____ (3) While personal computers have enabled people to respond to inquiries quickly and efficiently through e-mail, the telephone is still a businessperson's most effective marketing tool. (4) There is nothing that compares to the personal connection that associates and clients feel when they hear someone's voice at the other end of a telephone. (5) The voice offers expression, spontaneity, and humor that e-mail cannot offer.

(B)

(6) Family members are often separated for hours or days due to the demands of work, school, and play. (7) The telephone allows family members to communicate information with each other, such as what time one will arrive at home. (8) It also allows family members to share stories, ask questions, or voice concerns when they are not physically together.

(C)

(9) Emergency service providers, such as police officers, fire fighters, and doctors, are all a few telephone numbers away. (10) Distressed callers can reach these providers directly, or they can make use of the 9-1-1 system to obtain access. (11) In this sense, telephones make people safer by giving them immediate access to help.

---

2. Which sentence would be most effective if inserted as sentence 2?

   (1) Personal computers are important communication devices.
   (2) Business clients often have inquiries that need to be addressed.
   (3) Telephones enhance business opportunities.
   (4) Business associates have several means for communicating with one another.
   (5) Personal contact is not an important element of a successful business.

3. Which sentence would be most effective if inserted at the beginning of paragraph B?

   (1) Telephones enhance communication among family members.
   (2) Family members should spend more time together.
   (3) Family members maintain contact through a number of methods.
   (4) Families need to establish routines for school, work, and play.
   (5) Communication is the key to a happy family.

4. Which sentence would be most effective if inserted at the beginning of paragraph C?

   (1) The 9-1-1 system revolutionized emergency services.
   (2) Police officers, fire fighters, and doctors are heroes.
   (3) People regularly need to access emergency services.
   (4) People sometimes abuse the 9-1-1 system.
   (5) Telephones enhance access to emergency services.

Directions: Choose the one best answer to each question.

Questions 5 through 7 refer to the following excerpt.

County High School
End-of-Year Staff Meeting Notes

(A)
(1) The English department announced improved reading and writing test scores. (2) They plan to open a language lab to build on this success. (3) The Math department reported success at the national math competition. (4) They plan to purchase new textbooks for the fall. (5) The textbook review process will begin shortly. (6) The Science department described a successful science fair. (7) They hope to hire an additional staff member next year. (8) The Social Studies department reported that they have revised their curriculum and plan to offer a psychology elective next year. (9) The Fine Arts and Physical Education departments reported increased enrollment and student attendance. (10) Both departments plan to offer increased performances and events in the coming year.

(B)
(11) Parents are pleased with test score results but would like to see a renewed emphasis on project-based education. (12) Parent representatives are planning field trips to several charter schools to observe this type of curriculum. (13) They will report their findings at a later meeting.

(C)
(14) She said that suspension and expulsion rates dropped this year. (15) She hopes to continue this trend by implementing a new policy that offers students and parents alternatives to suspension for misconduct.

---

5. Which sentence would be most effective if inserted at the beginning of paragraph A?

   (1) The head of each department reported on successes of the past school year and goals for the coming year.
   (2) The Math department remains fixated on competition.
   (3) The English department does not have the budget to open a Language Lab.
   (4) The Science department plans to extend Science Fair eligibility to the middle school.
   (5) The Physical Education department needs to attract more students.

6. Which sentence would be most effective if inserted at the beginning of paragraph B?

   (1) Teachers resent having parents at staff meetings.
   (2) The community is highly involved in the workings of the school.
   (3) Several parents attended the meeting to provide community feedback regarding the school.
   (4) Charter schools will eventually replace public schools.
   (5) Parents in the community are unhappy with the school system.

7. Which sentence would be most effective if inserted at the beginning of paragraph C?

   (1) Principal Chaney plans to form a discipline committee.
   (2) Discipline issues remain a focus of school improvement.
   (3) Discipline issues increased during the past school year.
   (4) Principal Chaney reported on discipline issues.
   (5) Parents are disappointed with the school's discipline policy.

UNIT 2

Directions: Choose the one best answer to each question.

Questions 8 through 10 refer to the following information.

**Top Ten Jobs That Will
Land You in the Middle of the Pack**

(A)

(1) In 2006, the U.S. Census Bureau reported that the average household income in America was about $48,000. (2) According to CNN and its affiliate Careerbuilder.com, if a person works 40 hours per week, he or she must earn about $23 per hour to make this salary. (3) Fortunately for readers, CNN and CareerBuilder went on to investigate which jobs pay $20 per hour or better. (4) As a result of this study, researchers offered up a "top ten jobs" list. (5) It's important to note that each of these industries expects growth through the year 2016. (6) So, if you're looking to change careers or begin your first career, here's some food for thought.

(B)

(7) If your interests lie in these areas, you might consider a career as a gaming supervisor, a curator, a subway operator, an urban planner, or a loan officer. (8) Professionals in these fields earn anywhere from $41,000 to $61,000 per year.

(C)

(9) If your interests lie in these areas, you might consider a career as a respiratory therapist, a health educator, an animator, a cartographer, or an arbitrator. (10) Professionals in these fields earn anywhere from $45,000 to $58,000 per year.

---

8. Which sentence would be most effective if inserted at the beginning of paragraph A?

   (1) The U. S. Census Bureau serves an important cultural function.
   (2) How much money does one have to earn to be part of the middle class in America?
   (3) What do you want to be when you grow up?
   (4) Most Americans work more than 40 hours per week.
   (5) CNN is an important news organization.

9. Which sentence would be most effective if inserted at the beginning of paragraph B?

   (1) Gaming supervisors work in casinos.
   (2) Museum curators manage large collections of art, animals, and so on.
   (3) Loan officers help people obtain money for large purchases such as homes or boats.
   (4) Urban planners help developers allocate land for purposes.
   (5) Entertainment, development and transportation, and banking are all growing fields.

10. Which sentence would be most effective if inserted at the beginning of paragraph C?

   (1) Respiratory therapists help people who suffer from breathing problems.
   (2) Animators must be skilled in computer graphics.
   (3) Arbitrators can save people legal costs.
   (4) Healthcare, technology, and criminal justice are also growing fields.
   (5) Cartographers make maps using sophisticated equipment.

Supporting Details
For use with student book pp. 26–27

UNIT 2

1 Review the Skill

Following the topic sentence, a writer provides **supporting details**. Think of the topic sentence as a statement and the supporting details as an explanation. Supporting details may take many forms, including facts, statistics, explanations, examples, or analysis.

2 Refine the Skill

Use a graphic organizer, like the one provided, to identify the topic sentence and supporting details of a paragraph. Carefully review the graphic organizer, paragraph, and accompanying callouts. Then answer the question that follows.

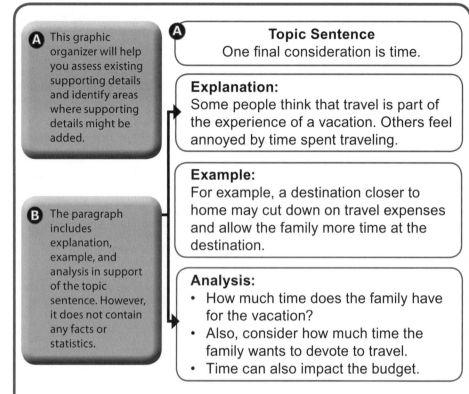

A This graphic organizer will help you assess existing supporting details and identify areas where supporting details might be added.

B The paragraph includes explanation, example, and analysis in support of the topic sentence. However, it does not contain any facts or statistics.

A
Topic Sentence
One final consideration is time.

Explanation:
Some people think that travel is part of the experience of a vacation. Others feel annoyed by time spent traveling.

Example:
For example, a destination closer to home may cut down on travel expenses and allow the family more time at the destination.

Analysis:
- How much time does the family have for the vacation?
- Also, consider how much time the family wants to devote to travel.
- Time can also impact the budget.

(D)
(1) One final consideration is time. (2) How much time does the family have for the vacation? (3) _____ (4) Be sure to consider how much time the family wants to devote to travel. (5) Some people think that travel is part of the experience of a vacation. (6) Others feel annoyed by time spent travel-ing. (7) Time can also impact the budget. (8) For example, a destination closer to home may cut down on travel expenses and allow the family more time at the destination.

✓ TEST-TAKING TIPS

A variety of supporting details create an effective paragraph. Read the passage and insert each answer option to see which supporting detail works best as sentence 3 in paragraph D.

1. Which sentence would be most effective if inserted as sentence 3?

   (1) Many families can find bargains if they vacation in off months.
   (2) Some families enjoy domestic vacations, while others enjoy foreign vacations.
   (3) It's interesting to note that about 51% of Americans did not engage in any leisure time in 2005.
   (4) Avoid the temptation to spend money on cheap souvenirs.
   (5) Repeated vacations to the same destination are often rewarding.

③ Master the Skill

Directions: Choose the <u>one best answer</u> to each question.

<u>Questions 2 through 4</u> refer to the following letter.

The Daily Article

Dear Editor:

(A)

(1) I am one of the many citizens who drive from the suburbs into the city for work every day. (2) The rising cost of gasoline has spurred me to a new awareness regarding the benefits of carpooling. (3) Ride-sharing is a transportation alternative that our city should embrace and support.

(B)

(4) The city should build Park and Ride lots at several key locations outside the city limits. (5) These lots would allow workers to meet at central locations and then ride into the city in single vehicles. (6) _____
(7) If three or more people carpool for a 20-mile round trip, each person can save $700 or more per year.

(C)

(8) The city should also add High Occupancy Vehicle (HOV) lanes to the major freeways that lead into the city. (9) Such lanes would reduce traffic congestion and reward citizens for making environmentally conscious choices. (10) _____.

(D)

(11) Americans can no longer afford the luxury of riding alone in large cars and SUVs. (12) _____ (13) However, if people are to begin making new choices, local governments must take steps to support these choices. (14) Please join me in urging local and state officials to ride together in making Arkansas a leader in green choices for a green future.

Sincerely,

Wendy Rothman

---

2. Which sentence would be most effective if inserted as sentence 6?

(1) The city needs to preserve green space rather than build parking lots.
(2) Park and Ride lots allow commuters to reduce money spent on parking fees and gasoline.
(3) Park and Ride lots may result in increased criminal activity.
(4) Police officers do not have time to survey Park and Ride lots.
(5) Park and Ride lots are great places for singles to meet potential spouses.

3. Which sentence would be most effective if inserted as sentence 10?

(1) Reducing the number of cars on the road also reduces air pollution.
(2) People who report violations of HOV lane rules are heroes.
(3) Three-lane freeways sufficiently handle the traffic flow into most cities.
(4) Two-passenger vehicles should not be allowed access to HOV lanes.
(5) Traffic congestion is not a problem in most major cities.

4. Which sentence would be most effective if inserted as sentence 12?

(1) Individual action will foster large-scale environmental change.
(2) Ride-sharing reduces the wear and tear on one's car.
(3) Carpooling will reduce stress levels and breed new friendships.
(4) Americans have a responsibility to protect the environment.
(5) These vehicles cost drivers between $7,000 and $8,000 per year.

Directions: Choose the <u>one best answer</u> to each question.

Questions 5 through 7 refer to the following information.

How to Become an Effective Public Speaker

(A)

(1) While success in any business is dependent on one's knowledge of a particular field, it is also dependent on one's ability to communicate effectively with associates and clients. (2) Follow these tips, and you, too, can become a great communicator.

(B)

(3) Don't forget the audience. (4) Think about what you want to say and how it will benefit the audience. (5) Then, make these benefits clear. (6) Also, interact with the audience. (7) _____

_____ (8) This interaction will create a connection with the audience and provide immediate feedback regarding the effectiveness of your message. (9) Additionally, encourage questions, and make sure to answer them all with direct, clear statements.

(C)

(10) Ensure that your opening and closing are memorable. (11) Use your opening to grab the attention of audience members. (12) _____

_____ (13) Let them know why they should stop everything else to listen to you. (14) Use your closing to reiterate your most important point. (15) It's the last thing the audience hears and probably the first thing they will remember.

(D)

(16) Be prepared and effective. (17) A prepared speaker is a speaker with credibility and commitment. (18) Preparation lets the audience know that they can trust what you're saying. (19) The effectiveness of a speech lies in its delivery. (20) Audiences respond to pacing, voice, eye contact, and body language. (21) Audiences also respond to images. (22) _____

_____ (23) Be conscious of these techniques and use them to convey your message.

5. Which sentence would be most effective if inserted as sentence 7?

   (1) Audiences are motivated to listen by self-interests.
   (2) Building personal connections is an ineffective speaking technique.
   (3) You can ask questions, suggest that listeners jot notes, or encourage people to talk with partners or small groups.
   (4) It is not polite to leave an audience during a speaker's presentation.
   (5) Good audience members listen actively, noting questions and personal connections.

6. Which sentence would be most effective if inserted as sentence 12?

   (1) Try using a question, story, or reference to a current event.
   (2) For example, greet the audience and state the purpose of your talk.
   (3) Provide the audience with a list of your credentials.
   (4) Tell the audience about your job.
   (5) Invite the audience to stand for the pledge of allegiance.

7. Which sentence would be most effective if inserted as sentence 22?

   (1) Divide your speech into talking points.
   (2) Speak from an outline rather than text.
   (3) Recommend suggested readings on the topic.
   (4) Make sure that your speech fits in an allotted time frame.
   (5) Utilize visuals, such as graphs, charts, and slide presentations.

Lesson 3 | **Supporting Details**

Directions: Choose the one best answer to each question.

Questions 8 through 10 refer to the following information.

Budget for Success

(A)

(1) Making and living by a budget is one of those tasks that everyone says he or she needs to do. (2) Yet, it seems that no one is really doing it. (3) However, if you follow these simple tips, you'll learn how empowering a budget can be.

(B)

(4) Get a travel size notebook with a pocket and carry it with you everywhere you go for a month. (5) Record every single item you purchase and keep the receipts. (6) _____ _____ (7) Place copies of your billing statements here, too. (8) At the end of the month, use this data to assess your spending habits.

(C)

(9) Separate needs from wants. (10) Record your necessary monthly expenses. (11) Determine monthly averages for bills that may change month to month or are not paid monthly. (12) _____ ____ (13) Then, subtract the total costs from your monthly income.

(D)

(14) Determine what you have learned. (15) Do you have money left over for savings? (16) Or, are you overspending? (17) If the latter is true, then make realistic budget cuts. (18) Now, strive to live by this budget. (19) _____ _____ (20) You'll be surprised when you learn that financial security is worth more than a month of $4.00 coffees.

8. Which sentence would be most effective if inserted as sentence 6?

(1) It is sufficient to write "$64 at grocery store."
(2) You need to know how much money you're spending on fast food, toilet paper, and laundry detergent.
(3) If you forget to write something down, just record an estimated figure for forgotten entries.
(4) Identifying spending habits is not as important as spending totals.
(5) Rather than making a budget, spend time trying to figure out how to earn extra income.

9. Which sentence would be most effective if inserted as sentence 12?

(1) Such bills may include insurance, utilities, or car registrations.
(2) You may be astounded to realize how much money you're spending on a particular item.
(3) If possible, use a spreadsheet to create a budget.
(4) Monthly expenses include housing, utilities, and food.
(5) Defining what is necessary can be a challenge for some budget makers.

10. Which sentence would be most effective if inserted as sentence 19?

(1) With extra money, you can buy movies.
(2) If you make mistakes, forgive yourself, but recommit to the budget.
(3) Make sure to use surplus funds to pay down debt.
(4) Don't forget to budget expenses for planned vacations.
(5) If you are unable to live according to a budget, join a support group.

Transitions

For use with student book pp. 28–29

UNIT 2

① Review the Skill

Transitions show the connections between ideas presented in a paragraph. Transitional words or phrases, such as *for example, for instance, then, on this occasion,* and *in this case,* are generally placed at the beginning of a sentence to indicate relationships. Check the glossary at the back of this book if you need help with unfamiliar terms.

② Refine the Skill

Use this graphic organizer and word/phrase bank to isolate two ideas, identify a connection, and choose an appropriate transitional word or phrase. Review the graphic organizer, paragraph, word bank, and accompanying callouts. Then answer the question that follows.

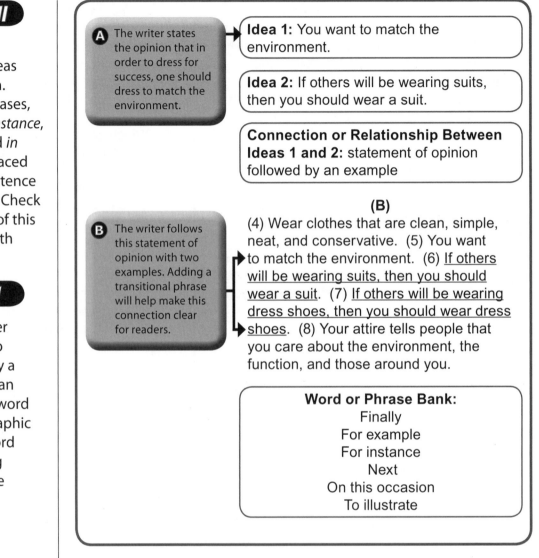

A The writer states the opinion that in order to dress for success, one should dress to match the environment.

Idea 1: You want to match the environment.

Idea 2: If others will be wearing suits, then you should wear a suit.

Connection or Relationship Between Ideas 1 and 2: statement of opinion followed by an example

(B)

B The writer follows this statement of opinion with two examples. Adding a transitional phrase will help make this connection clear for readers.

(4) Wear clothes that are clean, simple, neat, and conservative. (5) You want to match the environment. (6) If others will be wearing suits, then you should wear a suit. (7) If others will be wearing dress shoes, then you should wear dress shoes. (8) Your attire tells people that you care about the environment, the function, and those around you.

Word or Phrase Bank:
Finally
For example
For instance
Next
On this occasion
To illustrate

✓ TEST-TAKING TIPS

The transition belongs at the beginning of the second sentence in a pairing of ideas. *My dog enjoys swimming at the dog park. To illustrate, he wags his tail and gets very excited as soon as he sees the lake when we pull into the park.*

1. Sentence 6: **If others will be wearing suits, then you should wear a suit.**

   Which word or phrase would be most effective if inserted at the beginning of sentence 6?

   (1) On the other hand,
   (2) As soon as
   (3) For instance,
   (4) However,
   (5) On the contrary,

③ Master the Skill

Directions: Choose the <u>one best answer</u> to each question.

<u>Questions 2 through 4</u> refer to the following information.

Writing a Résumé

(A)

(1) A résumé has one primary function: getting you an interview. (2) You want a résumé to grab the attention of a potential employer among stacks of other résumés. (3) You want the information to cause this tired, overworked employer to think, *I've got to meet this person*. (4) Follow these tips, and set your datebook by the telephone to start scheduling interviews.

(B)

(5) A résumé has two aspects: design and content. (6) You want the design of a résumé to be clean, neat, and relevant. (7) Employers have neither the time nor the inclination to sift through information. (8) You should choose the information that is most relevant to a particular job or career field and make this information easily accessible through sequencing and text features such as bullets, bold-faced type, headings, subheadings, and so on.

(C)

(9) Regarding the content of a résumé, use descriptive, powerful language to tell potential employers about your skills and qualifications. (10) Point out how you will meet an employer's needs and the benefits of hiring you. (11) Don't try to cram a résumé with everything you've ever thought, said, or done. (12) Choose relevant information and present it in active, dynamic language in a design that is reader friendly and accessible.

---

2. Sentence 4: **Follow these tips, and set your datebook by the telephone to start scheduling interviews.**

Which correction should be made to sentence 4?

(1) insert <u>as a result</u> after <u>interviews</u>
(2) insert <u>in summary</u> after <u>and</u>
(3) remove <u>Follow these tips</u>
(4) insert <u>In short,</u> before <u>Follow</u>
(5) no correction is necessary

3. Sentence 8: **<u>You should</u> choose the information that is most relevant to a particular job or career field and make this information easily accessible through sequencing and text features such as bullets, bold-faced type, headings, subheadings, and so on.**

Which is the best way to write the underlined portion of sentence 8? If the original is the best way, choose option (1).

(1) You should
(2) Consequently, you should
(3) Farther on, you should
(4) On the whole, you should
(5) For example, you should

4. Sentence 12: **Choose relevant information and present it in active, dynamic language in a design that is reader friendly and accessible.**

Which word or phrase would be most effective if inserted at the beginning of sentence 12?

(1) Thereafter,
(2) In summary,
(3) To illustrate,
(4) In fact,
(5) Furthermore,

Directions: Choose the <u>one best answer</u> to each question.

Questions 5 through 7 refer to the following letter.

July 6, 2009

Ms. Christine Churchman
Human Resources, Aspen Architecture
2323 Colorado Drive
Aspen, CO 91223

Dear Ms. Churchman:

(A)

(1) I am responding to your listing with *Aspen Architecture* for a draftsperson. (2) I am currently an architectural student at a local technical college. (3) I am due to graduate in one semester. (4) I am interested in beginning employment in an apprentice capacity as I finish my education.

(B)

(5) Prior to beginning my education, I worked in home and commercial construction. (6) This experience has proven quite useful in drafting, as I understand the end result of my drafting work. (7) I have a portfolio of both my construction and drafting work that I would like to share with you.

(C)

(8) I am a punctual, hardworking person. (9) You are likely to find that I am the first to arrive at your office in the morning and among the last to leave. (10) My passion and my energy for this field will certainly benefit your company. (11) Please contact me for an interview.

Sincerely,

Bob Bower

5. Sentence 4: **I am interested in beginning employment in an apprentice capacity as I finish my education.**

Which correction should be made to sentence 4?

(1) insert <u>Later</u> after <u>interested</u>
(2) insert <u>For this reason,</u> before <u>I am</u>
(3) remove <u>as I finish my education</u>
(4) insert <u>formerly,</u> after <u>capacity</u>
(5) no correction is necessary

6. Sentence 7: <u>**I have**</u> **a portfolio of both my construction and drafting work that I would like to share with you.**

Which is the best way to write the underlined portion of sentence 7? If the original is the best way, choose option (1).

(1) I have
(2) Farther on, I have
(3) Formerly, I have
(4) To illustrate, I have
(5) Thereafter, I have

7. Sentence 10: **My passion and my energy for this field will certainly benefit your company.**

Which word or phrase would be most effective if inserted at the beginning of sentence 10?

(1) Finally,
(2) In addition,
(3) Consequently,
(4) Similarly,
(5) Furthermore,

UNIT 2

Directions: Choose the <u>one best answer</u> to each question.

<u>Questions 8 through 10</u> refer to the following information.

Staging an Effective Job Interview

(A)

(1) An interview really begins once you answer the telephone or respond to an email and agree to be interviewed. (2) A successful interview is dependent on preparation. (3) You need to research the company. (4) Find out what they do, how they do it, how successful they are, who their clients are, and who they hire. (5) Think about your qualifications for the job, including descriptions and anecdotes. (6) Practice answering relevant questions with a friend.

(B)

(7) Gather and make copies of relevant documents to carry to the interview. (8) Such documents might include transcripts, licenses, certifications, or a portfolio. (9) Bring a copy of your résumé as well, in case the interviewer is ill prepared. (10) Your preparation will reflect well on you.

(C)

(11) During the interview, do what your mother always taught you: be polite. (12) Learn the names of the interviewers. (13) Make eye contact. (14) Shake hands. (15) Say "Please" and "Thank you." (16) Speak clearly, loudly, and properly. (17) Use facial expression and body language to engage interest and showcase your communication skills. (18) Keep your answers to questions short and direct. (19) Make sure to follow up an interview with a telephone call or a written note.

---

8. Sentence 6: **Practice answering relevant questions with a friend.**

   Which correction should be made to sentence 6?

   (1) Insert <u>Finally,</u> before <u>Practice</u>
   (2) insert <u>subsequently</u> after <u>friend</u>
   (3) remove <u>relevant</u>
   (4) insert <u>in contrast,</u> before <u>with</u>
   (5) no correction is necessary

9. Sentence 8: **Such documents might include transcripts, licenses, certifications, or a portfolio.**

   Which word or phrase would be most effective if inserted at the beginning of sentence 8?

   (1) Likewise,
   (2) In addition,
   (3) Specifically,
   (4) In summary,
   (5) At the same time,

10. Sentences 12, 13, and 14: **Learn the names of the interviewers. Make eye contact. Shake hands.**

    Which of the following is the most effective revision of sentences 12, 13, and 14?

    (1) Learn the names of the interviewers. In summary, make eye contact and shake hands.
    (2) On the whole, learn the names of the interviewers. Make eye contact. Shake hands.
    (3) Learn the names of the interviewers. In contrast, make eye contact. Thereafter, shake hands.
    (4) In conclusion, learn the names of the interviewers. In other words, make eye contact and shake hands.
    (5) First, learn the names of interviewers. Meanwhile, make eye contact and shake hands.

Unity and Coherence
For use with student book pp. 30–31

① Review the Skill

A paragraph has **unity** and **coherence** when one sentence leads to the next and all of the sentences relate to the topic sentence. As a writer, you must make certain that you do not introduce unnecessary or irrelevant information.

② Refine the Skill

Use sentence strips, like the ones provided, to achieve unity and coherence by identifying the topic sentence and experimenting with the order of the supporting details. Eliminate any sentences that are unnecessary or irrelevant. Review the sentence strips and accompanying callouts. Then answer the question that follows.

☑ TEST-TAKING TIPS

A sentence that relates to the topic sentence but appears illogical should be repositioned rather than removed. Imagine you are writing a story about your dog. First you describe the dog's appearance, such as his floppy ears and big brown eyes. If later in the paragraph you describe his red coat, it would not fit. You should move that information to where you describe his appearance.

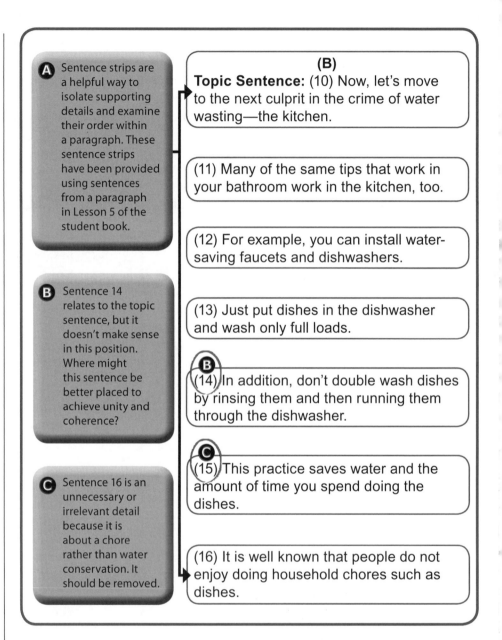

A Sentence strips are a helpful way to isolate supporting details and examine their order within a paragraph. These sentence strips have been provided using sentences from a paragraph in Lesson 5 of the student book.

B Sentence 14 relates to the topic sentence, but it doesn't make sense in this position. Where might this sentence be better placed to achieve unity and coherence?

C Sentence 16 is an unnecessary or irrelevant detail because it is about a chore rather than water conservation. It should be removed.

(B)
Topic Sentence: (10) Now, let's move to the next culprit in the crime of water wasting—the kitchen.

(11) Many of the same tips that work in your bathroom work in the kitchen, too.

(12) For example, you can install water-saving faucets and dishwashers.

(13) Just put dishes in the dishwasher and wash only full loads.

B (14) In addition, don't double wash dishes by rinsing them and then running them through the dishwasher.

C (15) This practice saves water and the amount of time you spend doing the dishes.

(16) It is well known that people do not enjoy doing household chores such as dishes.

1. Sentence 14: **In addition, don't double wash dishes by rinsing them and then running them through the dishwasher.**

   Which revision should be made to the placement of sentence 14?

   (1) move sentence 14 to follow sentence 10
   (2) move sentence 14 to the beginning of paragraph B
   (3) move sentence 14 to the end of paragraph B
   (4) move sentence 14 to follow sentence 12
   (5) remove sentence 14

Directions: Choose the one best answer to each question.

Questions 2 through 4 refer to the following information.

Rid Your Garden of Weeds

(A)

(1) Before beginning to weed your garden, make sure that conditions are ripe for success. (2) You can wet the ground yourself with a hose or watering can, or you can weed immediately following a good rain. (3) Wet ground is preferable. (4) The wet, soft ground makes it easier to uproot these garden pests.

(B)

(5) You also need the right tools. (6) If the weeds haven't sprouted, you can smother them somewhat with a thick layer of mulch. (7) Once the weeds have sprouted, you'll need a hoe to dig the weeds out by their roots. (8) You can also kill some weeds with boiling water. (9) Before purchasing gardening tools, make sure to compare prices at several of your local hardware stores.

(C)

(10) In addition, you need the right attitude toward weeds. (11) You will find that a good attitude will help you in most areas of your life. (12) Regardless of your best efforts, weeds will grow. (13) Therefore, don't worry about a few weeds in the garden, and don't try to get rid of all the weeds at once. (14) You'll be happier and more relaxed about this gardening task if you attack weeds for a few minutes every day or so.

---

2. Sentence 2: **You can wet the ground yourself with a hose or watering can, or you can weed immediately following a good rain.**

   Which revision should be made to the placement of sentence 2?

   (1) remove sentence 2
   (2) move sentence 2 to follow sentence 4
   (3) move sentence 2 to the beginning of paragraph A
   (4) move sentence 2 to the beginning of paragraph B
   (5) no correction is necessary

3. Sentence 9: **Before purchasing gardening tools, make sure to compare prices at several of your local hardware stores.**

   Which revision should be made to the placement of sentence 9?

   (1) remove sentence 9
   (2) move sentence 9 to follow sentence 5
   (3) move sentence 9 to the beginning of paragraph B
   (4) move sentence 9 to the beginning of paragraph A
   (5) no correction is necessary

4. Sentence 11: **You will find that a good attitude will help you in most areas of your life.**

   Which revision should be made to the placement of sentence 11?

   (1) move sentence 11 to the end of paragraph C
   (2) move sentence 11 to follow sentence 13
   (3) move sentence 11 to the beginning of paragraph C
   (4) remove sentence 11
   (5) no correction is necessary

Directions: Choose the one best answer to each question.

Questions 5 through 7 refer to the following information.

Community Recycling Report

(A)

(1) In general, community recycling efforts have maintained a gradual state of growth over the past few years. (2) However, national recycling efforts have declined slightly. (3) Almost 50% of the community's paper products, made up in large part of newspapers and cardboard, are being recycled. (4) In addition, nearly 50% of aluminum cans are being recycled.

(B)

(5) One exciting aspect of the community's recycling effort is the *Plant a Tree, Recycle a Tree* program. (6) In addition to weed control, mulched areas retain moisture, which conserves water. (7) Residents have been asked to tag tree trimmings or used Christmas trees with city-approved green tags, which are available at all local nurseries with the purchase of a tree of any size.
(8) Appropriately-tagged tree waste is picked up from curbsides free of charge and recycled into mulch for city parks and medians.

(C)

(9) Due to promising results, the city has plans to expand this program in the near future.
(10) Finally, the city has provided some residents with composting sheds for grass, leaves, and food waste that would ordinarily be sent to landfills. (11) The city selected one hundred volunteers to participate in this program that is now in its trial stage. (12) In return for the supplies, the volunteers agreed to provide the city with requested data.

5. Sentence 2: **However, national recycling efforts have declined slightly.**

   Which revision should be made to the placement of sentence 2?

   (1) remove sentence 2
   (2) move sentence 2 to follow sentence 3
   (3) move sentence 2 to the beginning of paragraph A
   (4) move sentence 2 to the end of paragraph A
   (5) no correction is necessary

6. Sentence 6: **In addition to weed control, mulched areas retain moisture, which conserves water.**

   Which revision should be made to the placement of sentence 6?

   (1) remove sentence 6
   (2) move sentence 6 to the beginning of paragraph B
   (3) move sentence 6 to the end of paragraph B
   (4) move sentence 6 to follow sentence 7
   (5) no correction is necessary

7. Sentence 9: **Due to promising results, the city has plans to expand this program in the near future.**

   Which revision should be made to the placement of sentence 9?

   (1) move sentence 9 to follow sentence 10
   (2) remove sentence 9
   (3) move sentence 9 to the beginning of paragraph B
   (4) move sentence 9 to follow sentence 12
   (5) no correction is necessary

Directions: Choose the one best answer to each question.

Questions 8 through 10 refer to the following information.

> **Save Energy Now**
>
> **(A)**
> (1) The trouble with asking people to save energy is that the task sounds daunting. (2) Sure, most people would like to save energy, but they're busy with work and their families. (3) In fact, many families are unable to engage in the traditional ritual of eating dinner together because their schedules are so complex. (4) What people need to get the ball rolling is a few simple tips that they can implement immediately—no money, no planning.
>
> **(B)**
> (5) For example, take a walk through your home right now. (6) You just saved energy! (7) Turn off every appliance or electrical gadget that no one is using. (8) Turn off lights, computer equipment, television sets, DVD players, and so on. (9) Guess what? (10) To make this task simpler the next time you do it, add power strips to your home so that you can turn off multiple machines with a single switch.
>
> **(C)**
> (11) While you're taking an energy tour of your home, adjust all the thermostats. (12) If it's summer, turn up the thermostat. (13) If it's winter, turn down the thermostat. (14) You don't need to be uncomfortable, but choose a temperature that is comfortable if you wear shorts or put on a sweater, respectively. (15) Also, don't forget to turn down the thermostat on the water heater to about 120 degrees. (16) You don't need to spend money heating water that's too hot for anyone to use. (17) Here's a tip for tomorrow: use the dishwasher and clothes washer only when they're full.

8. Sentence 3: **In fact, many families are unable to engage in the traditional ritual of eating dinner together because their schedules are so complex.**

   Which revision should be made to the placement of sentence 3?

   (1) move sentence 3 to the end of paragraph A
   (2) move sentence 3 to follow sentence 4
   (3) remove sentence 3
   (4) move sentence 3 to the beginning of paragraph A
   (5) no correction is necessary

9. Sentence 6: **You just saved energy!**

   Which revision should be made to the placement of sentence 6?

   (1) remove sentence 6
   (2) move sentence 6 to follow sentence 9
   (3) move sentence 6 to the end of paragraph C
   (4) move sentence 6 to the beginning of paragraph B
   (5) no correction is necessary

10. Sentence 17: **Here's a tip for tomorrow: use the dishwasher and clothes washer only when they're full.**

    Which revision should be made to the placement of sentence 17?

    (1) move sentence 17 to follow sentence 12
    (2) move sentence 17 to follow sentence 13
    (3) move sentence 17 to the beginning of paragraph C
    (4) remove sentence 17
    (5) no correction is necessary

Complete Sentences

For use with student book pp. 40–41

① Review the Skill

A **complete sentence** has a subject, a verb, a complete idea, and end punctuation: *Joe read the book*. The subject tells who or what the sentence is about, and the verb tells what the subject is doing. A complete idea can stand alone. End punctuation includes a period, exclamation point, or question mark. Check the glossary at the back of this book if you need help with unfamiliar terms.

② Refine the Skill

To identify the parts of a complete sentence, create a simple graphic organizer, like the one provided, to help you visualize how a sentence is structured. Draw a box around each of the four elements of a complete sentence. Review the organizer and the accompanying callouts. Then answer the question that follows.

☑ TEST-TAKING TIPS

Read each answer option and select the sentence that best fits in the paragraph. Try reading the paragraph several times, each time replacing sentence 7 with one of the answer options.

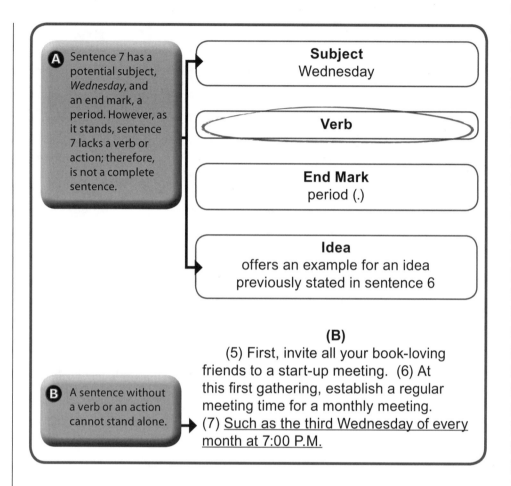

A Sentence 7 has a potential subject, *Wednesday*, and an end mark, a period. However, as it stands, sentence 7 lacks a verb or action; therefore, is not a complete sentence.

Subject
Wednesday

Verb

End Mark
period (.)

Idea
offers an example for an idea previously stated in sentence 6

B A sentence without a verb or an action cannot stand alone.

(B)
(5) First, invite all your book-loving friends to a start-up meeting. (6) At this first gathering, establish a regular meeting time for a monthly meeting. (7) <u>Such as the third Wednesday of every month at 7:00 P.M.</u>

1. Sentence 7: **Such as the third Wednesday of every month at 7:00 P.M.**

   Which revision makes sentence 7 a complete sentence?

   (1) A good time for the book club to meet is 7:00 P.M. on the third Wednesday of every month.
   (2) For instance, the third Wednesday of every month at 7:00 P.M.
   (3) The third Wednesday of every month such as 7:00 P.M.
   (4) The book club meets regularly, such as every month at 7:00 P.M.
   (5) no correction is necessary

③ Master the Skill

Directions: Choose the <u>one best answer</u> to each question.

<u>Questions 2 through 4</u> refer to the following information.

Let's Clean House

(A)

(1) While cleaning one's home is not among most people's favorite activities, the right tools do make the job less loathsome. (2) If you're in the market for a new vacuum cleaner, here are some features to consider.

(B)

(3) Categorize the surfaces of your home. (4) Do you need a vacuum that will clean primarily carpets, floors, stairways, or some combination of these surfaces? (5) Upright vacuums are good for large carpeted areas but clumsy on stairways? (6) Canisters are good for floors and stairways but clumsy in spacious areas.

(C)

(7) Understand the aspects of the machine. (8) A vacuum cleaner can be described in terms of airflow, lift, filtration, and design. (9) Airflow describes the volume of air moving through the machine. (10) Lift indicates how well a machine picks up dust. (11) Filtration keeps dust out of the machine's system. (12) Design affects airflow, lift, and filtration. (13) Also affects whether the machine is manageable.

(D)

(14) Be wary of bells and whistles. (15) Consider which attachments you really need, such as a dusting brush, crevice tool, upholstery tool, microfilter, and so on. (16) Remember that you're paying for these extras, and you will have to store them.

---

2. Sentence 5: **Upright vacuums are good for large carpeted areas but clumsy on stairways?**

Which correction should be made to sentence 5?

(1) remove <u>Upright vacuums</u>
(2) change <u>?</u> to <u>.</u>
(3) remove <u>on stairways</u>
(4) remove <u>?</u>
(5) no correction is necessary

3. Sentence 13: **Also affects whether the machine is manageable.**

Which correction should be made to sentence 13?

(1) change <u>Also</u> to <u>Design also</u>
(2) insert a comma after <u>whether</u>
(3) change <u>machine is</u> to <u>machine. Is</u>
(4) insert a comma after <u>also</u>
(5) no correction is necessary

4. Sentences 15: **Consider which attachments you really need, such as a dusting brush, crevice tool, upholstery tool, microfilter, and so on.**

Which correction should be made to sentence 15?

(1) remove <u>, such as</u>
(2) remove <u>Consider which attachments you really need</u>
(3) remove <u>and</u>
(4) remove <u>attachments</u>
(5) no correction is necessary

Directions: Choose the one best answer to each question.

Questions 5 through 7 refer to the following information.

Stargazing

(A)

(1) To the untrained eye, the starry sky may seem disorganized or chaotic. (2) However, you will remember that ancient sailors were able to navigate their ships according to the stars. (3) Suggesting an order behind the apparent chaos. (4) To begin deciphering the starry sky, it's best to begin with a simple task, such as finding the North Star.

(B)

(5) To begin, you need a compass and a dark location. (6) Bright, artificial lights will obscure your view. (7) Once you find a good location, use the compass to determine which direction is north.

(C)

(8) Now, while facing north, find the horizon, or the point where Earth and sky meet. (9) Then, move your eyes upward about one-third of the way between the horizon and the zenith, or the point directly above you. (10) Here, you should locate the North Star. (11) Which is fairly bright. (12) Note, however, that it is not the brightest star in the sky.

(D)

(13) If you've achieved success, you're ready to locate your first asterism. (14) Throughout the year, the Big Dipper rotates around the North Star. (15) Therefore, the position of the Dipper in relation to the North Star changes as it rotates. (16) Nonetheless, always aligns with the two stars that make up the far edge of the Dipper's cup.

---

5. Sentences 2 and 3: **However, you will remember that ancient sailors were able to navigate their ships according to the stars. Suggesting an order behind the apparent chaos.**

Which is the best way to write the underlined portion of sentences 2 and 3? If the original is the best way, choose option (1).

(1) stars. Suggesting
(2) stars; Suggesting
(3) stars, but suggesting
(4) stars and suggesting
(5) stars, suggesting

6. Sentences 10 and 11: **Here, you should locate the North Star. Which is fairly bright.**

Which is the best way to write the underlined portion of sentences 10 and 11? If the original is the best way, choose option (1).

(1) North Star. Which is
(2) North Star? Which is
(3) North Star. However, is
(4) North Star, which is
(5) North Star and is

7. Sentence 16: **Nonetheless, always aligns with the two stars that make up the far edge of the Dipper's cup.**

Which correction should be made to sentence 16?

(1) change Nonetheless to In contrast
(2) change Nonetheless to Such as
(3) insert the North Star before always
(4) remove the comma after Nonetheless
(5) no correction is necessary

Questions 8 through 10 refer to the following memorandum.

> **Johnson Engineering**
> **Office Management**
> **Corporate Headquarters**
> 111 First Street
> Volcano, CA 92221
> (555) 555-5555
>
> **To:** All Employees
> **From:** Tonya Smith
> **Subject:** Correspondence
>
> **(A)**
> (1) As business activity increases, we need to remind all employees of the procedure for sending correspondence. (2) All correspondence, whether it is delivered electronically or via hard copy.
>
> **(B)**
> (3) The letter of transmittal contains the following information: company contact information, a description of the attached documents, and an explanation of what we expect the recipient to do with the attached documents. (4) You may also include remarks as necessary.
>
> **(C)**
> (5) Each letter of transmittal must also by the appropriate supervisor. (6) Copies of each letter of transmittal should be filed in the appropriate project folder.
>
> **(D)**
> (7) Copies of the company letter of transmittal are available in hard copy and electronically through the manager of each department.

8. Sentence 2: **All correspondence, whether it is delivered electronically or via hard copy.**

   Which correction should be made to sentence 2?

   (1) replace the period with a question mark
   (2) remove the comma after correspondence
   (3) replace correspondence with letters
   (4) insert , requires a letter of transmittal after copy
   (5) no correction is necessary

9. Sentence 5: **Each letter of transmittal must also by the appropriate supervisor.**

   Which correction should be made to sentence 5?

   (1) remove also
   (2) insert be signed after also
   (3) remove letter of transmittal
   (4) insert signed after also
   (5) no correction is necessary

10. Sentence 7: **Copies of the company letter of transmittal are available in hard copy and electronically through the manager of each department.**

    Which correction should be made to sentence 7?

    (1) insert a comma before through
    (2) change letter of transmittal to letter and transmittal
    (3) replace and with but
    (4) replace through with although
    (5) no correction is necessary

UNIT 3

Sentence Fragments

For use with student book pp. 42–43

① **Review the Skill**

A **sentence fragment** lacks a subject, a verb, or a complete idea. To correct this problem, add a subject, verb, or end punctuation: *Joe's cold*. Insert the verb *worsened* to the end of the fragment in order to make a complete sentence: *Joe's cold worsened*. In some cases, you will need to re-attach one clause to another to create a complete idea. You can do this by adding a conjunction, semicolon, or comma between clauses: *Unfortunately for him, Joe's cold worsened*.

② **Refine the Skill**

To identify and correct a sentence fragment that has become detached from the independent clause, use a graphic organizer, like the one provided, to label the sentence parts. Review the organizer, paragraph, and accompanying callouts. Then answer the question that follows.

✎ WRITING STRATEGIES

A sentence fragment, or dependent clause, cannot stand alone as a complete sentence: *Although, a cold of this nature*. It must be attached to an independent clause: *Although, a cold of this nature may take some time to overcome.*

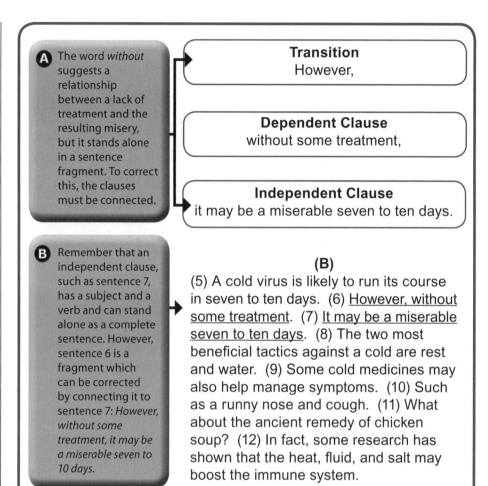

A The word *without* suggests a relationship between a lack of treatment and the resulting misery, but it stands alone in a sentence fragment. To correct this, the clauses must be connected.

Transition
However,

Dependent Clause
without some treatment,

Independent Clause
it may be a miserable seven to ten days.

B Remember that an independent clause, such as sentence 7, has a subject and a verb and can stand alone as a complete sentence. However, sentence 6 is a fragment which can be corrected by connecting it to sentence 7: *However, without some treatment, it may be a miserable seven to 10 days.*

(B)

(5) A cold virus is likely to run its course in seven to ten days. (6) <u>However, without some treatment</u>. (7) <u>It may be a miserable seven to ten days</u>. (8) The two most beneficial tactics against a cold are rest and water. (9) Some cold medicines may also help manage symptoms. (10) Such as a runny nose and cough. (11) What about the ancient remedy of chicken soup? (12) In fact, some research has shown that the heat, fluid, and salt may boost the immune system.

1. Sentence 10: **Such as a runny nose and cough**.

   Which correction should be made to sentence 10?

   (1) connect sentences 9 and 10 with a comma
   (2) change <u>Such</u> as to <u>However</u>
   (3) replace <u>and</u> with <u>but</u>
   (4) remove sentence 10
   (5) no correction is necessary

UNIT 3

Directions: Choose the <u>one best answer</u> to each question.

<u>Questions 2 through 4</u> refer to the following information.

Slap! Getting Rid of Those Pesky Mosquitoes

(A)

(1) The onset of summer brings with it visions of swimming pools, outdoor barbecues, and gardening. (2) It also brings the return of the dreaded mosquitoes. (3) In addition to creating bothersome, itchy bumps on human skin. (4) The mosquito also carries diseases such as the West Nile virus. (5) Most people would willingly and gleefully give up this sure sign of summer if they knew how to rid their yards of this pesky creature. (6) Try combining the summer pastime of gardening with pest control. (7) That's right—you can plant a garden that mosquitoes won't want to visit.

(B)

(8) Fill your garden with lemongrass and geraniums. (9) They contain citronella oils. (10) You have probably seen displays of citronella candles lining the aisles at the supermarket or hardware store during the summer months. (11) Citronella oils repel mosquitoes. (12) To double your efforts. (13) You can also place potted lemongrass or geraniums near doorways and windows to keep mosquitoes from entering your home.

(C)

(14) You can also plant chamomile, lavender, and basil. (15) In addition to repelling mosquitoes. (16) These herbs create a fragrant garden. (17) You can also use essential oils from lavender, tea trees, or lemon eucalyptus directly on the skin to repel mosquitoes.

---

2. Which of the following sentences is a fragment?

   (1) The onset of summer brings with it visions of swimming pools, outdoor barbecues, and gardening.
   (2) It also brings the return of the dreaded mosquitoes.
   (3) In addition to creating bothersome, itchy bumps on human skin.
   (4) The mosquito also carries diseases such as the West Nile virus.
   (5) Most people would willingly and gleefully give up this sure sign of summer if they knew how to rid their yards of this pesky creature.

3. Sentences 12 and 13: **To double <u>your efforts. You can</u> also place potted lemongrass or geraniums near doorways and windows to keep mosquitoes from entering your home.**

   Which is the best way to write the underlined portion of sentences 12 and 13? If the original is the best way, choose option (1).

   (1) your efforts. You can
   (2) your efforts you can
   (3) your efforts, you can
   (4) your efforts? You can
   (5) your efforts and you can

4. Sentences 15 and 16: **In addition to repelling mosquitoes. These herbs create a fragrant garden.**

   Which correction should be made to sentences 15 and 16?

   (1) swap sentences 15 and 16
   (2) change <u>mosquitoes. These</u> to <u>mosquitoes, these</u>
   (3) insert a comma after <u>addition</u>
   (4) change <u>These herbs</u> to <u>Herbs</u>
   (5) no correction is necessary

Directions: Choose the <u>one best answer</u> to each question.

<u>Questions 5 through 7</u> refer to the following excerpt.

It's Magic!

(A)

(1) If you're looking to impress your friends or colleagues at the next social gathering. (2) Try a few magic tricks. (3) They're easy to learn and fun to share. (4) You may even find that you begin receiving an increased number of invitations to parties.

(B)

(5) The first trick involves jumping paper clips. (6) To prepare for the trick. (7) Take a rectangular sheet of paper and fold it into an "S" shape without creasing the paper. (8) Use two paper clips to secure the "S" shape at each rounded bend. (9) Now, it's time for a little magic. (10) Take hold of each end of the "S" with your thumbs and forefingers. (11) Pull the two ends in opposite directions with a firm, quick tug. (12) Watch as the paper clips "jump" from the paper and join together in mid air.

(C)

(13) Keeping with the theme of jumping, let's move to the jumping coin trick. (14) Hold a quarter in the palm of each hand. (15) Make sure that the quarter in your right hand is slightly off center and nearer to your thumb than the quarter in your left hand. (16) Hold the quarters out for the audience to view. (17) Then, rotate both hands quickly inward and downward toward a table so that the backs of your hands are facing upward. (18) The quarter in your right hand will have "jumped" to the left. (19) When you lift your hands. (20) There will be two quarters under the left hand and no quarter under the right hand.

---

5. Which of the following sentences is a fragment?

   (1) If you're looking to impress your friends or colleagues at the next social gathering.
   (2) Try a few magic tricks.
   (3) They're easy to learn and fun to share.
   (4) You may even find that you begin receiving an increased number of invitations to parties.
   (5) The first trick involves jumping paper clips.

6. Sentence 6: **To prepare for the trick.**

   Which correction should be made to sentence 6?

   (1) insert a comma after <u>prepare</u>
   (2) remove <u>for</u>
   (3) replace the period after <u>trick</u> with a comma
   (4) remove sentence 6
   (5) no correction is necessary

7. Sentences 19 and 20: **When you lift <u>your hands. There will be</u> two quarters under the left hand and no quarters under the right hand.**

   Which is the best way to write the underlined portion of sentences 19 and 20? If the original is the best way, choose option (1).

   (1) your hands. There will be
   (2) your hands, there will be
   (3) there will be in your hands
   (4) your hands there will be
   (5) your hands? There will be

UNIT 3

Directions: Choose the one best answer to each question.

Questions 8 through 10 refer to the following information.

**Request for Proposal:
Project Overview**

(A)
(1) The project involves installing two emergency power generator sets to provide back-up power to serve a health care facility. (2) The generator sets provide emergency power to administrative offices, facility support buildings, and resident quarters. (3) The generator sets are replacement sets. (4) Which are being installed to serve additional loading that has been or is being connected to the system. (5) In the same location where the existing service pads are located. (6) Two replacement foundations will need to be installed. (7) To determine the current stability conditions and existing concrete depth. (8) Core soil samples are needed. (9) A report shall be developed detailing the condition and stability of the existing soil and any corrections that will need to be made to accommodate the anticipated foundation loading.

Scope of Work

(B)
(10) The scope of work for this project shall include, but not necessarily be limited to, the following items:

- site visitations
- soil samples and testing
- drilling and repair of concrete
- preparation and transmittal of reports
- recommendations for surface support

---

8. Sentences 3 and 4: **The generator sets are replacement <u>sets. Which</u> are being installed to serve additional loading that has been or is being connected to the system.**

   Which is the best way to write the underlined portion of sentences 3 and 4? If the original is the best way, choose option (1).

   (1) sets. Which
   (2) sets, which
   (3) set. Which
   (4) sets, yet they
   (5) set, but

9. Which of the following sentences is a fragment?

   (1) In the same location where the existing service pads are located.
   (2) A report shall be developed detailing the condition and stability of the existing soil and any corrections that will need to be made to accommodate the anticipated foundation loading.
   (3) Core samples are needed.
   (4) The project involves installing two emergency power generator sets to provide back-up power to serve a health care facility.
   (5) The generator sets are replacement sets.

10. Which of the following sentences is <u>not</u> a fragment?

    (1) Emergency power to administrative offices.
    (2) To determine current stability conditions and existing concrete depth.
    (3) The scope of this work shall include.
    (4) Preparation and transmittal of reports.
    (5) Two replacement foundations are being installed.

LESSON 3 FOCUS ON...

S imple Sentences

For use with student book pp. 44–45

① Review the Skill

A **simple sentence** is one type of complete sentence. It contains a subject, a verb, and a single idea. Writers may use simple sentences to emphasize particular points. However, too many simple sentences in a passage can make the writing choppy and repetitive. Try to use them sparingly. Check the glossary at the back of this book if you need help with unfamiliar terms.

② Refine the Skill

To practice writing and identifying simple sentences, use a series of word banks like the ones provided. Choose an entry from each word bank to form a simple sentence. Review the word banks, paragraph, and accompanying callouts. Then answer the question that follows.

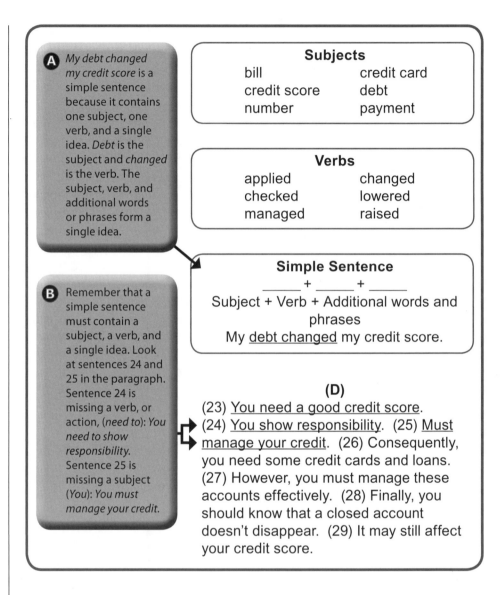

A My debt changed my credit score is a simple sentence because it contains one subject, one verb, and a single idea. Debt is the subject and changed is the verb. The subject, verb, and additional words or phrases form a single idea.

Subjects	
bill	credit card
credit score	debt
number	payment

Verbs	
applied	changed
checked	lowered
managed	raised

Simple Sentence

_____ + _____ + _____

Subject + Verb + Additional words and phrases

My <u>debt changed</u> my credit score.

B Remember that a simple sentence must contain a subject, a verb, and a single idea. Look at sentences 24 and 25 in the paragraph. Sentence 24 is missing a verb, or action, (need to): You need to show responsibility. Sentence 25 is missing a subject (You): You must manage your credit.

(D)

(23) <u>You need a good credit score</u>. (24) <u>You show responsibility</u>. (25) <u>Must manage your credit</u>. (26) Consequently, you need some credit cards and loans. (27) However, you must manage these accounts effectively. (28) Finally, you should know that a closed account doesn't disappear. (29) It may still affect your credit score.

✎ WRITING STRATEGIES

Simple sentences tend to be short sentences. After writing, identify the parts of each sentence to ensure that you have not left out the subject or the verb.

1. Sentence 23: **You need a good credit score.**

    The underlined portion of this simple sentence contains which of the following?

    (1) a verb
    (2) one idea
    (3) a subject
    (4) an end mark
    (5) a complete idea

Directions: Choose the one best answer to each question.

Questions 2 through 4 refer to the following memorandum.

Energetic Electrical Design
Office Management
Corporate Headquarters
444 South Dixie Drive
Natchez, MS 34593

To: All Engineers
From: Ray Burnice, Office Manager
Subject: Responding to Client Comments

(A)
(1) Effective immediately, we will implement a new procedure for responding to client comments on electrical design drawings. (2) Each engineer will be provided with an electronic "Review Comments" form. (3) This form will accompany all revised drawings when such drawings are returned to the clients for review.

(B)
(4) The form contains four columns. (5) In the first column, you will note the drawing number, or you will note the page number. (6) In the second column, you will note the client comment number, and you will note whether you concur with the comment. (7) In the third column, you will transcribe the actual client comment, or you will provide an accurate summary. (8) In the fourth column, you will write your response to the comment, and you will record the action to be taken.

(C)
(9) File a copy of this form in the project folder. (10) Please see your supervisor to address any questions or concerns.

---

2. Sentence 2: **Each engineer will be provided with an electronic "Review Comments" form.**

   Which is the best way to describe sentence 2?

   (1) a fragment
   (2) a simple sentence
   (3) a question
   (4) an incomplete idea
   (5) an exclamation

3. Which of the following sentences is a simple sentence?

   (1) This form will accompany all revised drawings when such drawings are returned to the clients for review.
   (2) The form contains four columns.
   (3) In the first column, you will note the drawing number, or you will note the page number.
   (4) In the second column, you will note the client comment number, and you will note whether you concur with the comment.
   (5) In the fourth column, you will write your response to the comment, and you will record the action to be taken.

4. Sentence 9: **File a copy of this form in the project folder.**

   Which of the following words from sentence 9 is the verb?

   (1) File
   (2) folder
   (3) this
   (4) form
   (5) project

Directions: Choose the <u>one best answer</u> to each question.

<u>Questions 5 through 7</u> refer to the following information.

Spring Cleaning the Medicine Cabinet

(A)

(1) After being shut in for the better part of winter, spring brings with it the opportunity to clean out, wipe down, and start anew. (2) One place that you don't want to forget during an annual spring cleaning of your home is the medicine cabinet.

(B)

(3) You should discard items that have expired. (4) In general, most medications expire in about a year's time; this expiration range applies to prescription medication. (5) In other words, if the medication was present during last year's spring cleaning, it's time to get rid of it now. (6) In addition, throw out any items that have labels that cannot be read, and throw out items with bottles that are broken. (7) Keeping such items may result in incorrect dosages, or such items may be mistakenly identified.

(C)

(8) You should also discard medications that no one in the family is currently taking. (9) Although high prescription costs make the idea of keeping extra medication for self-dosing at a later date appealing, it's a dangerous practice. (10) The convenience is not worth the life of a family member.

(D)

(11) Although it is tempting to discard medication by simply throwing it away or dumping it down the drain, this practice is dangerous because sewers and land fills may contaminate the water supply. (12) In general, you should mash pills, pull apart capsules, and mix liquids with cat litter or flour. (13) Then, seal these mixtures in containers such as coffee cans to be discarded.

---

5. Which of the following sentences is a simple sentence?

   (1) You should discard items that have expired.
   (2) In general, most medications expire in about a year's time; this expiration range applies to prescription medication.
   (3) In other words, if the medication was present during last year's spring cleaning, it's time to get rid of it now.
   (4) In addition, throw out any items that have labels that cannot be read, and throw out items with bottles that are broken.
   (5) Keeping such items may result in incorrect dosages, or such items may be mistakenly identified.

6. Which of the following sentences is <u>not</u> a simple sentence?

   (1) You should also discard unused medications.
   (2) It's a dangerous practice.
   (3) Such activities may result in a contaminated water supply.
   (4) In general, you should mash pills, pull apart capsules, and mix liquids with cat litter or flour.
   (5) Seal these mixtures in containers.

7. Sentence 10: **The convenience is not worth the life of a family member.**

   Which of the following words from sentence 10 is the subject?

   (1) is
   (2) family member
   (3) worth
   (4) life
   (5) convenience

UNIT 3

Directions: Choose the <u>one best answer</u> to each question.

<u>Questions 8 through 10</u> refer to the following information.

Soccer for All

(A)
(1) Soccer is a great sport for young athletes. (2) It involves physical skill and teamwork. (3) Also, the rules don't have to be modified significantly for young players; they are easy to understand. (4) With the increasing popularity of soccer in the United States, it's likely that your community has a local recreational league. (5) Consider registering your children or nieces or nephews. (6) Most leagues accept children as young as three or four years old. (7) You might also consider coaching a team or volunteering as a referee. (8) There's nothing like a Saturday morning soccer team to bring families and communities together.

(B)
(9) In general, two teams with eleven players each meet on a field with a goal at each end. (10) Players clad in shin guards and cleats move the ball toward the opposing team's goal with any part of their bodies except the arms or hands. (11) Players score points by kicking the ball into the opposing team's goal, past the goalie or goal keeper.

(C)
(12) At the recreational level, players alternate among three positions: fullback, midfielder or halfback, and forward or striker. (13) Forwards are responsible for scoring. (14) Fullbacks are responsible for defense. (15) Midfielders assist with both offense and defense.

---

8. Sentence 2: **It involves physical skill and teamwork.**

   Which of the following words from sentence 2 is the subject?

   (1) It
   (2) involves
   (3) physical
   (4) skill
   (5) teamwork

9. Sentence 14: **Fullbacks are responsible for defense.**

   Which of the following words from sentence 14 is the verb?

   (1) for
   (2) Fullbacks
   (3) responsible
   (4) are
   (5) defense

10. Which of the following sentences is a simple sentence?

    (1) Also, the rules don't have to be modified significantly for young players; they are easy to understand.
    (2) Soccer is a great sport for young athletes.
    (3) With the increasing popularity of soccer in the United States, it's likely that your community has a local recreational league.
    (4) Players score points by kicking the ball into the opposing team's goal, past the goalie or goal keeper.
    (5) At the recreational level, players alternate among three positions: fullback, midfielder or halfback, and forward or striker.

Compound Sentences

For use with student book pp. 46–47

① Review the Skill

A **compound sentence** is a sentence with two independent clauses that are connected by a coordinating conjunction, such as *and*, *but*, and *or*; a conjunctive adverb, such as *however* and *finally*; or a semicolon. These sentences create a relationship between the ideas expressed in two independent clauses: *Tigers are strong, beautiful creatures, and their numbers are decreasing.* Check the glossary at the back of this book if you need help with unfamiliar terms.

② Refine the Skill

To identify a compound sentence, use a graphic organizer, like the one provided, to label the clauses, relationship between the clauses, and the compound structure (best way to combine the two clauses). Review the organizer, paragraph, and accompanying callouts. Then answer the question that follows.

✎ WRITING STRATEGIES

To show contrast, the writer might also choose to use a coordinating conjunction, such as *but* or *yet*. In this case, the conjunction should come after a comma.

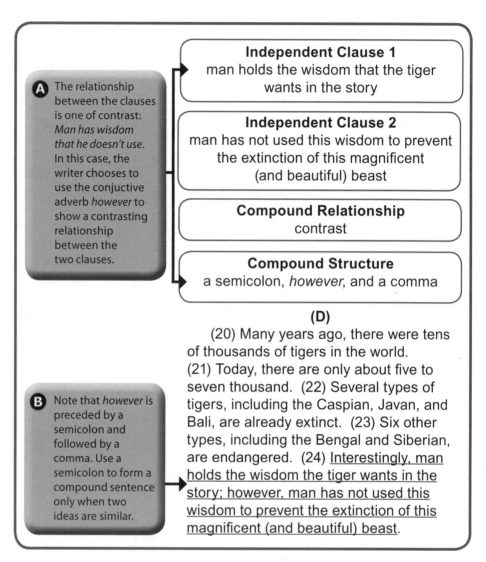

A The relationship between the clauses is one of contrast: *Man has wisdom that he doesn't use.* In this case, the writer chooses to use the conjuctive adverb *however* to show a contrasting relationship between the two clauses.

Independent Clause 1
man holds the wisdom that the tiger wants in the story

Independent Clause 2
man has not used this wisdom to prevent the extinction of this magnificent (and beautiful) beast

Compound Relationship
contrast

Compound Structure
a semicolon, *however*, and a comma

(D)
(20) Many years ago, there were tens of thousands of tigers in the world. (21) Today, there are only about five to seven thousand. (22) Several types of tigers, including the Caspian, Javan, and Bali, are already extinct. (23) Six other types, including the Bengal and Siberian, are endangered. (24) Interestingly, man holds the wisdom the tiger wants in the story; however, man has not used this wisdom to prevent the extinction of this magnificent (and beautiful) beast.

B Note that *however* is preceded by a semicolon and followed by a comma. Use a semicolon to form a compound sentence only when two ideas are similar.

1. Sentence 24: **Interestingly, man holds the wisdom the tiger wants in the story; however, man has not used this wisdom to prevent the extinction of this magnificent (and beautiful) beast.**

   Which is another way to write the underlined portion of this sentence and maintain the compound structure?

   (1) ; finally,
   (2) ; similarly
   (3) , yet
   (4) , and
   (5) ;

③ Master the Skill

<u>Directions</u>: Choose the <u>one best answer</u> to each question.

<u>Questions 2 through 4</u> refer to the following information.

Holiday Traditions

(A)

(1) Whether you celebrate Christmas, Hanukkah, or Kwanzaa, the holiday season revolves around traditions that bring families and friends together. (2) Sometimes the joy of a holiday is found in maintaining these traditions; sometimes the joy of a holiday is found in developing new traditions. (3) A gratitude tray is an activity that will please the old and young alike.

(B)

(4) Find a special serving tray, or make one of your own. (5) You can purchase something unique at a garage sale or thrift store. (6) You can also use images cut from magazines, photographs, and glue to make a collage of family symbols or memories on a plain tray.

(C)

(7) Next, gather the following items for the tray: a bone for a hound; hay for a horse; a coat for a traveler; berries for someone who has been caged; bread crumbs for a bird; and something sweet for a child. (8) Arrange these items on the tray.

(D)

(9) Finally, choose a special night when family and friends are gathered to take the tray to the curb or sidewalk outside your home. (10) Ask the participants to gather around the tray. (11) Invite each person to state something for which he or she is grateful in life and something he or she would like to share with others. (12) The following morning, check the tray. (13) You may find the items still in place, or you may find that someone in need has helped himself or herself to your gifts.

---

2. Sentence 2: **Sometimes the joy of a holiday is found in maintaining these traditions; sometimes the joy of a holiday is found in developing new traditions.**

   Which strategy did the writer use to form this compound sentence?

   (1) a coordinating conjunction
   (2) simple sentences
   (3) a conjunctive adverb
   (4) a semicolon
   (5) fragments

3. Sentence 4: **Find a special serving tray, or make one of your own.**

   Which strategy did the writer use to form this compound sentence?

   (1) a coordinating conjunction
   (2) simple sentences
   (3) a conjunctive adverb
   (4) a semicolon
   (5) fragments

4. Which of the following sentences is a compound sentence?

   (1) Finally, choose a special night when family and friends are gathered to take the tray to the curb or sidewalk outside your home.
   (2) Ask the participants to gather around the tray.
   (3) Invite each person to state something for which he or she is grateful in life.
   (4) The following morning, check the tray.
   (5) You may find the items still in place, or you may find that someone in need has helped himself or herself to your gifts.

Directions: Choose the <u>one best answer</u> to each question.

<u>Questions 5 through 7</u> refer to the following information.

It's Allergy Season

(A)

(1) If you suffer from allergies, you may find yourself making weekly visits to a doctor's office for an allergy shot. (2) Working out of St. Mary's Hospital in London, England, in 1911, Leonard Noon and John Freeman experimented with the first allergy shots. (3) These researchers extracted pollen from grass, and they used these extracts to treat people who suffered from hay fever. (4) Noon and Freeman administered low doses of the extract through shots. (5) Patients received shots every three to four days. (6) Noon and Freeman gradually increased the extract dosage over a series of shots consequently they found that they were able to relieve hay fever symptoms with these first experiments in immunotherapy.

(B)

(7) Noon and Freeman's pioneering work still helps many allergy sufferers there are those who cannot be helped because the risks are too great. (8) For example, people who suffer from allergies to eggs or peanuts are not able to take allergy shots. (9) Researchers, such as Andy Saxon, are trying to develop fused proteins that will eliminate allergic responses in the immune system.

---

5. Sentence 3: **These researchers extracted pollen from grass, and they used these extracts to treat people who suffered from hay fever.**

   Which strategy did the writer use to form this compound sentence?

   (1) a semicolon
   (2) a coordinating conjunction
   (3) a conjunctive adverb
   (4) simple sentences
   (5) fragments

6. Sentence 6: **Noon and Freeman gradually increased the extract dosage over a series of <u>shots consequently they</u> found that they were able to relieve hay fever symptoms with these first experiments in immunotherapy.**

   Which is the best way to write the underlined portion of sentence 6? If the original is the best way, choose option (1).

   (1) shots consequently they
   (2) shots. They
   (3) shots, consequently they
   (4) shots; consequently, they
   (5) shots? Consequently, they

7. Sentence 7: **Noon and Freeman's pioneering work still helps many allergy sufferers there are those who cannot be helped because the risks are too great.**

   Which correction should be made to sentence 7?

   (1) insert <u>and</u> after <u>sufferers</u>
   (2) remove <u>pioneering</u>
   (3) insert <u>, but</u> after <u>sufferers</u>
   (4) replace <u>because</u> with <u>however</u>
   (5) insert a semicolon after <u>helps</u>

Questions 8 through 10 refer to the following letter.

Savannah News Gazette

Dear Editor,

(A)

(1) With the presidential election approaching in November, there has been a lot of political analysis on television. (2) Experts in many fields are engaging in unlimited speculation regarding the effect on the election of a particular group's votes. (3) Candidates hire advisors to help them capture the votes of women they also hire advisors to help them capture the votes of particular religious or cultural groups. (4) Yet, it seems that each time an election comes and goes, only a fraction of potential voters actually make their way to the polls.

(B)

(5) Perhaps political analysts should cease speculation about the effect of votes that will never be cast instead they should focus their attention on motivating people—regardless of gender, beliefs, or skin color—to vote. (6) It is embarrassing to live in a country that speaks loudly and forcefully about the benefits of democracy when the majority of citizens do not exercise the most basic right in a democracy.

(C)

(7) I will make my way to the polls in November and I will cast my vote. (8) However, I fear that I will again find myself in the minority of Americans who actually vote.

---

8. Sentence 3: **Candidates hire advisors to help them capture the votes of women they also hire advisors to help them capture the votes of particular religious or cultural groups.**

   Which correction should be made to sentence 3?

   (1) insert a semicolon after <u>women</u>
   (2) remove <u>particular</u>
   (3) replace <u>they also</u> with <u>however they</u>
   (4) insert <u>but</u> after <u>women</u>
   (5) no correction is necessary

9. Sentence 5: **Perhaps political analysts should cease speculation about the effect of votes that will never be <u>cast instead they</u> should focus their attention on motivating people—regardless of gender, beliefs, or skin color—to vote.**

   Which is the best way to write the underlined portion of sentence 5? If the original is the best way, choose option (1).

   (1) cast instead they
   (2) cast and instead, they
   (3) cast; instead, they
   (4) cast. Instead they
   (5) cast? Instead they

10. Sentence 7: **I will make my way to the polls in <u>November and I</u> will cast my vote.**

    Which is the best way to write the underlined portion of sentence 7? If the original is the best way, choose option (1).

    (1) November and I
    (2) November; and, I
    (3) November? And I
    (4) November. And I
    (5) November, and I

Complex Sentences

For use with student book pp. 48–49

① Review the Skill

A **complex sentence** contains one independent clause and one dependent clause connected by a subordinating conjunction, such as *before*, *after*, *since*, or *if*: *Before you begin, make sure you have the necessary supplies*. A dependent clause 'depends' on an independent clause, and an independent clause can stand alone. Check the glossary at the back of this book if you need help with unfamiliar terms.

② Refine the Skill

To identify a complex sentence, use a graphic organizer, like the one provided, to label the clauses, the relationship between the clauses, and the subordinating conjunction.

☑ TEST-TAKING TIPS

A subordinating conjunction begins a dependent clause. In the case of question 1, *when* and *the* are the two words that begin the clauses. First, determine which clause cannot stand alone as a complete sentence, then identify which word is the subordinating conjunction.

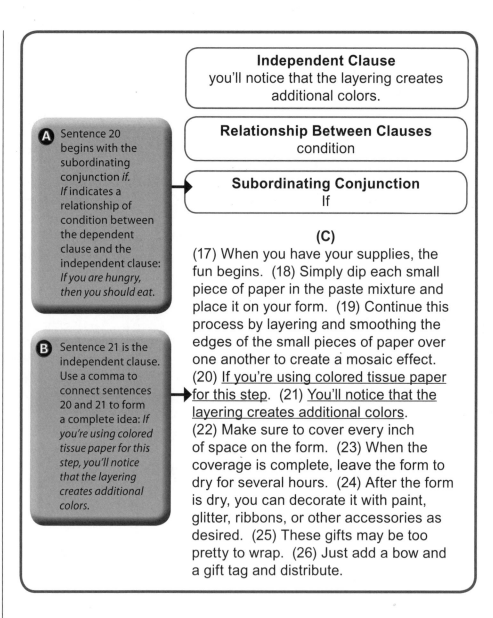

Independent Clause
you'll notice that the layering creates additional colors.

A Sentence 20 begins with the subordinating conjunction *if*. *If* indicates a relationship of condition between the dependent clause and the independent clause: *If you are hungry, then you should eat.*

Relationship Between Clauses
condition

Subordinating Conjunction
If

B Sentence 21 is the independent clause. Use a comma to connect sentences 20 and 21 to form a complete idea: *If you're using colored tissue paper for this step, you'll notice that the layering creates additional colors.*

(C)
(17) When you have your supplies, the fun begins. (18) Simply dip each small piece of paper in the paste mixture and place it on your form. (19) Continue this process by layering and smoothing the edges of the small pieces of paper over one another to create a mosaic effect. (20) <u>If you're using colored tissue paper for this step</u>. (21) <u>You'll notice that the layering creates additional colors</u>. (22) Make sure to cover every inch of space on the form. (23) When the coverage is complete, leave the form to dry for several hours. (24) After the form is dry, you can decorate it with paint, glitter, ribbons, or other accessories as desired. (25) These gifts may be too pretty to wrap. (26) Just add a bow and a gift tag and distribute.

1. Sentence 17: **When you have your supplies, the fun begins.**

    Which word in sentence 17 is a subordinating conjunction that shows a time relationship?

    (1) fun
    (2) begins
    (3) your
    (4) when
    (5) the

UNIT 3

Directions: Choose the <u>one best answer</u> to each question.

<u>Questions 2 through 4</u> refer to the following information.

Art Lesson

(A)

(1) Wandering the halls of any museum can be intimidating. (2) One wonders how artists such as Picasso and Van Gogh began their art careers. (3) Did they begin with doodles in the margins of school tablets? (4) How did they eventually learn to express ideas using lines, shapes, and color? (5) While art critics and students wallow in possible answers to these questions, you may want to turn your attention to the less difficult task of drawing a simple farm animal, such as the distinguished pig.

(B)

(6) Before you can begin drawing, you need to gather your supplies: a sheet of paper, a pencil, and some crayons or markers. (7) Draw a large circle on the paper. (8) Add two pointy ovals at the top of the large circle that will serve as ears. (9) Next, draw another oval just below the center of the circle that will serve as the nose. (10) Add two small circles that will serve as eyes, and add two more small circles that will serve as nostrils. (11) Draw two W shapes at the bottom of the large circle that will serve as feet. (12) Then, add a curly line that will serve as the tail.

(C)

(13) After your drawing is complete. (14) Add color to your pig. (15) You can use realistic colors, such as pinks and browns, or you can use imaginary pig colors, such as oranges and yellows. (16) You can also add scenery and a food trough to complete your masterpiece.

---

2. Which of the following sentences is a complex sentence?

   (1) Wandering the halls of any museum can be intimidating.
   (2) One wonders how artists such as Picasso and Van Gogh began their art careers.
   (3) Did they begin with doodles in the margins of school tablets?
   (4) How did they eventually learn to express ideas using lines, shapes, and color?
   (5) While art critics and students wallow in possible answers to these questions, you may want to turn your attention to the less difficult task of drawing a simple farm animal, such as the distinguished pig.

3. Sentence 6: **Before you can begin drawing, you need to gather your supplies: a sheet of paper, a pencil, and some crayons or markers.**

   Which part of sentence 6 is the dependent clause?

   (1) Before you can begin drawing
   (2) you need to gather your supplies
   (3) a sheet of paper, a pencil, and some crayons or markers
   (4) you can begin drawing
   (5) gather your supplies

4. Sentences 13 and 14: **After your drawing is <u>complete. Add</u> color to your pig.**

   Which is the best way to write the underlined portion of sentences 13 and 14? If the original is the best way, choose option (1).

   (1) complete. Add
   (2) complete; add
   (3) complete add
   (4) complete, add
   (5) complete? Add

Directions: Choose the <u>one best answer</u> to each question.

<u>Questions 5 through 7</u> refer to the following information.

Why Do Leaves Change Color in the Fall?

(A)
(1) In the fall, people enjoy gazing at the trees as the leaves shift from summer green to varying shades of yellow, orange, and red. (2) These changes inspire poets to reflect on the process of aging and death. (3) However, scientists know that these leaves are finally getting the opportunity to show their true colors.

(B)
(4) Plants make their own nutrients as they use sunlight to transform water from the Earth and carbon dioxide from the air into food. (5) A green chemical called chlorophyll helps plants with this food-making process. (6) The green color of spring and summer leaves comes from chlorophyll.

(C)
(7) Because the days grow shorter in the fall. (8) There is less sunlight. (9) Since plants know that there will not be enough water or sunlight during the winter months to continue the food-making process, they stop producing food. (10) The chlorophyll disappears, and other chemicals that have been inside the leaves begin to show. (11) Consequently, the leaves change from green to orange, yellow, or red.

---

5. Sentence 1: **In the fall, people enjoy gazing at the trees as the leaves shift from summer green to varying shades of yellow, orange, and red.**

   Which part of sentence 1 is an independent clause?

   (1) people enjoy gazing at the trees as the leaves shift from summer green to varying shades of yellow, orange, and red
   (2) as the leaves shift from summer green to varying shades of yellow, orange, and red
   (3) gazing at the trees as the leaves shift
   (4) In the fall
   (5) varying shades of yellow, orange, and red

6. Which of the following sentences is a complex sentence?

   (1) These changes inspire poets to reflect on the process of aging and death.
   (2) A green chemical called chlorophyll helps plants with this food-making process.
   (3) The green color of spring and summer leaves comes from chlorophyll.
   (4) Since plants know that there will not be enough water or sunlight during the winter months to continue the food-making process, they stop producing food.
   (5) Consequently, the leaves change from green to orange, yellow, or red.

7. Sentences 7 and 8: **Because the days grow shorter in the fall. There is less sunlight.**

   Which correction should be made to sentences 7 and 8?

   (1) remove <u>Because</u>
   (2) replace <u>less</u> with <u>more</u>
   (3) insert a semicolon after <u>fall</u>
   (4) change <u>fall. There</u> to <u>fall, there</u>
   (5) no correction is necessary

Directions: Choose the <u>one best answer</u> to each question.

<u>Questions 8 through 10</u> refer to the following information.

Science Lab Instructions

(A)

(1) Use this simple experiment to find the fall colors hiding inside green leaves.

Prepare the Experiment
(B)

(2) First, gather green leaves from a tree. (3) Make sure that all the leaves come from the same type of tree. (4) Use a sharp knife to chop the leaves into small pieces so that they resemble the fresh-chopped herbs that you might use for cooking. (5) Then, place the leaves in a glass jar, and soak them with alcohol. (6) Seal the jar with a lid. (7) Next, sit the jar in a shallow bath of hot water.

Conduct the Experiment
(C)

(8) Let the jar sit for 30 minutes or more. (9) Meanwhile, use coffee filters to cut rectangular strips of paper. (10) When the alcohol in the jar shows a dark color, remove the jar from the water bath and take off the lid. (11) Place only the tip of a strip of filter paper in the alcohol and tape the other end to the jar. (12) The colored alcohol will soak into the filter paper.

Learn the Results
(D)

(13) When the alcohol evaporates, you will see the colors that were contained inside the leaves. (14) You will see green, but you should also see yellow, orange, or red. (15) These additional colors tell you what color the leaves from this type of tree turn in the fall.

---

8. Sentence 4: **Use a sharp knife to chop the leaves into small pieces so that they resemble the fresh-chopped herbs that you might use for cooking.**

   Which part of sentence 4 is the dependent clause?

   (1) Use a sharp knife to chop the leaves into small pieces
   (2) chop the leaves into small pieces
   (3) so that they resemble the fresh-chopped herbs that you might use for cooking
   (4) you might use for cooking
   (5) they resemble the fresh-chopped herbs

9. Sentence 10: **When the alcohol in the jar shows a dark color, remove the jar from the water bath and take off the lid.**

   Which of the following words from sentence 10 is a subordinating conjunction?

   (1) remove
   (2) when
   (3) in
   (4) from
   (5) shows

10. Which of the following sentences is a complex sentence?

    (1) First, gather green leaves from a tree.
    (2) Then, place the leaves in a glass jar, and soak them with alcohol.
    (3) Meanwhile, use coffee filters to cut rectangular strips of paper.
    (4) The colored alcohol will soak into the filter paper.
    (5) When the alcohol evaporates, you will see the colors that were contained inside the leaves.

Combining Sentences

For use with student book pp. 50–51

① Review the Skill

Combining sentences is a method used to avoid repeating words and phrases. Use conjunctions, such as *and*, *but*, *or*, *because*, *when*, *if*, and *although*; conjunctive adverbs, such as *however* and *consequently*; and semicolons to combine shorter sentences into compound or complex sentences: *Because emergencies happen, plan an escape route and meeting place.* You can also insert commas to create a series: *I like basketball. I like baseball. I like soccer. = I like basketball, baseball, and soccer.*

② Refine the Skill

Mark the text by eliminating repeated words or phrases. Then, consider which strategy will help you combine the remaining ideas into a single sentence without changing the meaning of the original sentences. Review the examples. Then answer the question that follows.

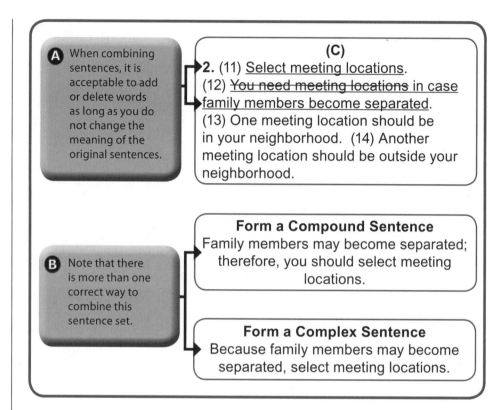

A When combining sentences, it is acceptable to add or delete words as long as you do not change the meaning of the original sentences.

(C)

2. (11) <u>Select meeting locations</u>.
(12) ~~You need meeting locations~~ <u>in case family members become separated</u>.
(13) One meeting location should be in your neighborhood. (14) Another meeting location should be outside your neighborhood.

B Note that there is more than one correct way to combine this sentence set.

Form a Compound Sentence
Family members may become separated; therefore, you should select meeting locations.

Form a Complex Sentence
Because family members may become separated, select meeting locations.

---

1. Sentences 13 and 14: **One meeting location should be in your neighborhood. Another meeting location should be outside your neighborhood.**

   Which of the following is the most effective revision of sentences 13 and 14?

   (1) One meeting location and another meeting location should be inside and outside your neighborhood.
   (2) Inside your neighborhood one meeting location should be. Outside your neighborhood another meeting location should be.
   (3) One meeting location should be in your neighborhood, and another one should be outside your neighborhood.
   (4) One meeting location in your neighborhood. One meeting location outside your neighborhood.
   (5) Meeting locations should be inside the neighborhood for family members outside of the neighborhood.

UNIT 3

Directions: Choose the <u>one best answer</u> to each question.

<u>Questions 2 and 3</u> refer to the following information.

Mapmaking

(A)

(1) In the age of Global Positioning System navigators that now come as standard features in many cars and on many cell phones, it may seem that the ability to read and understand a map is a skill of the past. (2) However, maps are still valuable tools in helping people visualize large land masses and helping people understand the relationships among land forms, bodies of water, climate, and human activity. (3) In addition, as many of you well know, a paper map still works even when technology fails. (4) You can encourage the young people in your life to familiarize themselves with the complexity and beauty of maps through a simple mapmaking activity that will feed the mind and the body.

(B)

(5) Use your favorite cookie recipe to prepare some dough. (6) Leave out of the dough any bulk ingredients such as chocolate chips, nuts, and so on. (7) Set bulk ingredients aside in small bowls. (8) In addition, gather blue-colored sugar, green frosting, gum drops, and any other treats that you might want to use as landforms, monuments, or bodies of water.

(C)

(9) Using a map of your state as a reference, ask the participants to shape the cookie dough into the form of your state. (10) Then, bake the cookie maps. (11) When the cookie maps are cool, tell the participants to decorate their cookie maps with geographical features. (12) They can use blue-colored sugar for bodies of water. (13) They can use green icing for forests. (14) They can use gum drops for mountains. (15) They can use chocolate chips for cities.

---

2. Sentences 6 and 7: **Leave out of the dough any bulk ingredients such as chocolate chips, nuts, and so on. Set bulk ingredients aside in small bowls.**

   Which of the following is the most effective revision of sentences 6 and 7?

   (1) Leave out of the dough any bulk ingredients such as chocolate chips or nuts, and set these items aside in small bowls.
   (2) Set chocolate chips and nuts aside in small bowls.
   (3) Set bulk ingredients such as chocolate chips and nuts aside outside of the dough.
   (4) Leave small bowls out of the dough after setting aside bulk ingredients such as chocolate chips and nuts.
   (5) Put the dough and bulk ingredients in small bowls.

3. Sentences 13, 14, and 15: **They can use green icing for forests. They can use gum drops for mountains. They can use chocolate chips for cities.**

   Which of the following is the most effective revision of sentences 13, 14, and 15?

   (1) They can use green icing, gum drops, and chocolate chips.
   (2) They can make forests, mountains, and cities.
   (3) They can use green icing for forests, gum drops for mountains, and chocolate chips for cities.
   (4) They can use green icing and gum drops for forests and mountains. They can use chocolate chips for cities.
   (5) Green icing, gum drops, and chocolate chips can be used.

UNIT 3

Questions 4 through 6 refer to the following information.

Pictographs

(A)

(1) Visual aides add interest to oral presentations. (2) You are required to speak in front of a group at work or at church. (3) Consider adding a pictograph to your presentation. (4) It will involve the audience in your speech.

(B)

(5) Draw a grid on a sheet of poster board. (6) Label each of the rows with topics that relate to your discussion. (7) You might list favorite fast foods. (8) You might list favorite music types. (9) You might list favorite sports. (10) Give each topic an icon. (11) For example, you might assign a hamburger icon to hamburgers. (12) Then, assign a number to each icon. (13) For example, one hamburger might represent five people. (14) Ask your audience how many of them prefer hamburgers to other types of fast food. (15) Ten people raise their hands. (16) Add two hamburgers to the hamburger row.

---

4. Sentences 2 and 3: **You are required to speak in front of a group at work or at church. Consider adding a pictograph to your presentation.**

   Which subordinating conjunction will help you combine sentences 2 and 3 to form a complex sentence?

   (1) when
   (2) in order that
   (3) wherever
   (4) whether
   (5) as

5. Sentences 7, 8, and 9: **You might list favorite fast foods. You might list favorite music types. You might list favorite sports.**

   Which sentence-combining strategy should you use to combine sentences 7, 8, and 9?

   (1) form a complex sentence
   (2) form a compound sentence
   (3) add commas to form a series
   (4) form a simple sentence
   (5) add a phrase

6. Sentences 15 and 16: **Ten people raise their hands. Add two hamburgers to the hamburger row.**

   Which of the following is the most effective revision of sentences 15 and 16?

   (1) Add two hamburgers, if ten people raise their hands, to the hamburger row.
   (2) Add ten hamburgers to the hamburger row; when ten people raise their hands.
   (3) Because ten people will raise their hands, you will need to add two hamburgers to the hamburger row.
   (4) If ten people raise their hands, add two hamburgers to the hamburger row.
   (5) Tell ten people to add their preferences to the hamburger row.

Directions: Choose the <u>one best answer</u> to each question.

<u>Questions 7 through 10</u> refer to the following information.

Apple Pie

(A)

(1) The family asks you to bring a dessert to a gathering. (2) Don't stop by the bakery at the grocery store on your way to the party. (3) Plan ahead. (4) Make a simple apple pie. (5) Your family will be impressed with your efforts. (6) You will feel good about the gesture.

(B)

(7) You're baking from scratch. (8) It's acceptable to cheat a little. (9) Go ahead and buy a prepared pie crust. (10) It's tasty. (11) It will save you time in the kitchen. (12) Make the pie filling. (13) Combine one half of a cup of sugar, one quarter of a cup of flour, a dash of nutmeg, cinnamon, salt, and a couple of tablespoons of butter in a bowl. (14) Add about eight cups of peeled, chopped apples to the bowl and toss. (15) Pour the filling into your pie crust. (16) Top the pie with a second crust. Cut slits into the second crust. (17) Bake for about 45 minutes at 425 degrees.

---

7. Sentences 3 and 4: **Plan ahead. Make a simple apple pie.**

   Which of the following is the most effective revision of sentences 3 and 4?

   (1) Plan ahead and make a simple apple pie.
   (2) Make a simple apple pie when you plan ahead.
   (3) Plan ahead so that you can bake.
   (4) If you plan ahead, apple pie you can make.
   (5) Because you plan ahead, you can bring apple pie.

8. Sentences 5 and 6: **Your family will be impressed with your efforts. You will feel good about the gesture.**

   Which coordinating conjunction can you use to combine sentences 5 and 6 into a compound sentence?

   (1) but
   (2) yet
   (3) and
   (4) or
   (5) nor

9. Sentences 7 and 8: **You're baking from scratch. It's acceptable to cheat a little.**

   Which of the following is the most effective revision of sentences 7 and 8?

   (1) Cheating is acceptable, but you're baking from scratch.
   (2) When you're baking from scratch, it's acceptable to cheat a little.
   (3) You're baking from scratch; furthermore, it's acceptable to cheat a little.
   (4) Cheating a little, it's acceptable to bake from scratch.
   (5) Cheating during baking is acceptable.

10. Sentences 10 and 11: **It's tasty. It will save you time in the kitchen.**

    Which of the following is the most effective revision of sentences 10 and 11?

    (1) It's tasty, and it will save you time in the kitchen.
    (2) It's tasty because it will save you time in the kitchen.
    (3) It will save you time and taste in the kitchen.
    (4) Saving time in the kitchen improves taste.
    (5) Tasty kitchens will save you time.

Run-On Sentences

For use with student book pp. 52–53

① Review the Skill

When two independent clauses are combined incorrectly, the result is a **run-on sentence**. To correct run-on sentences, insert commas, semicolons, or conjunctions (*and*, *but*, *or*) as appropriate. However, be careful not to create a **comma splice** (such as sentence 7), which happens when two independent clauses are connected incorrectly by a comma. To correct a comma splice, you can insert a semicolon, a coordinating conjunction (such as *and*), or a subordinating conjunction (such as *when*), or create two independent clauses.

② Refine the Skill

To identify a run-on sentence, isolate the independent clauses. Then, experiment with the strategies for correcting the run-on sentence without changing the meaning of the sentence. Review the paragraph and accompanying callouts. Then answer the question that follows.

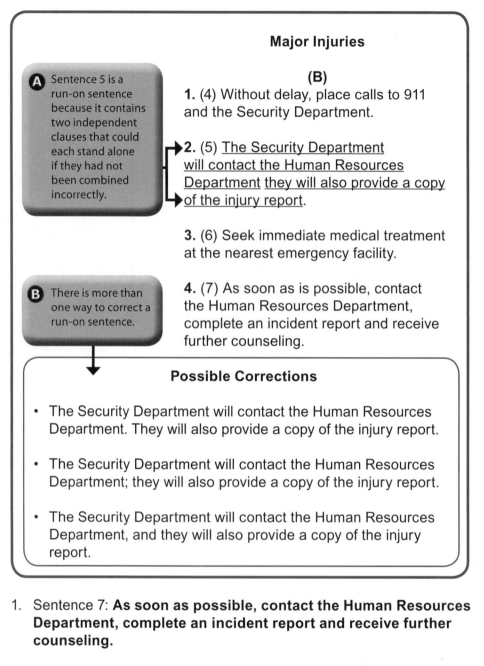

Major Injuries

(B)

A Sentence 5 is a run-on sentence because it contains two independent clauses that could each stand alone if they had not been combined incorrectly.

1. (4) Without delay, place calls to 911 and the Security Department.

2. (5) <u>The Security Department will contact the Human Resources Department</u> <u>they will also provide a copy of the injury report</u>.

3. (6) Seek immediate medical treatment at the nearest emergency facility.

B There is more than one way to correct a run-on sentence.

4. (7) As soon as is possible, contact the Human Resources Department, complete an incident report and receive further counseling.

Possible Corrections

• The Security Department will contact the Human Resources Department. They will also provide a copy of the injury report.

• The Security Department will contact the Human Resources Department; they will also provide a copy of the injury report.

• The Security Department will contact the Human Resources Department, and they will also provide a copy of the injury report.

1. Sentence 7: **As soon as possible, contact the Human Resources Department, complete an incident report and receive further counseling.**

Which is the best way to write the underlined portion of sentence 7? If the original is the best way, choose option (1).

(1) Department, complete an incident report
(2) Department. Complete an incident report
(3) Department complete an incident report
(4) Department; and complete an incident report
(5) Department and complete an incident report

③ *Master the Skill*

Directions: Choose the <u>one best answer</u> to each question.

<u>Questions 2 through 4</u> refer to the following information.

Heart Disease and Diet

(A)

(1) Heart disease is a serious problem in the United States. (2) Heart disease occurs as the result of fatty plaque deposits in the arteries that deliver blood to the heart these plaque deposits cause the arteries to become narrow and hard. (3) This condition does not allow the heart to receive the blood it needs for healthy functioning. (4) However, there is good news for American men and women. (5) You may be able to eat your way to a healthy heart, avoiding the complications that come with heart disease such as chest pain, stroke, or heart attack.

(B)

(6) There are several foods that you should eat to keep your heart healthy. (7) These foods include fruits, vegetables, grains, low-fat dairy products, fish, chicken, turkey, beans, eggs, and nuts. (8) You should also eat polyunsaturated and monounsaturated fats these "good" fats occur in vegetable oils, fish, and nuts.

(C)

(9) There are several foods that you should limit or avoid to keep your heart healthy. (10) These foods include salt, sugar, processed foods that contain trans fat, and cholesterol found in some meats and fatty dairy products. (11) You should also avoid saturated fat, this so-called "bad" fat is found in some meats and dairy products.

---

2. Sentence 2: **Heart disease occurs as the result of fatty plaque deposits in the arteries that deliver blood to the heart these plaque deposits cause the arteries to become narrow and hard.**

   Which correction should be made to sentence 2?

   (1) change <u>heart these</u> to <u>heart. These</u>
   (2) insert <u>but</u> after <u>heart</u>
   (3) change <u>these</u> to <u>and</u>
   (4) insert a comma after <u>blood to the heart</u>
   (5) no correction is necessary

3. Sentence 8: **You should also eat polyunsaturated and <u>monounsaturated fats these</u> "good" fats occur in vegetable oils, fish, and nuts.**

   Which is the best way to write the underlined portion of sentence 8? If the original is the best way, choose option (1).

   (1) monounsaturated fats these
   (2) monounsaturated fats these,
   (3) monounsaturated fats; these
   (4) monounsaturated fats; and these
   (5) monounsaturated fats, these

4. Sentence 11: **You should also avoid saturated fat, this so-called "bad" fat is found in some meats and dairy products.**

   Which correction should be made to sentence 11?

   (1) replace <u>You</u> with <u>Although, you</u>
   (2) change <u>saturated fat, this</u> to <u>saturated fat. This</u>
   (3) replace <u>fat, this</u> with <u>fat this,</u>
   (4) insert a semicolon after <u>this</u>
   (5) no correction is necessary

Directions: Choose the one best answer to each question.

Questions 5 through 7 refer to the following information.

It's Time for Hot Chocolate

(A)
(1) It's cold and snowy outside. (2) Your fingers and toes are cold, you're looking for just the thing to warm yourself from the inside to the outside. (3) Nothing accomplishes this task better than a steaming mug of hot chocolate.

(B)
(4) First, pour cold, milk into a tea kettle.
(5) Place the kettle over a warm, burner.
(6) Wait for the milk to warm, make sure it doesn't boil. (7) While waiting for the milk to warm, pour dark brown chocolate sugar in a large ceramic mug.

(C)
(8) When the milk is ready, pour it over the sugar. (9) Mix the milk and sugar with a long spoon. (10) When the ingredients are mixed, drop marshmallows on top of the steaming liquid. (11) Also, squirt whipped cream on top of the marshmallows. (12) The hot, steaming chocolate will melt the marshmallows and whipped cream into a gooey yumminess.

(D)
(13) Slurp the hot chocolate from the mug, creating a foamy, white mustache. (14) Let the steamy chocolate slide down your throat into your belly, thawing your fingers and toes.
(15) There may be snow outside, but you'll be warm.

---

5. Sentence 2: **Your fingers and toes are cold, you're looking for just the thing to warm yourself from the inside to the outside.**

   Which problem in sentence 2 needs to be corrected?

   (1) a comma splice
   (2) a sentence fragment
   (3) an incomplete idea
   (4) a missing subject
   (5) a run-on sentence

6. Sentence 6: **Wait for the milk to <u>warm, make</u> sure it doesn't boil.**

   Which is the best way to write the underlined portion of sentence 6? If the original is the best way, choose option (1).

   (1) warm, make
   (2) warm. For instance, make
   (3) warm, but make
   (4) warm. And make
   (5) warm; for example, make

7. Sentence 15: **There may be snow outside, but you'll be warm.**

   Which correction should be made to sentence 15?

   (1) insert a semicolon after <u>outside</u>
   (2) remove the comma before <u>but</u>
   (3) remove <u>but</u>
   (4) change <u>but</u> to <u>or</u>
   (5) no correction is necessary

Directions: Choose the <u>one best answer</u> to each question.

<u>Questions 8 through 10</u> refer to the following information.

It's Moving Time

(A)

(1) You've decided to move. (2) You've located a new place to live, you've found a new job. (3) You've made arrangements to leave your old home. (4) Now, it's time to pack. (5) As you know, the importance of having the right tools for a job cannot be overstated. (6) Packing, like any other job, is a task that requires the right tools.

(B)

(7) The first and most important tool for packing your belongings is boxes, of course. (8) You can buy boxes, shop around for the best prices. (9) Internet companies may offer better deals than local retailers. (10) If you've hired a moving company, they may provide you with some boxes for self-packing. (11) You can also ask local businesses such as liquor stores, grocery stores, or hair salons to save boxes for you.

(C)

(12) Next, you will need to seal and label the boxes after they're packed. (13) Use clear or brown packing tape in a dispenser rather than masking tape to seal the boxes packing tape adheres better than masking tape, particularly if the boxes will get hot or cold during the move. (14) Use colored permanent markers to label every box with its contents, location in the new home, and the name of a family member. (15) You can also assign a different color to each room of the home for easy identification during the unloading process.

---

8. Sentence 2: **You've located a new place to live, you've found a new job.**

    Which correction should be made to sentence 2?

    (1) insert <u>and</u> after <u>live,</u>
    (2) remove the comma after <u>live</u>
    (3) remove <u>to live</u>
    (4) change <u>live, you've</u> to <u>live. You've</u>
    (5) no correction is necessary

9. Sentence 8: **You can buy <u>boxes, shop</u> around for the best prices.**

    Which method is the best way to correct the underlined comma splice in this sentence?

    (1) add the conjunctive adverb <u>similarly</u>
    (2) insert the subordinating conjunction <u>Because</u>
    (3) insert the coordinating conjunction <u>but</u>
    (4) create a dependent clause
    (5) change the comma to a period

10. Sentence 13: **Use clear or brown packing tape in a dispenser rather than masking tape to seal the boxes packing tape adheres better than masking tape, particularly if the boxes will get hot or cold during the move.**

    Which correction should be made to sentence 13?

    (1) change <u>rather than</u> to <u>yet</u>
    (2) replace <u>if</u> with <u>when</u>
    (3) replace <u>the boxes packing</u> to <u>the boxes. Packing</u>
    (4) remove the comma before <u>particularly</u>
    (5) no correction is necessary

Misplaced Modifiers

For use with student book pp. 54–55

① Review the Skill

A **misplaced modifier** is a descriptive word or phrase that is incorrectly placed within a sentence. It creates confusion regarding which item is being described: *The tacos were on the table that the guests ate.* A modifier may be an adjective, an adverb, or a phrase. To correct the problem, move the modifier closer to its intended subject: *The tacos that the guests ate were on the table.* Check the glossary at the back of this book if you need help with unfamiliar terms.

② Refine the Skill

To correct misplaced modifiers, isolate the modifier and its possible subjects. Then, select the subject that makes the most sense within the context of the text. Review the paragraph and accompanying callouts. Then answer the question that follows.

☑ TEST-TAKING TIPS

Carefully read the sentence and question to determine the intended subject. Does the writer mean that the decorations are colorful, or does he or she mean that the entertainment is colorful?

(B)

(4) You provide the menu basics: an appetizer of fried or baked tortilla chips and an array of salsas; hard and soft taco shells; and a meat filling such as ground beef or chicken or both. (5) You are also responsible for the decorations and entertainment, which are colorful. **Ⓐ** (6) <u>In the background</u>, consider using cactuses as centerpieces and playing Salsa music.

Ⓐ The introductory phrase "In the background" is a misplaced modifier because, in its present location, the intended subject of the modifier is unclear.

Ⓑ A misplaced modifier must be repositioned in a sentence to clarify the intended subject. Examine the context of the sentence to determine the possible subjects.

Review the Context
The cactuses are sitting on the tables as centerpieces or focal points. Music is often discussed as being part of a setting that provides the background for action.

Possible Subject 1
cactuses as centerpieces

Possible Subject 2
Salsa music

1. Sentence 5: **You are also responsible for the decorations and entertainment, which are colorful.**

   Which of the following is the most effective revision of sentence 5?

   (1) You are responsible for the decorations and colorful entertainment.
   (2) You are responsible for the colorful decorations and entertainment.
   (3) Colorful decorations and entertainment you are responsible for.
   (4) Entertainment and colorful decorations you are responsible for.
   (5) Entertainment you are responsible for, and colorful decorations.

③ Master the Skill

Directions: Choose the <u>one best answer</u> to each question.

<u>Questions 2 through 4</u> refer to the following information.

Vacation on a Budget

(A)

(1) When you're pinching pennies, it's difficult to make the decision to take a vacation. (2) However, it's possible to vacation without emptying your savings account or winding up with debt. (3) It just takes a little careful planning and a willingness to think outside the box.

(B)

(4) One aspect of many vacations that is overlooked during the budgeting phase is transportation, which is often. (5) You have to get from one site or activity to another. (6) However, the cost of gas, a rental car, or a tour bus can break your budget. (7) Instead of these costly options, plan to use public transportation. (8) It's available in most large cities for less than $10 per day.

(C)

(9) Next, consult a tour guide or Internet travel site to identify free attractions. (10) For instance, in New York City, you might walk through Central Park, ice skate at Rockefeller Center, or visit Times Square. (11) In addition, many city parks host free summer concerts. (12) There may also be a lively parade or exhibit to attend.

(D)

(13) Another consideration is food. (14) This expense alone can make going on vacation impossible. (15) In a large city, you can find hot dogs, at a street vendor's cart, steaming. (16) You can also ask locals to recommend good, cheap places to eat that are not located near the city's popular tourist attractions.

---

2. Sentence 4: **One aspect of many vacations that is overlooked during the budgeting phase is transportation, which is often.**

Which part of sentence 4 contains a misplaced modifier?

(1) One aspect of many vacations
(2) that is overlooked
(3) during the budgeting phase
(4) is transportation
(5) which is often

3. Sentence 12: **There may also be a lively parade or street fair to attend.**

Which of the following is the most effective revision of sentence 12?

(1) There may also be an exhibit or lively parade to attend.
(2) There may also be a parade lively or exhibit to attend.
(3) There may also be a parade or exhibit lively to attend.
(4) There may also be a parade or an exhibit to attend lively.
(5) Also to attend, may be a lively exhibit or parade.

4. Sentence 15: **In a large city, you can find hot dogs, at a street vendor's cart, steaming.**

Which of the following is the most effective revision of sentence 15?

(1) You can find hot dogs at a street vendor's cart in a large city, steaming.
(2) In a large city, you can find steaming hot dogs at a street vendor's cart.
(3) In a large city, you can find hot dog's at a steaming street vendor's cart.
(4) At a street vendor's cart, steaming hot dogs you can find, in a large city.
(5) In a large city, you can find hot dogs at a street vendor's steaming cart.

Directions: Choose the <u>one best answer</u> to each question.

<u>Questions 5 through 7</u> refer to the following information.

Fruit Kabobs

(A)

(1) Every talk show and evening news program in America bombards viewers with facts and statistics about the obesity problem nearly affecting all young people. (2) School cafeterias send home menus with items such as "wheat crust pizza" to try to bridge the gap between adolescent eating preferences and doctors' dietary recommendations. (3) Teachers send home notes saying that only children may bring "healthy snacks and bottles of water" to school. (4) Where does this information leave those of us who still have to plan birthday parties, pack lunches, or babysit for a living? (5) How do we maintain interest, create some fun, and teach kids to eat right? (6) There are no easy answers. (7) However, we may be able to solve this dilemma one recipe at a time. (8) Here's one to get us started: fruit kabobs.

(B)

(9) The beauty of the fruit kabob is that it's an activity and a snack all in one. (10) Simply place bowls of clean fruit on a table. (11) Offer strawberries, banana slices, blueberries, Mandarin orange slices, grapes, and so on. (12) Then, give each child a wooden skewer. (13) Make sure to caution children with the skewers about responsible and safe behavior. (14) Then, show children how to select pieces of fruit and thread them onto the skewers, creating beautiful patterns of color and texture.

---

5. Sentence 1: **Every talk show and evening news program in America bombards viewers with facts and statistics about the obesity problem nearly affecting all young people.**

   Which part of sentence 1 contains a misplaced modifier?

   (1) Every talk show and evening news program
   (2) in America bombards viewers
   (3) with facts and statistics
   (4) about the obesity problem
   (5) nearly affecting all young people

6. Sentence 3: **Teachers send home notes saying that only children may bring "healthy snacks and bottles of water" to school.**

   Which correction should be made to sentence 3?

   (1) move <u>only</u> to follow <u>Teachers</u>
   (2) remove <u>may</u>
   (3) insert a comma after <u>water</u>
   (4) move <u>only</u> to follow <u>bring</u>
   (5) no correction is necessary

7. Sentence 13: **Make sure to caution children with the skewers about responsible and safe behavior.**

   Which part of sentence 13 contains a misplaced modifier?

   (1) Make sure
   (2) caution children
   (3) with the skewers
   (4) about responsible
   (5) safe behavior

Lesson 8 | Misplaced Modifiers

Directions: Choose the one best answer to each question.

Questions 8 through 10 refer to the following information.

> **Request for Proposal**
>
> **Project Overview**
>
> **(A)**
>
> (1) For the purpose of this project, a bidder shall be described as a field services and reporting supplier with a license to work in Arkansas, having insurance. (2) Evans Engineering will issue a performance contract to the bidder to supply field services and engineering reporting for the project. (3) The bidder will supply background information concerning the individuals performing field work and will be subject to a security verification review. (4) The bidder shall submit a list and shall also submit a statement of availability to perform contract services. (5) Bidder should submit verification of insurance and show evidence of ability to perform work in the state of Arkansas. (6) The bidder will be selected, after supplying the criteria, above-mentioned.
>
> **(B)**
>
> (7) Selection of bidder will be made within five business days of receipt of complete package and all inquiries shall be made to Ms. Anna Smith at Evans Engineering, 5685 Main Street, Little Rock, Arkansas, 11834.
>
> **Statement of Purpose**
>
> **(C)**
>
> (8) The purpose and objective of this contract is to provide engineering services to verify or make design-ready the subsurface for the installation of generator equipment only. (9) Reports detailing conditions and recommendations, current, are required.

8. Sentence 1: **For the purpose of this project, a bidder shall be described as a field services and reporting supplier with a license to work in Arkansas, having insurance.**

   In sentence 1, who must have insurance?

   (1) license
   (2) Arkansas
   (3) project
   (4) supplier
   (5) services

9. Sentence 6: **The bidder will be selected, after supplying the criteria, above-mentioned.**

   Which of the following is the most effective revision of sentence 6?

   (1) Selected the bidder will be, supplying the criteria above-mentioned.
   (2) The bidder will be selected after supplying the above-mentioned criteria.
   (3) Supplying the above-mentioned bidder, the criteria will be selected.
   (4) The bidder will be, after supplying the above-mentioned criteria, selected.
   (5) The bidder will be selected and supplied the above-mentioned criteria.

10. Sentence 9: **Reports detailing conditions and recommendations, current, are required.**

    Which of the following is the most effective revision of sentence 9?

    (1) Reports are required detailing conditions and recommendations, which are current.
    (2) Current reports are required. Details conditions and recommendations.
    (3) Required reports detail condition and recommendations currently.
    (4) Reports current detailing conditions and recommendations are required.
    (5) Reports detailing current conditions and recommendations are required.

Dangling Modifiers

For use with student book pp. 56–57

① Review the Skill

A **dangling modifier** is a word or phrase in a sentence that describes a missing subject. Dangling modifiers are often introductory clauses that contain verb+*ing* (*visiting*) words or *to*+verb phrases: *To obtain physicals, doctors must be visited*. To correct the problem, form a dependent clause or replace the subject in the independent clause: *To obtain physicals, patients must visit doctors*. Check the glossary at the back of this book if you need help with unfamiliar terms. Check the glossary at the back of this book if you need help with unfamiliar terms.

② Refine the Skill

To correct dangling modifiers, isolate the modifier and its stated and intended subjects. Then, select the subject that makes the most sense within the context of the text. Review the paragraph and accompanying callouts. Then answer the question that follows.

☑ TEST-TAKING TIPS

Carefully read each sentence of a passage to identify dangling modifiers. Practice identifying the missing, or intended, subject of a sentence.

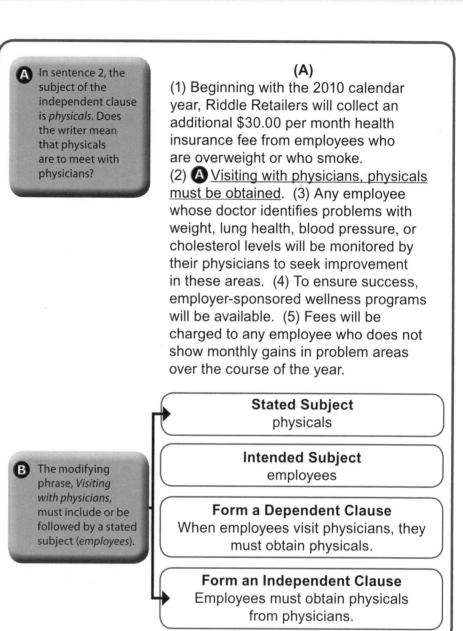

Ⓐ In sentence 2, the subject of the independent clause is *physicals*. Does the writer mean that physicals are to meet with physicians?

(A)

(1) Beginning with the 2010 calendar year, Riddle Retailers will collect an additional $30.00 per month health insurance fee from employees who are overweight or who smoke. (2) **Ⓐ** <u>Visiting with physicians, physicals must be obtained.</u> (3) Any employee whose doctor identifies problems with weight, lung health, blood pressure, or cholesterol levels will be monitored by their physicians to seek improvement in these areas. (4) To ensure success, employer-sponsored wellness programs will be available. (5) Fees will be charged to any employee who does not show monthly gains in problem areas over the course of the year.

Ⓑ The modifying phrase, *Visiting with physicians*, must include or be followed by a stated subject (*employees*).

Stated Subject
physicals

Intended Subject
employees

Form a Dependent Clause
When employees visit physicians, they must obtain physicals.

Form an Independent Clause
Employees must obtain physicals from physicians.

1. Sentence 4: <u>**To ensure success**</u>**, employer-sponsored wellness programs will be available.**

What is the intended subject of the underlined modifying phrase?

(1) programs
(2) employer
(3) employees
(4) wellness
(5) success

UNIT 3

③ *Master the Skill*

Directions: Choose the <u>one best answer</u> to each question.

<u>Questions 2 through 4</u> refer to the following information.

Food Budget

(A)

(1) Working on a family budget, the money you're spending at the grocery store may surprise you. (2) Many money experts caution people against eating out too often. (3) Yet, the grocery store can also be a money drain. (4) To reduce the financial pain of the check-out line, simple strategies will help.

(B)

(5) The best grocery shopping strategy is simple: plan ahead. (6) Spend a little time each week gathering coupons. (7) These gems can save you a significant amount of money over time. (8) However, be careful not to buy items because you have coupons. (9) Rather, use coupons for items that you intend to buy anyway.

(C)

(10) Following through on rebate offers, companies will pay you to buy their products. (11) Companies offer rebates because they expect that the offer will increase sales, and they don't really expect many people to follow through on collection. (12) Sometimes, companies make the criteria for collection so complicated that many people give up. (13) Don't give up. (14) Read the directions, gather the required documentation, and mail your rebates within one week of purchase. (15) Then, wait for the checks to arrive in the mail.

(D)

(16) Finally, shop the sales. (17) When an item that you buy regularly goes on sale at the grocery store, buy enough of the item that you won't have to purchase it again until the next sale. (18) There's nothing wrong with a well-stocked pantry or a freezer full of menu options.

---

2. Sentence 1: <u>**Working on a family budget,** the money you're spending at the grocery store will surprise you.</u>

   Which subject does the underlined portion of sentence 1 *intend* to modify?

   (1) money
   (2) grocery
   (3) you
   (4) store
   (5) surprise

3. Sentence 4: <u>**To reduce the financial pain of the check-out line,** simple strategies will help.</u>

   Which subject does the underlined portion of sentence 4 *actually* modify?

   (1) you
   (2) strategies
   (3) help
   (4) pain
   (5) line

4. Sentence 10: **Following through on rebate offers, companies will pay you to buy their products.**

   Which is the most effective revision of sentence 10?

   (1) Companies, following through on rebate offers, will pay you to buy their products.
   (2) Companies will pay you to buy their products, following through on rebate offers.
   (3) Following through, companies will pay you to buy their products, on rebate offers.
   (4) When you follow through on rebate offers, companies will pay you to buy their products.
   (5) If you follow through, on rebates, companies will pay you to buy products, of theirs.

Directions: Choose the one best answer to each question.

Questions 5 through 7 refer to the following information.

> ### Don't Fall For It!
>
> **(A)**
> (1) How many times have you entered a store for the purpose of buying a particular item or a particular set of items, yet you exited the store with additional items? (2) It's probably more times than you can count, and retailers are counting on you to continue this habit. (3) To prolong this habit, encouragement is everywhere.
>
> **(B)**
> (4) Product placement encourages people to buy impulsively. (5) For example, basic necessities such as milk and peanut butter are located in the back of the grocery store or in the middle of an aisle so that you are forced to pass additional items. (6) Grocery store designers intentionally place expensive items at eye level. (7) Forcing frequent stops, it is difficult for shoppers to maneuver quickly. (8) They also make sure that goodies are placed near the check-out counter. (9) Product placement is based on the assumption that you will buy what you see.
>
> **(C)**
> (10) Shopping accessories make it easy to buy. (11) After all, there are always plenty of over-sized shopping carts located near the front of a store, but you can never find one of those plastic, hand-held baskets. (12) Helping customers shop, convenient, bright yellow stickers appear on store shelves. (13) Yet, they price items so that it's difficult for most people to engage in comparison shopping.

5. Sentence 3: **To prolong this habit, encouragement is everywhere.**

   Which is the best way to write the underlined portion of sentence 3? If the original is the best way, choose option (1).

   (1) encouragement is everywhere
   (2) everywhere there is encouragement
   (3) everywhere, encouragement can be found
   (4) retailers provide encouragement everywhere
   (5) encouragement abounds

6. Sentence 7: **Forcing frequent stops, it is difficult for shoppers to maneuver quickly.**

   Which of the following is the most effective revision of sentence 7?

   (1) It is difficult for shoppers to maneuver quickly, forcing stops.
   (2) To force frequent stops, difficult maneuvering for shoppers.
   (3) Store designers make it difficult for shopping.
   (4) Stores are crowded, and shoppers stop frequently.
   (5) Store designers make it difficult for shoppers to maneuver quickly by forcing frequent stops.

7. Sentence 12: **Helping customers shop, convenient, bright yellow stickers appear on store shelves.**

   Which is the most effective revision of sentence 12?

   (1) Convenient, bright yellow stickers appear on store shelves helping customers shop.
   (2) Employees place convenient, bright yellow stickers on store shelves to help customers shop.
   (3) Convenient, bright yellow stickers, helping customers shop, appear on store shelves.
   (4) On store shelves, customers appear with convenient, bright yellow stickers.
   (5) To help customers, when shopping, store shelves have convenient, yellow stickers.

Directions: Choose the one best answer to each question.

Questions 8 through 10 refer to the following information.

Whose Night Is It To Do the Dishes?

(A)

(1) Who does the dishes in your home? (2) Who takes out the trash? (3) Who does the laundry? (4) Who does the yard work? (5) Proving that your family is like many American families, chores are defined according to gender. (6) Do the women in your home do the dishes and the laundry? (7) Do the men in your home take out the trash and do the yard work? (8) Is there any crossover? (9) For example, do the men do dishes on occasion, or do the women ever take out the trash?

(B)

(10) What do such gender-based chores say about American culture? (11) Are we still living in a society that views women as caretakers and men as breadwinners? (12) Are women's or men's skill sets particularly suited to certain types of chores? (13) Having observed the habits in several households, conclusions are difficult to form.

(C)

(14) These questions provide the basis for an interesting gender study. (15) If we form the hypothesis that domestic chores are based on gender-related skill sets, how do we prove or disprove this theory? (16) To test this theory, studies of role reversal must take place.

---

8. Sentence 5: **Proving that your family is like many American families, chores are defined according to gender.**

   Which of the following is the most effective revision of sentence 5?

   (1) Your answers suggest that chores, proving that your family is like many American families, are defined according to gender.
   (2) Your answers suggest that chores are defined according to gender, proving that your family is like many American families.
   (3) Chores are defined by gender, your answers suggest, like any American families.
   (4) Proving that your family is like many American families. Your answers suggest chores are defined according to gender.
   (5) Chores are defined according to gender; proving that your family is like many American families, your answers suggest.

9. Sentence 13: **Having observed the habits in several households, conclusions are difficult to form.**

   The most effective revision of sentence 13 would include which group of words?

   (1) I find it difficult to form conclusions
   (2) difficulty forming conclusions follows
   (3) forming conclusions is difficult
   (4) conclusions, as always, are difficult to form
   (5) to form conclusions, as always, is difficult

10. Sentence 16: **To test this theory, studies of role reversal must take place.**

    Which of the following is the most effective revision of sentence 16?

    (1) Studies of role reversal must take place to test this theory.
    (2) Studies, to test this theory, must take place.
    (3) To test this theory, men and women must reverse gender roles and study the results.
    (4) To test this theory, role reversal must take place and be studied.
    (5) Role reversal must take place, to test this theory, and studied.

Parallel Structure

For use with student book pp. 58–59

① Review the Skill

When writers present ideas of equal importance in a sentence, they should use the same word form and sentence structure: *Brows<u>ing</u>, compar<u>ing</u>, and budget<u>ing</u> are important.* This technique is called **parallel structure**. Parallel structure may be used when forming a compound sentence or creating a series of words or ideas. Check the glossary at the back of this book if you need help with unfamiliar terms.

② Refine the Skill

To correct a lack of parallel structure, isolate the words or ideas and coordinating conjunctions (*and*; *or*). Then, examine and correct the word form. Review the sentences, examples, and accompanying callouts. Then answer the question that follows.

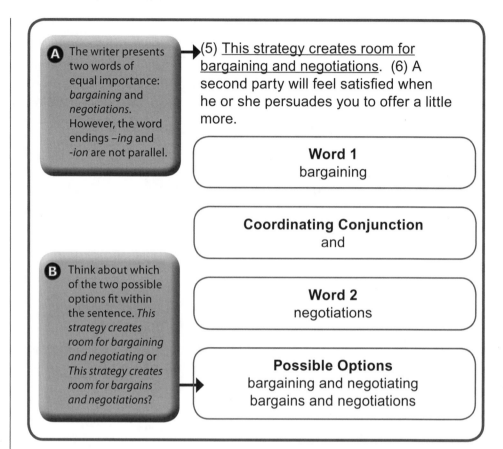

A The writer presents two words of equal importance: *bargaining* and *negotiations*. However, the word endings –*ing* and –*ion* are not parallel.

(5) <u>This strategy creates room for bargaining and negotiations</u>. (6) A second party will feel satisfied when he or she persuades you to offer a little more.

Word 1
bargaining

Coordinating Conjunction
and

B Think about which of the two possible options fit within the sentence. *This strategy creates room for bargaining and negotiating* or *This strategy creates room for bargains and negotiations?*

Word 2
negotiations

Possible Options
bargaining and negotiating
bargains and negotiations

TEST-TAKING TIPS

A coordinating conjunction, such as *and*, *but*, or *or*, suggests equal importance. Carefully read the question and answer options. Remember what you have learned about using the same word form or sentence structure.

1. Sentence 5: **This strategy creates room for bargaining and negotiations.**

   If you want to add the word *compromise* to sentence 5, which is the best revision of the sentence?

   (1) This strategy creates room for bargaining, negotiating, and compromising.
   (2) This strategy creates room for bargains, negotiations, and compromising.
   (3) This strategy creates room for bargaining, negotiating, and compromise.
   (4) This strategy creates room for bargains, negotiating, and compromising.
   (5) This strategy creates room for bargaining, negotiations, and compromise.

Directions: Choose the <u>one best answer</u> to each question.

<u>Questions 2 through 4</u> refer to the following information.

What's For Lunch?

(A)

(1) It never fails. (2) Whatever you pack your kids for lunch isn't good enough. (3) They don't like peanut butter. (4) Sally had pretzels in her lunch. (5) Jimmy had a dessert. (6) After this argument, comes the inevitable question: What's for lunch tomorrow? (7) What are parents who want their kids to eat healthy lunches supposed to do? (8) It's not healthy to pack chips and candy bars. (9) However, it's not healthy to pack turkey sandwiches if the kids don't eat them. (10) Try these tips for healthy and happier eating.

(B)

(11) Allow your kids to feel ownership over their diets by contributing to the grocery list. (12) For example, ask: Do you want apple slices, peaches, or bananas for lunch next week? (13) If kids feel ownership over a selection, they're more likely to eat it.

(C)

(14) Pack dips such as low-fat salad dressing or peanut butter. (15) Dipping is interactive and fun. (16) Kids enjoy dipping apple slices in peanut butter or to plunge carrot sticks in salad dressing.

(D)

(17) Add fiber and calcium to the lunches in interesting ways. (18) For example, create your own trail mix with bran flakes. (19) Offer low-fat cheese sticks as a side item or low-fat yogurt cups for dessert. (20) Pack whole fruits instead of juice.

---

2. Sentence 10: **Try these tips for healthy and happier eating.**

   Where does sentence 10 lack parallel structure?

   (1) Try these tips
   (2) these tips for
   (3) healthy and happier
   (4) happier eating
   (5) tips for healthy

3. Sentence 12: **For example, ask: Do you want apple slices, peaches, or bananas for lunch next week?**

   Which correction should be made to sentence 12?

   (1) insert <u>grapes</u> after <u>peaches</u>
   (2) replace <u>apple slices</u> with <u>apples</u>
   (3) remove the comma after <u>example</u>
   (4) change <u>next</u> to <u>this</u>
   (5) no correction is necessary

4. Sentence 16: **Kids enjoy dipping apple slices in peanut butter <u>or to plunge</u> carrot sticks in salad dressing.**

   Which is the best way to write the underlined portion of sentence 16? If the original is the best way, choose option (1).

   (1) or to plunge
   (2) or plunging
   (3) or to plunging
   (4) and to plunge
   (5) and to plunging

UNIT 3

Directions: Choose the <u>one best answer</u> to each question.

<u>Questions 5 through 7</u> refer to the following information.

Yard Sale Buying Guide: Part One

(A)

(1) The lady who lives next door and spends every Saturday morning driving from yard sale to yard sale knows something that you don't know. (2) Some items are better used. (3) Sure, it's nice to sleep late on a weekend morning, but keeping a little money in one's pocket is nicer. (4) Next weekend, maybe you should join your next-door neighbor. (5) Keep your eyes open for the following items.

(B)

(6) Buy used entertainment. (7) That's right—shop for books, DVDs, CDs, computer software, and video games. (8) The retail mark-up on these items is astronomical, and most people tire of them before they wear them out. (9) Ask yourself this question: After buying this book new, how many times will I read it? (10) If the answer is once, why spend $10 to $25? (11) You can spend one dollar on the same book used, and end up spending the other nine dollars on snacks.

(C)

(12) Stock up on supplies for home projects. (13) You can buy used office furniture and non-electric tools. (14) Why pay full price for items that are well-made and difficult to break? (15) A sturdy desk, an office chair, or a cabinet for filing will last for years. (16) A used hammer or screwdriver looks and functions similarly to a new hammer or screwdriver.

(D)

(17) Look for fun and games. (18) You can buy used toys and sporting equipment. (19) Again, people tire of these items before they wear them out. (20) Think about how many kids you know who played baseball for a summer or two before moving on to basketball or swimming. (21) Guess what? (22) That leather baseball mitt will still catch a pop-up fly.

5. Sentence 3: **Sure, it's nice to sleep late on a weekend morning, <u>but keeping a little money in one's pocket is nicer.</u>**

   Which is the best way to write the underlined portion of sentence 3? If the original is the best way, choose option (1).

   (1) but keeping a little money in one's pocket is nicer
   (2) but nicer to keep a little money in one's pocket
   (3) but one should keep a little money in one's pocket
   (4) but keep a little money in one's pocket
   (5) but it's nicer to keep a little money in one's pocket

6. Sentence 11: **You can spend one dollar on the same book used, <u>and end up spending</u> the other nine dollars on snacks.**

   Which is the best way to write the underlined portion of sentence 11? If the original is the best way, choose option (1).

   (1) and end up spending
   (2) and ending up spending
   (3) and you can spend
   (4) and spending
   (5) and you end up spending

7. Sentence 15: **A sturdy desk, an office chair, or a <u>cabinet for filing</u> will last for years.**

   Which is the best way to write the underlined portion of sentence 15? If the original is the best way, choose option (1).

   (1) cabinet for filing
   (2) filing cabinet
   (3) cabinets for filing
   (4) cabinets for filing papers
   (5) filing cabinets

Directions: Choose the <u>one best answer</u> to each question.

<u>Questions 8 through 10</u> refer to the following information.

Yard Sale Buying Guide: Part Two

(A)

(1) Now that I've convinced you to join your neighbor in a Saturday morning hunt for used items of value, I owe you a warning. (2) Not everything at a yard sale is a good deal.
(3) Let's face it; some things are better new.
(4) The trick to smart yard sale shopping is knowing when to buy used and when buying new is the better deal.

(B)

(5) While it's good to buy used entertainment, it's not good to buy used electronics. (6) That's right—buy used DVDs or computer software, but buying used players or computers is a bad idea. (7) People use and abuse these items, generally not throwing them out until something starts to malfunction. (8) There's no reason to buy someone else's problem.

(C)

(9) It's good to purchase used toys and sporting equipment, but purchasing used safety equipment is a bad idea. (10) Again, people use and abuse safety equipment such as car seats or bicycle helmets. (11) You don't want to take the chance that the safety equipment isn't really safe anymore. (12) After all, it's the health of you and your loved ones that's at risk. (13) Also, newer technology is better when it comes to safety.

---

8. Sentence 4: **The trick to smart yard sale shopping is knowing when to buy used and <u>when buying new is the better deal</u>.**

Which is the best way to write the underlined portion of sentence 4? If the original is the best way, choose option (1).

(1) when buying new is the better deal
(2) when to buy new
(3) when buying new
(4) when having bought new is the better deal
(5) when buy new is the better deal

9. Sentence 6: **That's right—buy used DVDs or computer software, <u>but buying used players or computers is a bad idea</u>.**

Which is the best way to write the underlined portion of sentence 6? If the original is the best way, choose option (1).

(1) but buying used players or computers is a bad idea
(2) but buy used players or computers
(3) but having bought used players or computers
(4) but do not buy used players or computers
(5) but used players or computers is a bad idea

10. Sentence 9: **It's good to purchase used toys and sporting equipment, but purchasing used safety equipment is a bad idea.**

Which is the best revision of sentence 9?

(1) It's good to purchase used toys, sporting equipment, and safety equipment.
(2) It's not good to purchase used toys, sporting equipment, or safety equipment.
(3) It's good to purchase used toys and equipment for sporting, but it's not good to purchase safety equipment.
(4) It's good to purchase used toys and sporting equipment, but it's not good to purchase used safety equipment.
(5) Purchasing used toys and sporting equipment, even though to purchase used safety equipment is bad, is a good purchase.

Nouns

For use with student book pp. 68–69

① Review the Skill

In general, **nouns** are used to identify people, places, and things, such as *fisherman*, *coast*, and *boats*. The most familiar nouns include common nouns and proper nouns. By identifying the different types of nouns and the places they appear in sentences, you can better understand the role that nouns play in helping to communicate your ideas through writing. Check the glossary at the back of this book if you need help with unfamiliar terms.

② Refine the Skill

Common nouns are used to identify people, places, or things. Proper nouns, unlike common nouns, represent the name of a person, a title, or a specific place. These proper nouns should always begin with a capital letter. Review the paragraphs and accompanying callouts. Then answer the question that follows.

✓ TEST-TAKING TIPS

The names of cities, states, and countries are all proper nouns. Like other nouns, proper nouns can be made up of more than one word.

A More than one noun can be found in a sentence. Sentence 1 contains the following nouns: *grandmother*, *adventures*, and *Europe*. In this case, childhood is not a noun because it is describing the time in which the adventure took place.

B In sentence 4, *Eiffel Tower* is a proper noun. For example, *I visited the monument in Paris* uses the common noun *monument*, but *I visited the Eiffel Tower in Paris*, uses a proper noun because *Eiffel Tower* is the name of the monument.

(A)

(1) After I learned about my grandmother's childhood adventures in Europe, I admired her more than ever. (2) We looked through her photo albums together, and she showed me pictures from when she was young. (3) We laughed as she told me stories about her journeys all over Italy, Spain, and France. (4) She visited the **B** Eiffel Tower when she was only 5 years old. (5) I couldn't believe how young she looked, and that the people standing beside her were her parents. (6) Grandmother's parents looked so strong and dignified.

(B)

(7) My grandmother lives in the United States now, but she has fond memories of her time abroad. (8) One day, we will take a trip from this small town in north dakota to see the Eiffel Tower. (9) Then we can take new pictures to add to grandmother's photo album.

1. Sentence 8: **One day, <u>we will take a trip from this small town in north dakota to see the Eiffel Tower</u>.**

   Which is the best way to write the underlined portion of sentence 8? If the original is the best way, choose option (1).

   (1) we will take a trip from this small town in north dakota to see the Eiffel Tower
   (2) we will take a trip from this small Town in North Dakota to see the Eiffel tower
   (3) we will take a trip from this small town in North Dakota to see the Eiffel Tower
   (4) we will take a trip from this small town in north dakota to see the eiffel tower
   (5) we will take a trip from this small town in north Dakota to see the Eiffel Tower

Master the Skill

Directions: Choose the <u>one best answer</u> to each question.

<u>Questions 2 through 5</u> refer to the following letter.

Dear Valued Customer,

(A)

(1) We have enclosed the following brochure so that you can review all the benefits of joining ez pay. (2) EZ Pay allows you to pay all of your monthly bills from your computer. (3) To sign up, call us today or return the attached from in the prepaid envelope.

(B)

(4) It's our goal to offer you an excellent program while providing you with dependable quality and service. (5) Many customers have already enrolled in EZ Pay because they have found that it is an effective way to manage their monthly bills. (6) We hope you will review the enclosed information and let us know your decision regarding the program as soon as possible.

Sincerely,

Mr. Owens
EZ Pay Management

---

2. Sentence 1: **We have enclosed the following brochure <u>so that you can review all the benefits of joining ez pay</u>.**

    Which is the best way to write the underlined portion of sentence 1? If the original is the best way, choose option (1).

    (1) so that you can review all the benefits of joining ez pay
    (2) so that we can review all the benefits of joining ez pay
    (3) so that you can review all the benefits of joining EZ PAY
    (4) so that you can review all the benefits of joining EZ Pay
    (5) so that you can review all the Benefits of joining EZ Pay

3. Sentence 3: **To sign up, call us today or return the attached from in the prepaid envelope.**

    Which correction should be made to sentence 3?

    (1) remove the comma after <u>up</u>
    (2) change <u>us</u> to <u>U.S.</u>
    (3) change <u>from</u> to <u>form</u>
    (4) change <u>prepaid envelope</u> to <u>Prepaid Envelope</u>
    (5) no correction is necessary

4. Sentence 5: **Many customers have already enrolled in EZ Pay because they have found that it is an effective way to manage their monthly bills.**

    Which correction should be made to sentence 5?

    (1) replace <u>customers</u> with <u>employees</u>
    (2) change <u>EZ Pay</u> to <u>ez pay</u>
    (3) replace <u>bills</u> with <u>Bills</u>
    (4) replace <u>because</u> with <u>yet</u>
    (5) no correction is necessary

5. Sentence 6: **We hope you will review the enclosed <u>information</u> and let us know your decision regarding the program as soon as possible.**

    Why is the underlined word a noun?

    (1) it is an action
    (2) it is a person
    (3) it is a place
    (4) it is a thing
    (5) it is the name of a specific place

Directions: Choose the <u>one best answer</u> to each question.

Questions 6 through 9 refer to the following document.

SUMMONS for JURY DUTY
Wednesday, April 28, 2009 at 8:15 AM
Alphaville District Court

(A)
(1) You have been called to jury service. (2) Most people complete their service in one day. (3) However, you should be prepared to serve three or more days. (4) If longer service is a problem for you, you will be able to tell the Judge before you are seated on a jury.

(B)
(5) You will be mailed a reminder notice about 10 days before your scheduled date to appear. (6) It will contain a map and directs to the courthouse. (7) Please notify us if your address changes. (8) You may also postpone your juror service, if necessary.

(C)
(9) Failing to obey this summons without a reasonable cause is A Crime, which is punishable by a maximum fine of $2,000 upon conviction.

6. Sentence 1: **You have been called to jury service.**

   Which correction should be made to sentence 1?

   (1) replace <u>jury</u> with <u>Jury</u>
   (2) replace <u>service</u> with <u>Service</u>
   (3) change <u>jury</u> to <u>juries</u>
   (4) change <u>service</u> to <u>services</u>
   (5) no correction is necessary

7. Sentence 4: **If longer service is a problem for you, you will be able to tell the Judge before you are seated on a jury.**

   Which correction should be made to sentence 4?

   (1) remove the comma after <u>you</u>
   (2) change <u>Judge</u> to <u>judge</u>
   (3) replace <u>before</u> with <u>after</u>
   (4) change <u>you, you</u> to <u>you. You</u>
   (5) change <u>jury</u> to <u>Jury</u>

8. Sentence 6: **It will contain a map and directs to the courthouse.**

   The most effective revision of sentence 6 would include which noun?

   (1) jury
   (2) information
   (3) judge
   (4) directions
   (5) vehicle

9. Sentence 9: **Failing to obey this summons without a <u>reasonable cause is A Crime,</u> which is punishable by a maximum fine of $2,000 upon conviction.**

   Which is the best way to write the underlined portion of sentence 9? If the original is the best way, choose option (1).

   (1) reasonable cause is A Crime
   (2) reasonable cause is a Crime
   (3) reasonable Cause is a crime
   (4) reasonable cause is a crime
   (5) reasonable crime

Lesson 1 | Nouns

Directions: Choose the one best answer to each question.

Questions 10 and 11 refer to the following memorandum.

To: All Employees of Fireside Manufacturing
From: Don Bridgewater, President
Subject: Coffee with the President

(1) I am delighted to inform you about a new program called "Coffee with don" that will begin this year. (2) About once a month, I will be hosting a coffee hour in my office. (3) During this time, employees can share their concerns about the companies and hear a few plan about our future expansion in Canada. (4) I look forward to meeting with you!

10. Sentence 1: **I am delighted to inform you about a new program called "Coffee with don" that will begin this year.**

    Which correction should be made to sentence 1?

    (1) change inform to information
    (2) change Coffee to coffee
    (3) change don to Don
    (4) change program to Program
    (5) no correction is necessary

11. Sentence 3: **During this time, employees can share their concerns about the companies and hear a few plan about our future expansion in Canada.**

    Which is the best way to write the underlined portion of sentence 3? If the original is the best way, choose option (1).

    (1) about the companies and hear a few plan
    (2) about the companys and hear a few plan
    (3) about the companies and hear a few plans
    (4) about the company and hear a few plans
    (5) about the companys and hear a few plans

Questions 12 and 13 refer to the following paragraphs.

(A)
(1) El Niño is an unusual change in the ocean's temperatures that happens when the warm waters of the Pacific flow towards the east. (2) Many climate scientists study El Niño. (3) _____ have been studying El Niño for many years. (4) What they know from their research is that it is a natural event that happens every four or five years, lasts nine to twelve months, and that no two are the same. (5) Depending on its strength, El Niño can have serious effects on the weather in many parts of the world.

(B)
(6) El Niño was named by fishermen in Peru and means "The Christ Child" in Spanish. (7) Its name refers to the time of the year when the condition peaks, which is usually around Christmas. (8) Warm water builds up off the coast of South America, and the rise in water temperature kills many nutrients that fish use for food.

12. Which noun would be most effective if inserted at the beginning of sentence 3?

    (1) People
    (2) Scientists
    (3) El Niño
    (4) Fishermen
    (5) Fish

13. Sentence 6: **El Niño was named by fishermen in Peru and means "The Christ Child" in Spanish.**

    Which is the best way to write the underlined portion of sentence 6? If the original is the best way, choose option (1).

    (1) El Niño was named by fishermen in Peru
    (2) el niño was named by fishermens in peru
    (3) El Niño was named by fishermens in peru
    (4) El Niño was named by fishermens in Peru
    (5) El Niño was named by fishermen in peru

Pronouns

For use with student book pp. 70–71

① **Review the Skill**

Pronouns, such as *he*, *she*, *it*, and *they*, take the place of nouns in a sentence. Subject, object, and possessive pronouns help ease the flow of text by replacing repetitive, or repeated, nouns.

② **Refine the Skill**

Subject pronouns (*I, you, she, he,* and *it*) take the place of a subject in a sentence: *she* instead of *grandmother*. When the subject is plural, use *we* or *they*. Object pronouns (*me, you, him, her,* and *it*) are used as the object of a verb: *My mother visited her in Italy.* When the object is plural, use *us* or *them*. Possessive pronouns (*my, mine, your, yours, his, hers,* and *its*) represent ownership: *The album is not mine, it is hers.* When the possessive pronoun is plural, use *theirs* or *them*. *I* and *we* are first-person pronouns. *You* is a second-person pronoun, and *he, she, it,* and *they* are third-person pronouns.

A In sentence 3, notice that *grandmother* has been replaced with the subject pronoun *she*, and *I* has been replaced with the object pronoun *me*.

B In sentence 6, the noun *grandmother* is used three times. Replacing *grandmother* with different types of pronouns makes the sentence easier to read: *I couldn't believe how young* <u>*she*</u> *looked, and that the people standing beside* <u>*her*</u> *were* <u>*her*</u> *parents.*

(A)

(1) After I learned about my grandmother's childhood adventures in Europe, I admired grandmother more than ever. (2) Grandmother and I looked through her photo albums together, and she showed me pictures from when she was young. (3) Grandmother and I laughed as <u>she</u> told <u>me</u> stories about her journeys all over Italy, Spain, and France. (4) Grandmother visited the Eiffel Tower when she was only 5 years old. (5) I couldn't believe how young <u>grandmother</u> looked, and that the people standing beside <u>grandmother</u> were <u>grandmother's</u> parents. (6) Grandmother's parents looked so strong and dignified.

(B)

(7) My grandmother lives in the United States now, but she has fond memories of her time abroad. (8) One day, we will take a trip from this small town in North Dakota to see the Eiffel Tower. (9) Then we can take new pictures to add to grandmother's photo album.

☑ **TEST-TAKING TIPS**

The way we write is often influenced by the way we hear people speak. If you are trying to determine which pronoun is the best to use in a sentence, say the sentence to yourself. For example, *I told her stories* or *I told she stories*?

1. Sentence 1: **After I learned about my grandmother's childhood adventures in Europe, <u>I admired grandmother more than ever</u>.**

   Which is the best way to write the underlined portion of sentence 1? If the original is the best way, choose option (1).

   (1) I admired grandmother more than ever
   (2) I admired her more than ever
   (3) she admired me more than ever
   (4) she admired her more than ever
   (5) I admired she more than ever

UNIT 4

③ Master the Skill

Directions: Choose the <u>one best answer</u> to each question.

<u>Questions 2 through 5</u> refer to the following memorandum.

To: All Students
From: Donna Buckley, State College President and Staff
Subject: Emergency Notification System

(A)

(1) As part of a statewide plan to inform students about major safety-related emergency news, our school has created a new Emergency Notification System. (2) From now on, your will receive alerts from this system regarding emergencies. (3) The alerts will be sent to your college e-mail address. (4) If you also want to receive these alerts as text messages, the alerts can be sent to your cell phone. (5) Please e-mail your cell phone number to the address at the bottom of this memo.

(B)

(6) We will be conducting tests of our new Emergency Notification System over the next several weeks. (7) Communicating important emergency information to our students, faculty, and staff is very important to the State College President and her staff. (8) We thank you for your support with this endeavor.

---

2. Sentence 2: **From now on, <u>your will receive alerts from this system</u> regarding emergencies.**

   Which is the best way to write the underlined portion of sentence 2? If the original is the best way, choose option (1).

   (1) your will receive alerts from this system
   (2) you will receive alerts from the Emergency Notification System
   (3) you will receive alerts from it
   (4) your will receive alerts from it
   (5) you will receive alerts from us

3. Sentence 4: **If you also want to receive alerts as text messages, <u>the alerts can be sent to your cell phone</u>.**

   Which is the best way to write the underlined portion of sentence 4? If the original is the best way, choose option (1).

   (1) the alerts can be sent to your cell phone
   (2) they can be sent to my cell phone
   (3) we can be sent to your cell phone
   (4) they can be sent to their cell phone
   (5) they can be sent to your cell phone

4. Sentence 7: **Communicating important emergency information <u>to our students, faculty, and staff is very important to the State College President and her staff</u>.**

   Which is the best way to write the underlined portion of sentence 7? If the original is the best way, choose option (1).

   (1) to our students, faculty, and staff is very important to the State College President and her staff
   (2) to our students, faculty, and staff is very important to us
   (3) to my students, faculty, and staff is very important to them
   (4) to your students, faculty, and staff is very important to me
   (5) to the students, faculty, and staff is very important to them

5. Sentence 8: **We thank you for your support with this endeavor.**

   Which correction should be made to sentence 8?

   (1) change <u>you</u> to <u>my</u>
   (2) replace <u>your</u> with <u>our</u>
   (3) change <u>you</u> to <u>their</u>
   (4) replace <u>your</u> with <u>my</u>
   (5) no correction is necessary

Directions: Choose the <u>one best answer</u> to each question.

<u>Questions 6 through 9</u> refer to the following letter.

Dear Potential First-time Home Buyers,

(A)

(1) On June 10, Ron Allenson will be presenting a talk on how you can buy your first house. (2) If you are interested, Ron Allenson would be delighted to have you attend as Ron Allenson's guest. (3) It should be a fun event!

(B)

(4) Space is limited so please RSVP to Ron Allenson and Ron Allenson will put your name on my guest list. (5) The talk will last about one hour, and there will be refreshments afterward. (6) Also, if you know anyone else who might be interested in attending, please let Ron Allenson know and pass this invitation along.

Sincerely,

Ron Allenson
Allenson Real Estate

---

6. Sentence 1: **On June 10, Ron Allenson will be presenting a talk on how you can buy your first house.**

    Which correction should be made to sentence 1?

    (1) change <u>Ron Allenson</u> to <u>I</u>
    (2) replace <u>Ron Allenson</u> with <u>they</u>
    (3) replace <u>you</u> with <u>they</u>
    (4) change <u>your</u> to <u>their</u>
    (5) replace <u>Ron Allenson</u> with <u>he</u>

7. Sentence 2: **If you are interested, <u>Ron Allenson would be delighted to have you attend as Ron Allenson's guest</u>.**

    Which is the best way to write the underlined portion of sentence 2? If the original is the best way, choose option (1).

    (1) Ron Allenson would be delighted to have you attend as Ron Allenson's guest
    (2) I would be delighted to have you attend as Ron Allenson's guest
    (3) I would be delighted to have you attend as my guest
    (4) He would be delighted to have you attend as Ron Allenson's guest
    (5) He would be delighted to have you attend as his guest

8. Sentence 4: **Space is limited so please RSVP to <u>Ron Allenson and Ron Allenson will put your name on my guest list</u>.**

    Which is the best way to write the underlined portion of sentence 4? If the original is the best way, choose option (1).

    (1) Ron Allenson and Ron Allenson will put your name on my guest list
    (2) Ron Allenson and he will put your name on my guest list
    (3) me and he will put your name on the guest list
    (4) me and I will put your name on my guest list
    (5) Ron Allenson and I will put your name on my guest list

9. Sentence 6: **Also, if you know anyone else who might be interested in attending, please let Ron Allenson know and pass this invitation along.**

    Which correction should be made to sentence 6?

    (1) replace <u>you</u> with <u>they</u>
    (2) change <u>Ron Allenson</u> to <u>me</u>
    (3) replace <u>you</u> with <u>we</u>
    (4) change <u>Ron Allenson</u> to <u>him</u>
    (5) no correction is necessary

Lesson 2 | Pronouns

Directions: Choose the one best answer to each question.

Questions 10 through 13 refer to the following document.

SUMMONS for JURY DUTY
Alphaville District Court

(A)
(1) You are being called to jury service. (2) Most people complete their service in one day. (3) However, you should be prepared to serve three or more days. (4) If longer service is a problem for you, they will be able to tell the judge before you are seated on a jury.

(B)
(5) You will be mailed a reminder notice about 10 days before their scheduled date to appear. (6) It will contain a map and directions to the courthouse. (7) Please notify this office if your address changes. (8) You may also postpone the person's juror service, if necessary.

(C)
(9) Failing to obey this summons without a reasonable cause is a crime, which is punishable by a maximum fine of $2,000 upon conviction.

---

10. Sentence 4: **If longer service is a problem for you, they will be able to tell the judge before you are seated on a jury.**

    Which is the best way to write the underlined portion of sentence 4? If the original is the best way, choose option (1).

    (1) they will be able to tell the judge before you are seated
    (2) they will be able to tell the judge before they are seated
    (3) you will be able to tell the judge before you are seated
    (4) you will be able to tell the judge before we are seated
    (5) you will be able to tell the judge before they are seated

11. Sentence 5: **You will be mailed a reminder notice about 10 days before their scheduled date to appear.**

    Which correction should be made to sentence 5?

    (1) change their to His
    (2) change their to your
    (3) change You to They
    (4) change You to I
    (5) no correction is necessary

12. Sentence 7: **Please notify this office if your address changes.**

    Which is the best way to write the underlined portion of sentence 7? If the original is the best way, choose option (1).

    (1) this office if your address changes
    (2) this office if their address changes
    (3) this office if her address changes
    (4) this office if my address changes
    (5) this office if you address changes

13. Sentence 8: **You may also postpone the person's juror service, if necessary.**

    Which correction should be made to sentence 8?

    (1) replace the person's with your
    (2) change You to They
    (3) change You to I
    (4) replace the person's with their
    (5) no correction is necessary

Pronoun Agreement

For use with student book pp. 72–73

① **Review the Skill**

Pronoun agreement is when a pronoun correctly agrees with its **antecedent** in terms of gender (*Tom = he/his; Mary = she/her*) and number. A singular pronoun needs to have a singular antecedent: *Tom* wore *his* favorite jeans. A plural pronoun needs to have a plural antecedent: *The students oppose the dress code because they want to express themselves.* Check the glossary at the back of this book if you need help with unfamiliar terms.

② **Refine the Skill**

It is important to first identify the subject or object of the sentence in order to use the correct pronoun. Be sure to carefully read each sentence in order to identify proper pronoun agreement. Review the paragraphs and accompanying callouts. Then answer the question that follows.

☑ TEST-TAKING TIPS

The antecedent (*Tom; Mary*) and pronoun (*he; she*) usually appear in the same sentence. However, it is possible for the antecedent to appear in a previous sentence.

To Whom It May Concern,

(A)

(1) I am writing to oppose the school dress code. (2) The school board recently proposed a mandatory dress code for the entire student body. (3) A dress code is a bad idea. (4) Not only does it limit individuality, but it also prohibits freedom of expression. (5) My <u>daughter</u> attends your school, and I know that the idea of a dress code will cause <u>her</u> added stress. (6) This dress code will also cause stress to her classmates. (7) How will the <u>students</u> express their interests or ideas through their clothes if <u>they</u> are all wearing the same clothes?

(B)

(8) A school-wide dress code is an easy way for school officials to get rid of ideas they don't like. (9) I request that the entire student body, parents, and faculty are invited to the meeting when this issue will be raised, so that we can have a say in this matter. (10) I will attend with my daughter. (11) They will bring her friends.

A Sentence 5 contains the singular object pronoun *her,* which agrees with the antecedent *daughter* at the beginning of the sentence. The singular pronoun agrees both in number (singular) and gender.

B Sentence 7 contains the plural subject pronoun *they,* which agrees with the antecedent *students* at the beginning of the sentence. The pronoun and antecedent agree because they are plural.

1. Sentence 11: **They will bring her friends.**

   Which correction should be made to sentence 11?

   (1) change <u>They</u> to <u>She</u>
   (2) change <u>her</u> to <u>their</u>
   (3) replace <u>They</u> with <u>Her</u>
   (4) replace <u>her</u> with <u>them</u>
   (5) no correction is necessary

UNIT 4

Directions: Choose the <u>one best answer</u> to each question.

<u>Questions 2 through 5</u> refer to the following letter.

Dear Valued Customer,

(A)

(1) We have enclosed the following brochure so that you can review all the benefits of joining EZ Pay. (2) It allows you to pay all the monthly bills from his computer. (3) To sign up, call us today or return the attached form in the prepaid envelope.

(B)

(4) Our goal is to offer an excellent and dependable program to good customers. (5) We are hard to find these days. (6) Many customers have already enrolled in it because we have found that it is an effective way to manage their monthly bills. (7) We hope you will review the enclosed form and send them back as soon as possible.

Sincerely,

Mr. Owens
EZ Pay Management

---

2. Sentence 2: **It allows you to pay all the monthly bills from his computer.**

Which is the best way to write the underlined portion of sentence 2? If the original is the best way, choose option (1).

(1) the monthly bills from his computer
(2) their monthly bills from their computer
(3) his monthly bills from your computer
(4) my monthly bills from my computer
(5) your monthly bills from your computer

3. Sentence 5: **We are hard to find these days.**

Which correction should be made to sentence 5?

(1) change <u>We</u> to <u>You</u>
(2) replace <u>We are</u> with <u>It is</u>
(3) change <u>these</u> to <u>those</u>
(4) replace <u>find</u> with <u>found</u>
(5) change <u>We</u> to <u>They</u>

4. Sentence 6: **Many customers have already <u>enrolled in it because we have found</u> that it is an effective way to manage their monthly bills.**

Which is the best way to write the underlined portion of sentence 6? If the original is the best way, choose option (1).

(1) enrolled in it because we have found
(2) enrolled in EZ Pay because they have found
(3) enrolled in EZ Pay because I have found
(4) enrolled in it because it has found
(5) enrolled in EZ Pay because we have found

5. Sentence 7: **We hope you will review the enclosed form and send them back as soon as possible.**

Which correction should be made to sentence 7?

(1) change <u>you</u> to <u>your</u>
(2) replace <u>We</u> with <u>They</u>
(3) change <u>them</u> to <u>it</u>
(4) change <u>you</u> to <u>they</u>
(5) no correction is necessary

Directions: Choose the <u>one best answer</u> to each question.

<u>Questions 6 through 9</u> refer to the following paragraphs.

(A)

(1) Welcome and thank you for joining the Hi-Lo Hotel Rewards program! (2) You are now part of a major reward program available at hundreds of hotels nationwide. (3) More than 100 comfortable rooms to fit your budget are available in each hotel. (4) It are newly redecorated, too! (5) You will earn points for qualifying stays. (6) They are good toward free stays and other rewards. (7) Or, you can earn 10 airline miles for each stay good on any airline. (8) The choice is up to you!

(B)

(9) You don't need to stay at the same hotel each time. (10) So you and his wife can visit the city, or enjoy a week at the beach with your children. (11) In most cases, after just ten nights, you will have enough points for one free night. (12) That's faster than any other rewards program. (13) Stay five more nights to earn more points, and it will add up to another free night! (14) See why it's the best deal around!

---

6. Sentence 4: **It are newly redecorated, too!**

    Which correction should be made to sentence 4?

    (1) change <u>It</u> to <u>We</u>
    (2) replace <u>It</u> with <u>Them</u>
    (3) change <u>It</u> to <u>They</u>
    (4) replace <u>It</u> with <u>Us</u>
    (5) no correction is necessary

7. Sentence 6: **They are good toward free stays and other rewards.**

    Which correction should be made to sentence 6?

    (1) change <u>They</u> to <u>It</u>
    (2) replace <u>They</u> with <u>We</u>
    (3) change <u>They</u> to <u>Us</u>
    (4) replace <u>They</u> with <u>Them</u>
    (5) no correction is necessary

8. Sentence 10: **<u>So you and his wife</u> can visit the city, or enjoy a week at the beach with your children.**

    Which is the best way to write the underlined portion of sentence 10? If the original is the best way, choose option (1).

    (1) So you and his wife
    (2) So he and his wife
    (3) So you and the wife
    (4) So you and your wife
    (5) So he and your wife

9. Sentence 13: **Stay five more nights to earn more points, and it will add up to another free night!**

    Which correction should be made to sentence 13?

    (1) change <u>it</u> to <u>they</u>
    (2) replace <u>points</u> with <u>point</u>
    (3) change <u>it</u> to <u>you</u>
    (4) change <u>nights</u> to <u>days</u>
    (5) no correction is necessary

Directions: Choose the <u>one best answer</u> to each question.

<u>Questions 10 through 13</u> refer to the following paragraph.

---

(1) A good voice teacher, such as Mrs. Shaver, is someone who isn't too strict and who loves singing. (2) Someone should be who makes singing fun and interesting, because that's what singing should be about. (3) Many voice teachers will ask a student, such as my brother, to rehearse several hours a week, because if they want to be a good singer, they need to rehearse. (4) However, if a student like him does not want to sing professionally, they may only need to rehearse once or twice a week. (5) If he rehearses too much they could strain their voice.

---

10. Sentence 2: **<u>Someone should be</u> who makes singing fun and interesting, because that's what singing should be about.**

Which is the best way to write the underlined portion of sentence 2? If the original is the best way, choose option (1).

(1) Someone should be
(2) She should be someone
(3) They should be someone
(4) You should be someone
(5) I should be someone

11. Sentence 3: **Many voice teachers will ask a student, such as my brother, to rehearse several hours a week, because <u>if they want to be a good singer, they need to rehearse</u>.**

Which is the best way to write the underlined portion of sentence 3? If the original is the best way, choose option (1).

(1) if they want to be a good singer, they need to rehearse
(2) if he wants to be a good singer, they need to rehearse
(3) if they want to be a good singer, he needs to rehearse
(4) if he wants to be a good singer, he needs to rehearse
(5) if he wants to be a good singer, you need to rehearse

12. Sentence 4: **However, if a student like him does not want to sing professionally, they may only need to rehearse once or twice a week.**

Which correction should be made to sentence 4?

(1) change <u>him</u> to <u>my brother</u>
(2) change <u>him</u> to <u>them</u>
(3) change <u>they</u> to <u>he</u>
(4) change <u>they</u> to <u>it</u>
(5) no correction is necessary

13. Sentence 5: **If he rehearses too much <u>they could strain their voice</u>.**

Which is the best way to write the underlined portion of sentence 5? If the original is the best way, choose option (1).

(1) they could strain their voice
(2) he could strain their voice
(3) he could strain his voice
(4) they could strain his voice
(5) he could strain their voices

Collective Nouns

For use with student book pp. 74–75

① Review the Skill

Some nouns refer to more than one person or thing. These **collective nouns** can take either singular or plural verbs: *The family wants dinner; The family members want dinner.* Practice determining which kind of verb a collective noun takes. Check the glossary at the back of this book if you need help with unfamiliar terms.

② Refine the Skill

Collective nouns can appear in many different places within a paragraph. When trying to determine if a noun is collective, try to figure out if it refers to a group of people or a group of things. Just about any group that includes members can be considered a collective noun. Review the paragraphs and accompanying callouts. Then answer the question that follows.

✓ TEST-TAKING TIPS

If a group functions together as a unit, you should use a singular verb. If a group has parts or members that might act differently, you should use a plural verb.

Ⓐ In sentence 4, the collective noun *group* takes the singular verb *comes* because it functions as a single group taking action.

Ⓑ In sentence 6, the collective noun *group* takes the plural verb *want* because it refers to a group of cats that could act or want differently.

(A)

(1) Have you ever watched a group of cats play outside? (2) Typically, the cats play by themselves. (3) One will chase a butterfly, while another uses a wooden fence as a balance beam. (4) After an hour or so of running around, the Ⓐgroup <u>comes</u> inside. (5) Some of the group heads for their food bowls, while some of the group meows for attention.

(B)

(6) It's often hard to know what a Ⓑgroup of cats <u>want</u>. (7) Some of the group perch on windowsills in the living room to watch for birds outside. (8) While others might settle down for an afternoon nap. (9) It's clear that even in a group, cats like to do their own thing.

---

1. Sentence 7: **Some of the group perch on windowsills in the living room to watch for birds outside.**

   Which correction should be made to sentence 7?

   (1) replace <u>group</u> with <u>groups</u>
   (2) replace <u>perch</u> with <u>perches</u>
   (3) replace <u>watch</u> with <u>watches</u>
   (4) change <u>birds</u> to <u>bird</u>
   (5) no correction is necessary

Directions: Choose the <u>one best answer</u> to each question.

<u>Questions 2 through 5</u> refer to the following memorandum.

To: All Students
From: Registrar's Office
Subject: Emergency Notification System

(A)

(1) As part of a statewide effort to inform different audiences about major, safety-related emergency news, State College plan to create a new Emergency Notification System. (2) From now on, students and staff will receive alerts from the new system regarding emergencies. (3) Department heads will be notified if staff chooses not to receive the alerts. (4) If the student body prefer to receive alerts as text messages, please e-mail the registrar's office.

(B)

(5) The campus police are conducting tests of our new Emergency Notification System over the next several weeks. (6) Communicating important emergency information to our students, faculty, and staff is very important to us. (7) We thank you for your support in our endeavor.

---

2. Sentence 1: **As part of a statewide effort to inform different audiences about major, safety-related emergency news, State College plan to create a new Emergency Notification System.**

   Which correction should be made to sentence 1?

   (1) replace <u>audiences</u> with <u>audience</u>
   (2) change <u>State College</u> to <u>State Colleges</u>
   (3) replace <u>plan</u> with <u>plans</u>
   (4) change <u>inform</u> to <u>informs</u>
   (5) no correction is necessary

3. Sentence 3: **Department heads will be notified if staff chooses not to receive the alerts.**

   Which correction should be made to sentence 3?

   (1) replace <u>chooses</u> with <u>choose</u>
   (2) change <u>be</u> to <u>is</u>
   (3) change <u>heads</u> to <u>head</u>
   (4) replace <u>alerts</u> with <u>alert</u>
   (5) no correction is necessary

4. Sentence 4: **If the student body prefer to receive alerts as text messages, please e-mail the registrar's office.**

   Which correction should be made to sentence 4?

   (1) replace <u>the student body</u> with <u>any student body</u>
   (2) replace <u>prefer</u> with <u>prefers</u>
   (3) insert a comma after <u>body</u>
   (4) change <u>alerts</u> to <u>alert</u>
   (5) no correction is necessary

5. Sentence 5: <u>**The campus police are conducting tests**</u> **of our new Emergency Notification System over the next several weeks.**

   Which is the best way to write the underlined portion of sentence 5? If the original is the best way, choose option (1).

   (1) The campus police are conducting tests
   (2) The Campus Police are conducting tests
   (3) The campus police is conducting tests
   (4) The Campus Police is conducting tests
   (5) The campus police are conducting testing

Directions: Choose the <u>one best answer</u> to each question.

<u>Questions 6 through 9</u> refer to the following information.

(A)

(1) Serving on a jury is an important civic duty. (2) Your service as a juror is one of the most valuable contributions you can make to the justice system. (3) Serving on a jury allows you to see how the justice system works, and allows you to gain a better understanding of how government work in general.

(B)

(4) The Constitution guarantees people the right to a trial by a jury of one's peer. (5) The juries make its decision based on the facts in a case. (6) The jury's decision must be fair and impartial in order to protect the rights of the person on trial.

(C)

(7) While serving on a jury, you will be asked to assume certain responsibilities. (8) You should always be on time, because a trial cannot begin or end until all jury members are present. (9) You should not try to research the case you are deciding in any way. (10) Finally, you should not discuss the case with anyone else. (11) This includes your friends, relatives, spouse, or other jurors. (12) After deliberations begin in the jury room, only the jury cans discuss the case until the verdict is agreed upon.

---

6. Sentence 3: **Serving on a jury allows you to see how the justice system works, and allows you to gain a better understanding of how government work in general.**

    Which correction should be made to sentence 3?

    (1) change <u>a jury</u> to <u>the juries</u>
    (2) replace <u>allows</u> with <u>allow</u>
    (3) change <u>government</u> to <u>governments</u>
    (4) replace <u>work</u> with <u>works</u>
    (5) no correction is necessary

7. Sentence 4: **The Constitution guarantees people the right to a trial by a jury of one's peer.**

    Which correction should be made to sentence 4?

    (1) replace <u>right</u> with <u>rights</u>
    (2) change <u>peer</u> to <u>peers</u>
    (3) replace <u>Constitution</u> with <u>constitution</u>
    (4) change <u>trial</u> to <u>trials</u>
    (5) no correction is necessary

8. Sentence 5: <u>**The juries make its decision**</u> **based on the facts in a case.**

    Which is the best way to write the underlined portion of sentence 5? If the original is the best way, choose option (1).

    (1) The juries make its decision
    (2) The jury make its decision
    (3) The jury make their decision
    (4) The juries make their decision
    (5) The jury makes its decision

9. Sentence 12: **After deliberations begin in the jury room, only the jury cans discuss the case until the verdict is agreed upon.**

    Which correction should be made to sentence 12?

    (1) replace <u>agreed</u> with <u>agree</u>
    (2) replace <u>begin</u> with <u>begins</u>
    (3) change <u>cans</u> to <u>can</u>
    (4) replace <u>verdict is</u> with <u>verdicts are</u>
    (5) no correction is necessary

Directions: Choose the one best answer to each question.

Questions 10 through 13 refer to the following information.

(A)

(1) Many fans want to know what's wrong with the Thunder this season. (2) The team are not playing well and are in danger of not making the playoffs. (3) We are passionate fans and demand excellence from our team because we really care whether they win or lose.

(B)

(4) Some players on the Thunder have been accused of not hustling this season. (5) They appear to not be trying as hard as they did in the past, and not playing up to their full abilities. (6) Fans show how they feel about this behavior by booing the players. (7) This is unfortunate because it does not take into account how the team feels, or the fact that some Thunder players might be injured.

(C)

(8) If we want the Thunder to win the championship this season, then the team have to be shown our support. (9) It's one thing if Thunder players puts its heads down and ignores what the fans think. (10) But our team really seems to care about the fans, and they say that booing bothers them and affects their performance. (11) So let's stop booing them and cheer the team on!

10. Sentence 2: **The team are not playing well and are in danger of not making the playoffs.**

Which is the best way to write the underlined portion of sentence 2? If the original is the best way, choose option (1).

(1) The team are not playing well and are in danger
(2) The team is not playing well and are in danger
(3) The team are not playing well and is in danger
(4) The team is not playing well and is in danger
(5) The teams are not playing well and are in danger

11. Sentence 7: **This is unfortunate, because it does not take into account how the team feels, or the fact that some Thunder players might be injured.**

Which is the best way to write the underlined portion of sentence 7? If the original is the best way, choose option (1).

(1) how the team feels
(2) how the team feel
(3) how teams feel
(4) how his team feels
(5) how our teams feel

12. Sentence 8: **If we want the Thunder to win the championship this season, then the team have to be shown our support.**

Which correction should be made to sentence 8?

(1) change Thunder to them
(2) replace to win with wins
(3) change have to has
(4) replace team with teams
(5) no correction is necessary

13. Sentence 9: **It's one thing if Thunder players puts its heads down and ignores what the fans think.**

Which is the best way to write the underlined portion of sentence 9? If the original is the best way, choose option (1).

(1) players puts its heads down and ignores
(2) player puts its head down and ignores
(3) players put its heads down and ignore
(4) player put their heads down and ignores
(5) players put their heads down and ignore

Simple Verb Tense

For use with student book pp. 76–77

1 Review the Skill

Use **simple verb tense** to show whether an action or condition occurs in the past, present, or future. For example, *We made a snowman* (past); *We are making a snowman* (present); and *We will make a snowman* (future) are actions. *Yesterday was snowy* (past); *It is snowing today* (present); and *It will snow next week* (future) are examples of conditions. Check the glossary at the back of this book if you need help with unfamiliar terms.

2 Refine the Skill

Past tense refers to events that have already taken place: *Grandmother told me stories.* Present tense refers to events that are taking place in the present: *Grandmother tells me stories.* Future tense refers to events that will happen in the future: *Grandmother will tell me stories.* Review the paragraphs and accompanying callouts. Then answer the question that follows.

TEST-TAKING TIPS

If you're trying to determine which tense is best to use in the sentence, ask yourself if the action *took* place in the *past*, is *taking* place in the *present*, or *will take* place in the *future*.

A Notice the use of *spent* in sentence 4. It is the past tense of the verb *spend*, which means this action took place in the past.

B *Includes* in sentence 5 indicates a present condition. However, the sentence also contains the word *will*, which indicates a future action. These two tenses are used in the same sentence to show the order in which the action (or condition) took place.

C Adding the helping verb *will* before a verb indicates future tense. Future tense means that the action (or condition) has not happened yet.

New Hit Movie to Premiere

(A)
(1) Do you like action movies? (2) Well, get ready, because the biggest action movie of all time will opened in theaters on May 20th! (3) If you like explosions, car chases, and hair-raising escapes, this is the movie for you!

(B)
(4) We have **A** spent millions of dollars making this movie, and we promise that it will not disappoint you! (5) It **B** includes some of the biggest stars in Hollywood and some of the best special effects you **C** will see! (6) So mark your calendars. (7) May 20th will be the first day to see the greatest action movie ever made.

1. Sentence 2: **Well, get ready, because the biggest action movie of all time will opened in theaters on May 20th!**

   Which correction should be made to sentence 2?

   (1) replace <u>get</u> with <u>be</u>
   (2) change <u>get</u> to <u>is</u>
   (3) change <u>opened</u> to <u>open</u>
   (4) remove <u>will</u>
   (5) no correction is necessary

UNIT 4

Directions: Choose the one best answer to each question.

Questions 2 through 5 refer to the following information.

(A)

(1) During an El Niño year, warm water builds up in the Pacific Ocean off the western coast of South America. (2) The rise in water temperature will kill many nutrients that fish eat for food. (3) This leads to a bad fishing period in Peru and other countries in South America.

(B)

(4) As the warmest water moves east, clouds and thunderstorms is formed over the Pacific. (5) The storms pass over places such as the island of Tahiti, which normally has a pleasant tropical climate. (6) Tahiti often experiences strong and damaging rainstorms during an El Niño year.

(C)

(7) The impact of El Niño will affect many places at the same time, and causes many problems. (8) Places that normally expect heavy rain, such as tropical rainforests, often have severe droughts and forest fires instead.

---

2. Sentence 2: **The rise in water temperature will kill many nutrients that fish eat for food.**

   Which correction should be made to sentence 2?

   (1) replace eat with eats
   (2) replace rise with rises
   (3) change will kill to kills
   (4) change eat to will eat
   (5) no correction is necessary

3. Sentence 4: **As the warmest water moves east, clouds and thunderstorms is formed over the Pacific.**

   Which is the best way to write the underlined portion of sentence 4? If the original is the best way, choose option (1).

   (1) is formed over the Pacific
   (2) form over the Pacific
   (3) forming over the Pacific
   (4) formed over the Pacific
   (5) is forming over the Pacific

4. Sentence 5: **The storms pass over places such as the island of Tahiti, which normally has a pleasant tropical climate.**

   What correction should be made to sentence 5?

   (1) replace pass with passed
   (2) replace pass with will pass
   (3) replace has with will have
   (4) replace has with had
   (5) no correction is necessary

5. Sentence 7: **The impact of El Nino will affect many places at the same time, and causes many problems.**

   Which is the best way to write the underlined portion of sentence 7? If the original is the best way, choose option (1).

   (1) The impact of El Niño will affect many places at the same time
   (2) The impact of El Niño affected many places at the same time
   (3) The impact of El Niño has affected many places at the same time
   (4) The impact of El Niño is an effect on many places at the same time
   (5) The impact of El Niño affects many places at the same time

Directions: Choose the one best answer to each question.

Questions 6 through 9 refer to the following information.

(A)

(1) A jury trial involves many people directly or indirectly. (2) As a juror, you are listen to the evidence that the prosecution and the defense will present in order to reach a decision in a case. (3) The judge conducts the trial and rules on questions of law raised by the attorneys. (4) At the end of the trial, he reviewed the applicable laws with the jury.

(B)

(5) The participants in the case bring their own attorneys or their attorneys will be appointed by the court. (6) The lawyers advise the participants on the law and represent them during the trial.

(C)

(7) Under oath, the witnesses give their testimony to the court. (8) They indicate what they saw at the time of the case. (9) They may also indicate what facts they know about the case.

---

6. Sentence 2: **As a juror, <u>you are listen to the evidence that the prosecution and the defense will present</u> in order to reach a decision in a case.**

   Which is the best way to write the underlined portion of sentence 2? If the original is the best way, choose option (1).

   (1) you are listen to the evidence that the prosecution and the defense will present
   (2) you listened to the evidence that the prosecution and the defense have presented
   (3) you will listen to the evidence that the prosecution and the defense presented
   (4) you will listen to the evidence that the prosecution and the defense will present
   (5) you listened to the evidence that the prosecution and the defense presented

7. Sentence 4: **At the end of the trial, he reviewed the applicable laws with the jury.**

   Which correction should be made to sentence 4?

   (1) change <u>end</u> to <u>ended</u>
   (2) change <u>reviewed</u> to <u>reviews</u>
   (3) replace <u>jury</u> with <u>juries</u>
   (4) remove <u>he</u>
   (5) no correction is necessary

8. Sentence 5: **The participants in the case bring their own attorneys or their attorneys will be appointed by the court.**

   Which correction should be made to sentence 5?

   (1) change <u>bring</u> to <u>brought</u>
   (2) insert <u>will</u> after <u>case</u>
   (3) replace <u>appointed</u> with <u>appoints</u>
   (4) replace <u>will be</u> with <u>have been</u>
   (5) no correction is necessary

9. Sentence 9: **They may also indicate <u>what facts they know about the case</u>.**

   Which is the best way to write the underlined portion of the sentence 9? If the original is the best way, choose option (1).

   (1) what facts they know about the case
   (2) what facts they have known about the case
   (3) what facts they will know about the case
   (4) what facts they are known about the case
   (5) what about the case they can know

Directions: Choose the one best answer to each question.

Questions 10 through 13 refer to the following information.

(A)

(1) It is important to checked the oil in your car often. (2) Checking the oil is very easy and can keep you from having major repair bills. (3) The first step is to park the car on a level surface, such as a driveway. (4) Then turn off the engine and open the hood while the engine is still warm.

(B)

(5) Next, find the dipstick, a long, thin piece of metal sticking out of the engine with a loop at one end. (6) After you located the dipstick, pull on the loop to pull it out of the part of the engine that stores the oil. (7) Wipe the oil off the dipstick with a paper towel and then replace the clean dipstick. (8) Made sure that you push it all the way into the engine. (9) Pull the dipstick out again, and look at the pointy end opposite the loop.

(C)

(10) If the oil on it was below the line marked "full," you needed to add a small amount of oil to your car. (11) You can use a funnel, but be sure not to add too much! (12) Otherwise, you will flood your engine.

---

10. Sentence 1: **It is important to checked the oil in your car often.**

Which correction should be made to sentence 1?

(1) replace <u>is</u> with <u>will be</u>
(2) change <u>checked</u> to <u>check</u>
(3) replace <u>is</u> with <u>was</u>
(4) insert <u>have</u> after <u>to</u>
(5) no correction is necessary

11. Sentence 6: **<u>After you located the dipstick,</u> pull it out of the part of the engine that stores the oil.**

Which is the best way to write the underlined portion of sentence 6? If the original is the best way, choose option (1).

(1) After you located the dipstick
(2) After you will locate the dipstick
(3) After you locate the dipstick
(4) After you will located the dipstick
(5) After you locating the dipstick

12. Sentence 8: **Made sure that you push it all the way into the engine.**

Which correction should be made to sentence 8?

(1) replace <u>Made</u> with <u>Make</u>
(2) change <u>push</u> to <u>pushes</u>
(3) change <u>push</u> to <u>pushed</u>
(4) replace <u>Made</u> with <u>Makes</u>
(5) no correction is necessary

13. Sentence 10: **If the oil on it <u>was below the line</u> marked "full," you needed to add** a small amount of oil to your car.

Which is the best way to write the underlined portion of sentence 10? If the original is the best way, choose option (1).

(1) was below the line marked "full," you needed to add
(2) was below the line marked "full," you need to add
(3) were below the line marked "full," you need to add
(4) is below the line marked "full," you need to add
(5) is below the line marked "full," you needed to add

Regular Verb Tense

For use with student book pp. 78–79

① Review the Skill

Regular verb tense indicates past and present by adding suffixes, or endings, to words. Suffixes include *–ed* (*create = created*), *–ied* (*cry = cried*), *–s* (*sing = sings*), *–ies* (*hurry = hurries*), and *–ing* (*eat = eating*). Check the glossary at the back of this book if you need help with unfamiliar terms.

② Refine the Skill

The verb tenses indicate when different actions occur at different times. This makes text easier to read: *Sally and Julie are eating ice cream, when a man approaches to ask the time. This was the second time they had seen this man at the shop.* The varied verb tenses tell us that Sally and Julie are eating ice cream in the present, and that they see a familiar man from the past. Review the paragraphs and accompanying callouts. Then answer the question that follows.

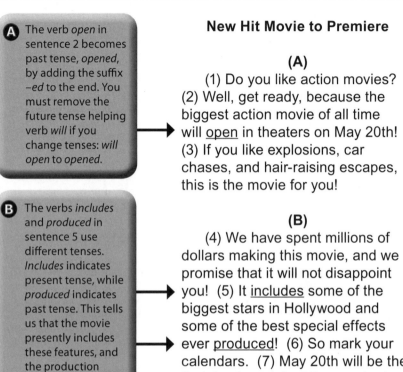

A The verb *open* in sentence 2 becomes past tense, *opened*, by adding the suffix *–ed* to the end. You must remove the future tense helping verb *will* if you change tenses: *will open* to *opened*.

B The verbs *includes* and *produced* in sentence 5 use different tenses. *Includes* indicates present tense, while *produced* indicates past tense. This tells us that the movie presently includes these features, and the production of the special effects has already happened.

New Hit Movie to Premiere

(A)
(1) Do you like action movies? (2) Well, get ready, because the biggest action movie of all time will <u>open</u> in theaters on May 20th! (3) If you like explosions, car chases, and hair-raising escapes, this is the movie for you!

(B)
(4) We have spent millions of dollars making this movie, and we promise that it will not disappoint you! (5) It <u>includes</u> some of the biggest stars in Hollywood and some of the best special effects ever <u>produced</u>! (6) So mark your calendars. (7) May 20th will be the first day to <u>watched the greatest action movie ever create</u>.

✓ TEST-TAKING TIPS

Note that the *to+verb* combination indicates the verb's original state (*to dance; to sing; to run*) and should not have a suffix.

1. Sentence 7: **May 20th will be the first day to <u>watched the greatest action movie ever create</u>.**

   Which is the best way to write the underlined portion of sentence 7? If the original is the best way, choose option (1).

   (1) watched the greatest action movie ever create
   (2) watching the greatest action movie ever create
   (3) watch the greatest action movie ever creating
   (4) watch the greatest action movie ever created
   (5) watches the greatest action movie ever created

③ Master the Skill

<u>Directions</u>: Choose the <u>one best answer</u> to each question.

<u>Questions 2 through 5</u> refer to the following letter.

Dear Potential First-time Home Buyers,

(1) On June 10, I will present a talk about how you can buy your first home. (2) If you are interesting, I would be delighted to have you attend as my guest. (3) It should be a fun event!

(4) Space is limited so please responded to my office and we will put your name on the guest list. (5) The talk will last about one hour, and there will be refreshments afterward. (6) Also, if you know anyone else who might be interested in attend, please let me know and pass this invitation along.

          Sincerely,

          Ron Allenson
          Allenson Real Estate

---

2. Sentence 1: **On June 10, I will present a talk about how you can buy your first home.**

   Which correction should be made to sentence 1?

   (1) replace <u>buy</u> with <u>buys</u>
   (2) remove <u>will present a</u>
   (3) replace <u>present</u> with <u>presenting</u>
   (4) change <u>talk</u> to <u>talking</u>
   (5) no correction is necessary

3. Sentence 2: <u>**If you are interesting, I would be delighted**</u> **to have you attend as my guest.**

   Which is the best way to write the underlined portion of sentence 2? If the original is the best way, choose option (1).

   (1) If you are interesting, I would be delighted
   (2) If you are interest, I would be delighted
   (3) If you are interested, I would be delighted
   (4) If interested, I would be delighted
   (5) If you have interest, I would be delighted

4. Sentence 4: **Space is limited so <u>please responded to my office</u> and we will put your name on the guest list.**

   Which is the best way to write the underlined portion of sentence 4? If the original is the best way, choose option (1).

   (1) please responded to my office
   (2) please responding to my office
   (3) please respond to your office
   (4) please responded to their office
   (5) please respond to my office

5. Sentence 6: **Also, if you know anyone else who might be <u>interested in attend</u>, please let me know and pass this invitation along.**

   Which is the best way to write the underlined portion of sentence 6? If the original is the best way, choose option (1).

   (1) interested in attend
   (2) interests in attended
   (3) interested in attending
   (4) interested in attends
   (5) interesting in attending

Directions: Choose the <u>one best answer</u> to each question.

<u>Questions 6 through 9</u> refer to the following information.

(A)

(1) Our manufacturing company has a long and distinguished history. (2) It start in the early 1920s, a time changing American business. (3) Electrical companies built power lines across the United States, and telephones link homes and businesses. (4) People worried about the future, especially after the end of World War I.

(B)

(5) As is the case with many other start-up businesses, the company's first product was a failure. (6) It will seem like a good idea at the time, but when it left our factory and went into people's homes, it didn't work!

(C)

(7) However, it opened the door to many other products that eventually worked much better. (8) In the more than 80 years since, the company has changed the course of American technology and history. (9) Today, our products are used in millions of homes, and we hope they will be used in millions more in the future.

---

6. Sentence 2: **It start in the early 1920s, a time changing American business.**

   The most effective revision to sentence 2 would include which group of words?

   (1) It starting in the early 1920s, a time changing American business.
   (2) It started in the early 1920s, a time changing American business.
   (3) It was started in the early 1920s, a time that changed American business.
   (4) It will start in the early 1920s, a time that will change American business.
   (5) It was started in the early 1920s, a time to change American business.

7. Sentence 3: **Electrical companies built power lines across the United States, and telephones link homes and businesses.**

   Which correction should be made to sentence 3?

   (1) replace <u>companies</u> with <u>company</u>
   (2) replace <u>link</u> with <u>linked</u>
   (3) change <u>power</u> to <u>powering</u>
   (4) change <u>link</u> to <u>links</u>
   (5) no correction is necessary

8. Sentence 6: **<u>It will seem like a good idea at the time</u>, but when it left our factory and went into people's homes, it didn't work!**

   Which is the best way to write the underlined portion of sentence 6? If the original is the best way, choose option (1).

   (1) It will seem like a good idea at the time
   (2) It seems like a good idea at the time
   (3) It was seeming like a good idea at the time
   (4) It seemed like a good idea at the time
   (5) It is seeming like a good idea at the time

9. Sentence 9: **Today, <u>our products are used in millions of homes</u>, and we hope they will be used in millions more in the future.**

   Which is the best way to write the underlined portion of sentence 9? If the original is the best way, choose option (1).

   (1) our products are used in millions of homes
   (2) our products be use millions of homes
   (3) our products is using in millions of homes
   (4) our products are in used millions of homes
   (5) our products is used in millions of homes

Lesson 6 | Regular Verb Tense

Directions: Choose the one best answer to each question.

Questions 10 through 13 refer to the following letter.

To Whom It May Concern,

(A)

(1) I do not think that school uniforms keep students from expressing themselves. (2) With uniforms, everyone comes to school looking neat and clean. (3) Uniforms help students get along with one another because they aren't tease about what they wear.

(B)

(4) For example, at my son's school they are not allowed to wear hats or baggy pants. (5) It's nice because they don't have to thinked about what they are going to wear. (6) Everyone wears the same clothes and doesn't bother to checking how others are dressed.

(C)

(7) Another reason that school uniforms are important is that they keep the students from getting in fights with parents about what to wear. (8) Uniforms help all students feel more like equals and keep them from being peer pressured to wearing cool or popular clothing.

Sincerely,

Mandy Tomkins

---

10. Sentence 3: **Uniforms help students get along with one another because they aren't tease about what they wear.**

Which is the best way to write the underlined portion of sentence 3? If the original is the best way, choose option (1).

(1) they aren't tease about what they wear
(2) they aren't teased about what they wear
(3) they teasing about what they wear
(4) they aren't teasing about what them wear
(5) they tease about what they wear

11. Sentence 5: **It's nice because they don't have to thinked about what they are going to wear.**

Which correction should be made to sentence 5?

(1) change they don't to they does
(2) change they are to they is
(3) replace thinked with think
(4) replace wear with wearing
(5) no correction is necessary

12. Sentence 6: **Everyone wears the same clothes and doesn't bother to checking how others are dressed.**

Which is the best way to write the underlined portion of sentence 6? If the original is the best way, choose option (1).

(1) to checking how others are dressed
(2) to checked how others are dressed
(3) to check how others are dressed
(4) to check how others are dresses
(5) to checking how others are dressing

13. Sentence 8: **Uniforms help all students feel more like equals and keep them from being peer pressured to wear cool or popular clothing.**

Which correction should be made to sentence 8?

(1) change help to helps
(2) replace pressured with pressures
(3) change help to helping
(4) replace pressured with pressuring
(5) no correction is necessary

Perfect Verb Tense

For use with student book pp. 80–81

① Review the Skill

Perfect verb tense shows actions that happened in the past, happen in the present, and will happen in the future. **Past perfect tense** is formed using the helping verb *had*: *She had spent the summer golfing.* **Present perfect tense** is formed using *has, have,* or *has/ have been*: *She has been golfing all summer.* **Future perfect tense** is formed using *will have* or *will have been*: *She will have been golfing all summer.*

② Refine the Skill

Using past perfect tense, writers describe events or actions that took place before other actions. Using present perfect tense, writers describe actions that began in the past and continue in the present. Using future perfect tense, writers describe events or actions that will take place in the future. Review the paragraphs. Then answer the question that follows.

A The verb *balanced* in sentence 4 is in past perfect tense because the helping verb *had* comes before it.

B The verb *learned* in sentence 8 is in present perfect tense because the helping verb *have* comes before it. Only *has* or *have* can be used to form the present perfect tense.

(A)

(1) Have you ever watched a group of cats play outside? (2) I have four cats that always play by themselves. (3) One time, I saw that one of my cats had chased a butterfly into a corner to play with it before releasing it. (4) It kept her busy for hours. (5) Another cat <u>had balanced</u> on a wooden fence, then pounced on a mouse. (6) After an hour or so of running around, the cats had come inside. (7) Some of them headed for their food bowls, while others meowed for attention.

(B)

(8) I <u>have learned</u> that it is often hard to know what a group of cats will want. (9) Some of them will want to perch on windowsills in the living room to watch the birds outside. (10) Others will want to settle down for an afternoon nap. (11) It is clear that even in a group, cats like to do their own thing.

> **TEST-TAKING TIPS**
>
> When using past perfect tense, remember that the helping verb *had* should describe the first action in the sentence: *After I had gone to the movies, I went to pick up dinner.*

1. Sentence 6: **After an hour or so of running around, the cats had come inside.**

   The most effective revision of sentence 6 would include which group of words?

   (1) The cats had come inside after an hour or so of running around.
   (2) The cats come inside after running around for an hour.
   (3) After having run around for an hour or so, the cats come inside.
   (4) The cats had came inside after running around for an hour.
   (5) After the cats had run around for an hour or so, they came inside.

UNIT 4

③ Master the Skill

Directions: Choose the <u>one best answer</u> to each question.

<u>Questions 2 through 5</u> refer to the following information.

(A)

(1) Our manufacturing company will have learned many lessons during its first 80 years. (2) The company was started in the late 1920s, a time that changed American business. (3) Electrical companies will have started to build power lines across the United States, then telephones started to link homes and businesses. (4) People were worried about the future, especially after the end of World War I.

(B)

(5) As is the case with many other start-up businesses, the company's first product was a failure. (6) It seemed like a good idea at the time, but when it left our factory and went into people's homes, it didn't work!

(C)

(7) Even though our founders did not know it at the time, that failure opened the door to many other products that has work much better. (8) In the more than 80 years since, the company has changed the course of American technology and history. (9) Today, our products have been used in millions of homes. (10) We hope that, by the time the company celebrates its next 80 years, they used by millions more.

---

2. Sentence 1: **Our manufacturing company will have learned many lessons during its first 80 years.**

   Which correction should be made to sentence 1?

   (1) replace <u>will have</u> with <u>had</u>
   (2) change <u>will have</u> to <u>has</u>
   (3) change <u>will</u> to <u>wants to</u>
   (4) replace <u>its</u> with <u>their</u>
   (5) no correction is necessary

3. Sentence 3: <u>**Electrical companies will have started to build power lines**</u> **across the United States, then telephones started to link homes and businesses.**

   Which is the best way to write the underlined portion of sentence 3? If the original is the best way, choose option (1).

   (1) Electrical companies will have started to build power lines
   (2) Electrical companies has started to build power lines
   (3) Electrical companies have started to build power lines
   (4) Electrical companies will had started to build power lines
   (5) Electrical companies had started to build power lines

4. Sentence 7: **Even though our founders did not know it at the time, that failure opened the door to many other products that has work much better.**

   Which correction should be made to sentence 7?

   (1) replace <u>has work</u> with <u>have worked</u>
   (2) replace <u>has</u> with <u>have</u>
   (3) change <u>work</u> to <u>worked</u>
   (4) replace <u>opened</u> with <u>has opened</u>
   (5) no correction is necessary

5. Sentence 10: **We hope that, by the time the company celebrates its next 80 years,** <u>**they used by millions more.**</u>

   Which is the best way to write the underlined portion of sentence 10? If the original is the best way, choose option (1).

   (1) they used by millions more
   (2) they will have used millions more
   (3) they had been used by millions more
   (4) they will have been used by millions more
   (5) they are using millions more

Directions: Choose the <u>one best answer</u> to each question.

<u>Questions 6 through 9</u> refer to the following editorial.

(A)

(1) *The City Chronicle* discover that riders of ATVs (All Terrain Vehicles) are supporting a new bill in the state legislature. (2) The bill would allow them to ride their ATVs in state parks. (3) It is important to stop this bill before it passes.

(B)

(4) A recently-conducted survey shown that walkers and hikers in these areas outnumber ATV riders by more than 2 to 1. (5) ATVs are loud and cause damage to trails even when people ride them responsibly.

(C)

(6) There are many other places where people can enjoy riding their ATVs. (7) For example, thousands of acres of old coal mines in the southern part of the state will have become a tourist destination for ATV riders from other states. (8) We should encourage our state's riders to use these areas rather than try to create new ones.

UNIT 4

6. Sentence 1: ___The City Chronicle___ **discover that riders of ATVs (All Terrain Vehicles) are supporting a new bill in the state legislature.**

   Which is the best way to write the underlined portion of sentence 1? If the original is the best way, choose option (1).

   (1) *The City Chronicle* discover
   (2) *The City Chronicle* had discovering
   (3) *The City Chronicle* has discovered
   (4) *The City Chronicle* have discovers
   (5) *The City Chronicle* will have discover

7. Sentence 4: **A recently-conducted survey shown that walkers and hikers in these areas outnumber ATV riders by more than 2 to 1.**

   Which correction should be made to sentence 4?

   (1) replace <u>conducted</u> with <u>conducting</u>
   (2) replace <u>shown</u> with <u>had shown</u>
   (3) insert <u>have</u> after <u>survey</u>
   (4) insert <u>has</u> before <u>shown</u>
   (5) no correction is necessary

8. Which sentence would be most effective if inserted before sentence 6?

   (1) ATVs have no trouble riding over rough surfaces.
   (2) People have learned to like ATVs.
   (3) Even if you don't like ATVs, they haven't been banned from state parks yet.
   (4) ATVs have been used to explore many rural parts of our state.
   (5) People in the survey have made it clear that they do not want to see ATVs in state parks.

9. Sentence 7: **For example, thousands of acres of old coal mines in the southern part of the state will have become a tourist destination for ATV riders from other states.**

   Which correction should be made to sentence 7?

   (1) remove <u>For example,</u>
   (2) replace <u>become</u> with <u>becoming</u>
   (3) remove <u>will</u>
   (4) change <u>have</u> to <u>have to</u>
   (5) no correction is necessary

Directions: Choose the one best answer to each question.

Questions 10 through 13 refer to the following information.

(A)

(1) Many things happen after a jury had agreed on a verdict. (2) The first thing is that the foreperson, or leader of the jury, returns to the courtroom. (3) The verdict is given to the judge, and read and recorded by the court clerk. (4) Jurors must keep their decision secret until the court have told the verdict.

(B)

(5) The judge will then call the jury and the participants in the case back into the courtroom. (6) If the jury has deliberated for several days, the participants have go home or to another location. (7) It could take several hours to get everyone together.

(C)

(8) After everyone is in the courtroom, the judge will ask the participants to stand. (9) The foreperson of the jury will be asked by the judge what verdict the jury will reach. (10) The foreperson will then read the verdict aloud in the courtroom.

10. Sentence 1: **Many things happen after a jury had agreed on a verdict.**

    Which correction should be made to sentence 1?

    (1) replace had with has
    (2) replace agreed with agrees
    (3) change happen to happens
    (4) remove had
    (5) no correction is necessary

11. Sentence 4: **Jurors must keep their decision secret until the court have told the verdict.**

    Which is the best way to write the underlined portion of sentence 4? If the original is the best way, choose option (1).

    (1) until the court have told the verdict
    (2) until the court has told the verdict
    (3) until the court will have been told the verdict
    (4) until the court has been told the verdict
    (5) until the court will tell the verdict

12. Sentence 6: **If the jury has deliberated for several days, the participants have go home or to another location.**

    Which is the best way to write the underlined portion of sentence 6? If the original is the best way, choose option (1).

    (1) the participants have go home or to another location
    (2) the participants will have to go home or to another location
    (3) the participants had go home or to another location
    (4) the participants to have go home or to another location
    (5) the participants had been at home or at another location

13. Sentence 9: **The foreperson of the jury will be asked by the judge what verdict the jury will reach.**

    Which is the best way to write the underlined portion of sentence 9? If the original is the best way, choose option (1).

    (1) what verdict the jury will reach
    (2) what verdict the jury will have reach
    (3) what verdict the jury had reached
    (4) what verdict the jury has reached
    (5) what verdict the jury will be reaching

Irregular Verbs

For use with student book pp. 82–83

① Review the Skill

Irregular verbs do not follow the rules of regular verbs that use the suffix *–ed*. They change form/letters: *write = wrote* (not *writed*). However, when an irregular verb changes to the past participle form, the suffix *-en* is added: *drive* (present); *drove* (past tense); *driven* (past participle). The best way to learn many irregular verbs is to memorize them.

② Refine the Skill

Even if you do not know the rules, remember that sometimes a sentence just sounds wrong. The past tense form of an irregular verb is used alone (*steal/stole, fall/fell, grow/grew, become/became*), while the past participle form is used with a helping verb (*had stolen, had fallen, have grown, have become*).

☑ TEST-TAKING TIPS

Even if you do not know the rules, remember that sometimes a sentence just sounds wrong. For example, *Not only did it limit individuality, she said the outfits were uncomfortable* sounds better than *Not only do it limit individuality, she say the outfits be uncomfortable.*

To Whom It May Concern,

(A)

(1) I am writing to oppose the school dress code. (2) The school board recently put a mandatory dress code for the entire student body into effect. (3) This dress code was a bad idea. (4) Not only did it limit individuality, but it also prohibited freedom of expression. (5) My daughter attended your school and become so stressed that she withdrew. (6) This dress code also caused unnecessary stress to her classmates.

(B)

(7) A school-wide dress code was an easy way for school officials to get rid of ideas they did not like. (8) I requested that the entire student body, parents, and faculty be invited to the meeting when this issue was raised so that we could have a say in this matter. (9) I <u>took</u> my daughter and her friends to this very important meeting, but we were out-voted. (10) I also <u>went</u> to the meeting that was held last week. (11) I continue to disagree with the decision to make the dress code mandatory, and I plan to fight it until you change your minds.

A *Had taken* is the past participle form of the verb *take*. The past tense, however, is *took*, as seen in sentence 9.

B In sentence 10, *went* is the past tense form of the verb *go*. The past participle, however, is *have gone*.

---

1. Sentence 5: **My daughter attended your school and become so stressed that she withdrew.**

   Which correction should be made to sentence 5?

   (1) change <u>become</u> to <u>became</u>
   (2) replace <u>attended</u> with <u>attends</u>
   (3) replace <u>attended</u> with <u>had attends</u>
   (4) change <u>become</u> to <u>had became</u>
   (5) no correction is necessary

UNIT 4

③ Master the Skill

Directions: Choose the <u>one best answer</u> to each question.

<u>Questions 2 through 5</u> refer to the following editorial.

(A)

(1) Many fans want to know what's wrong with the Thunder this season. (2) The team has not taken care of business this season and is in danger of not making the playoffs. (3) We are passionate fans and demand excellence from the Thunder because we grow up with this team. (4) We really care whether the Thunder wins or loses.

(B)

(5) Some players on the Thunder have been accused of not hustling this season. (6) They appear not to be trying as hard as they did in the past and not playing as well as they have in the past. (7) Fans showed how they felt about this behavior by booing the players last Friday night. (8) This was sad, because it do not take into account how the team felt.

(C)

(9) If we want the Thunder to win the championship this season, then we have to show our support. (10) It would be one thing if the team know it had no chance and give up on the season. (11) However, our players really seem to care, and they said that booing bothers them and has affected their performance. (12) So let's stop booing the Thunder and cheer the team on!

---

2. Sentence 3: **We are passionate fans and demand excellence from the Thunder <u>because we grow up with this team</u>.**

   Which is the best way to write the underlined portion of sentence 3? If the original is the best way, choose option (1).

   (1) because we grow up with this team
   (2) because we grew up with this team
   (3) because we are grown up with this team
   (4) because we growed up with this team
   (5) because we grown up this team

3. Sentence 8: **This was sad, because it do not take into account how the team felt.**

   Which correction should be made to sentence 8?

   (1) replace <u>felt</u> with <u>feels</u>
   (2) change <u>do</u> to <u>does</u>
   (3) change <u>do</u> to <u>did</u>
   (4) replace <u>felt</u> with <u>feeling</u>
   (5) no correction is necessary

4. Sentence 10: **It would be one thing if the team <u>know it had no chance and give up</u> on the season.**

   Which is the best way to write the underlined portion of sentence 10? If the original is the best way, choose option (1).

   (1) know it had no chance and give up
   (2) knows it has no chance and given up
   (3) knew it had no chance and gave up
   (4) knew it had no chance and give up
   (5) know it had no chance and had given up

5. Sentence 11: **However, our players really seem to care, and they said that booing bothers them and has affected their performance.**

   Which correction should be made to sentence 11?

   (1) change <u>However</u> to <u>Similarly</u>
   (2) change <u>players</u> to <u>player</u>
   (3) replace <u>has affected</u> with <u>will have affected</u>
   (4) replace <u>has affected</u> with <u>affecting</u>
   (5) no correction is necessary

Directions: Choose the <u>one best answer</u> to each question.

<u>Questions 6 through 9</u> refer to the following information.

(A)

(1) Your job as a member of the jury is to be a fact finder. (2) Jurors have chose to judge how reliable the witnesses are and must decide how valuable the testimony of each witness is. (3) The jury must listen carefully to all the evidence that gives in the case.

(B)

(4) You may not take notes during the trial unless the judge allows it. (5) If you take notes without the judge's permission, they can be taken away and you may be removed from the jury. (6) You must listen carefully to all the evidence, including what the witnesses say they see, and use your best judgment to reach a decision. (7) As a juror, you should use your common sense and what your adult experience will teach you to arrive at a verdict. (8) You may not rely on private or outside sources of information about the case.

---

6. Sentence 2: **Jurors have chose to judge how reliable the witnesses are and must decide how valuable the testimony of each witness is.**

   Which correction should be made to sentence 2?

   (1) change <u>have chose</u> to <u>have been chosen</u>
   (2) replace <u>are</u> with <u>be</u>
   (3) replace <u>chose</u> with <u>chosed</u>
   (4) change <u>chose</u> to <u>choose</u>
   (5) no correction is necessary

7. Sentence 3: **The jury must listen carefully to all <u>the evidence that gives in the case</u>.**

   Which is the best way to write the underlined portion of sentence 3? If the original is the best way, choose option (1).

   (1) the evidence that gives in the case
   (2) the evidence that gave the case
   (3) the evidence that was given in the case
   (4) the evidence that is given in the case
   (5) the evidence that the case gives

8. Sentence 6: **You must listen carefully to all the evidence, including what <u>the witnesses say they see</u>, and use your best judgment to reach a decision.**

   Which is the best way to write the underlined portion of sentence 6? If the original is the best way, choose option (1).

   (1) the witnesses say they see
   (2) the witnesses said they seen
   (3) the witnesses say they saw
   (4) the witnesses say they will see
   (5) the witnesses said they saw

9. Sentence 7: **As a juror, you should use your common sense and what your adult experience will teach you to arrive at a verdict.**

   The most effective revision to sentence 7 would include which group of words?

   (1) you should use your common sense and what your experience as an adult has taught you
   (2) you should use your common adult sense to teach yourself
   (3) you should be an adult even if you haven't been taught how
   (4) you should use your common sense and adult experience to teach you
   (5) you should have been taught how to be an adult juror

Directions: Choose the <u>one best answer</u> to each question.

<u>Questions 10 through 13</u> refer to the following information.

(A)

(1) Located within walking distance of Hilltop Beach, Breezy Inn and Resort takes you back to another time and place. (2) Our inn recalls the Victorian beach era, when people eat, drink, and first fall in love with the ocean. (3) Today, Breezy Inn has grown into a modern and comfortable hotel.

(B)

(4) A free continental breakfast is served every day, as well as lunch and dinner in our restaurant. (5) Because we treat our guests as we would want to be treated, we have ensured that every guestroom is smoke free. (6) Also, don't forget to get your feet wet in our large outdoor pool, which is open 24 hours and heated all year. (7) Just sit back, relax, and leave your worries at the door.

(C)

(8) Come as you are, or with your family or friends. (9) You can even organize a family reunion. (10) We are approved by travel agents who give us their business year after year. (11) Make your next trip a great one and stay at Breezy Inn and Resort. (12) You will be glad you do!

---

10. Sentence 2: **Our inn recalls the Victorian beach era, when people <u>eat, drink, and first fall in love with the ocean</u>.**

    Which is the best way to write the underlined portion of sentence 2? If the original is the best way, choose option (1).

    (1) eat, drink, and first fall in love with the ocean
    (2) ate, drank, and first fall in love with the ocean
    (3) ate, drunk, and first fell in love with the ocean
    (4) ate, drank, and first fell in love with the ocean
    (5) eating, drinking, and first falling in love with the ocean

11. Sentence 3: **Today, Breezy Inn has grown into a modern and comfortable hotel.**

    Which correction should be made to sentence 3?

    (1) replace <u>has</u> with <u>been</u>
    (2) change <u>grown</u> to <u>grows</u>
    (3) replace <u>has grown</u> with <u>grew</u>
    (4) change <u>has</u> to <u>have</u>
    (5) no correction is necessary

12. Sentence 10: **We are approved by travel agents <u>who give us their business year after year</u>.**

    Which is the best way to write the underlined portion of sentence 10? If the original is the best way, choose option (1).

    (1) who give us their business year after year
    (2) who have given us their business year after year
    (3) who has given us their business year after year
    (4) who give us its business year after year
    (5) who are giving us their business year after year

13. Sentence 12: **You will be glad you do!**

    The most effective revision to sentence 12 would include which group of words?

    (1) You have been glad you do
    (2) You will be glad you did
    (3) You will be glad to do
    (4) You will be glad you have done
    (5) You will have been glad to do

Subject-Verb Agreement
For use with student book pp. 84–85

① **Review the Skill**

Subject-verb agreement is defined by a subject agreeing with its verb in number (singular or plural). When two or more subjects share a verb, it is called a **compound subject**. Compound subjects joined by *and* take a plural verb: *Joe and Jane enjoy watching movies*. Compound subjects joined by *or* agree with the part of the subject closest to the verb: *Joe or his friends enjoy watching movies; The Smiths or Jane enjoys watching movies*.

② **Refine the Skill**

If the subject is singular, the verb should be singular: *He purchases a cell phone*. If the subject is plural, the verb should be plural: *They purchase cell phones*. Review the paragraphs and accompanying callouts. Then answer the question that follows.

☑ **TEST-TAKING TIPS**

When writing, be sure to reread your sentences in order to identify proper subject-verb agreement. Pay special attention to compound subjects by determining whether the subject uses *and* or *or*. Remember that *and* is always plural.

(A)

(1) Thank you for purchasing your new AirWave cell phone. (2) Your new AirWave cell phone is also a radio transmitter and receiver. (3) Be sure to carefully review the manual before you or the phone's recipient begin operating this new AirWave phone. (4) It is important that you understand how to operate your new phone, so be sure to stop by the store with any questions you may have regarding the special features offered to you. (5) If you cannot make it into our store during store hours, please call the customer service number that has been provided to you.

A The singular subject *cell phone* takes the singular verb *is*. If the subject were *cell phones* (plural), then *is* would be the plural form *are*.

(B)

(6) Your new AirWave phone was designed and manufactured not to exceed certain limits set by the U.S. Government. (7) Scientists and phone technicians have tested all AirWave phones, including the one you recently purchased, to make sure they are safe for everyone who will use them. (8) You will get more information about your new phone's safeguards in the mail within a few weeks.

B In sentence 7, the compound subject is *Scientists and phone technicians*. This compound subject is joined by *and*, therefore, the verb must be plural: *have tested*.

1. Sentence 3: **Be sure to carefully review the manual before you or the phone's recipient begin operating this new AirWave phone.**

Which correction should be made to sentence 3?

(1) change <u>review</u> to <u>reviews</u>
(2) replace <u>begin</u> with <u>begins</u>
(3) change <u>begin</u> to <u>began</u>
(4) replace <u>this</u> with <u>these</u>
(5) no correction is necessary

UNIT 4

③ Master the Skill

<u>Directions</u>: Choose the <u>one best answer</u> to each question.

<u>Questions 2 through 5</u> refer to the following editorial.

(A)

(1) *The City Chronicle* has discovered that riders of ATVs (All Terrain Vehicles) is supporting a new bill in the state legislature. (2) The bill would allow them to ride their ATVs in state parks. (3) It is important to stop this bill before it passes.

(B)

(4) Walkers and hikers in these areas outnumbers ATV riders by more than 2 to 1, according to a survey conducted last year. (5) People in the survey have made it clear that they do not want to see ATVs in state parks. (6) Even when people riding them responsibly, loud ATVs causes damage to trails.

(C)

(7) Many other places are available where people can enjoy riding their ATVs. (8) For example, thousands of acres of old coal mines in the southern part of the state have become a tourist destination for ATV riders from other states. (9) We should encourage our state's riders to use these areas rather than try to create new ones.

---

2. Sentence 1: *The City Chronicle* **has discovered that riders of ATVs (All Terrain Vehicles) is supporting a new bill in the state legislature.**

Which correction should be made to sentence 1?

(1) change <u>has</u> to <u>have</u>
(2) change <u>has</u> to <u>had</u>
(3) replace <u>is</u> with <u>are</u>
(4) replace <u>is</u> with <u>were</u>
(5) no correction is necessary

3. Sentence 4: **Walkers and hikers in these areas outnumbers ATV riders by more than 2 to 1, according to a survey conducted last year.**

Which correction should be made to sentence 4?

(1) replace <u>Walkers and hikers</u> with <u>Walker and hiker</u>
(2) replace <u>these</u> with <u>this</u>
(3) replace <u>outnumbers</u> with <u>outnumber</u>
(4) replace <u>year</u> with <u>years</u>
(5) no correction is necessary

4. Sentence 6: **Even when people riding them responsibly, loud ATVs causes damage to trails.**

The most effective revision to sentence 6 would include which group of words?

(1) Loud ATVs causing damage to trails even when people riding them responsibly.
(2) ATVs are loud and causes damage to trails even when people riding them responsibly.
(3) Even when the people rode them responsibly, loud ATVs damage trails.
(4) Loud ATVs cause trail damage if people responsible for riding them
(5) Even when people ride them responsibly, ATVs are loud and cause damage to trails.

5. Sentence 7: <u>**Many other places are**</u> **available where people can enjoy riding their ATVs.**

Which is the best way to write the underlined portion of sentence 7? If the original is the best way, choose option (1).

(1) Many other places are
(2) Many other places be
(3) Many other places is
(4) Many other places were
(5) Many other places been

Directions: Choose the <u>one best answer</u> to each question.

Questions 6 through 9 refer to the following letter.

To All My Readers,

(A)

(1) I want to thank you for reading my latest book. (2) I am grateful for your time and the attention you pay to my works. (3) As an author, it were often hard for me to connect with individual readers. (4) It seems that many people would like to connect, since they have often asked for a way to write to me directly. (5) I am happy to announce that there is a new way. (6) You can now e-mail your thoughts and comments about my work through my new Web site.

(B)

(7) News and information about my books is also going to be on the Web site. (8) It will also offer links to other books that you may be interested in. (9) You will be able to buy these books directly from those Web sites.

(C)

(10) Thanks again for all your support and for reading this book. (11) If you would like to write to me directly, please feel free to do so! (12) I looks forward to hearing from you!

Sincerely,

Joan Tyler

6. Sentence 2: **I am grateful for your time and the attention you pay to my works.**

   Which is the best way to write the underlined portion of sentence 2? If the original is the best way, choose option (1).

   (1) I am grateful for your time
   (2) I was grateful for your time
   (3) You are grateful for my time
   (4) I were grateful for your time
   (5) You is grateful for my time

7. Sentence 3: **As an author, it were often hard for me to connect with individual readers.**

   Which correction should be made to sentence 3?

   (1) replace <u>connect</u> with <u>connects</u>
   (2) change <u>were</u> to <u>is</u>
   (3) change <u>readers</u> to <u>reader</u>
   (4) remove <u>were</u>
   (5) no correction is necessary

8. Sentence 7: **News and information about my books is also going to be on the Web site.**

   Which is the best way to write the underlined portion of sentence 7? If the original is the best way, choose option (1).

   (1) News and information about my books is also
   (2) News and information about my books will
   (3) News and information about my book be also
   (4) News and information about my books are also
   (5) News and information about my book is also

9. Sentence 12: **I looks forward to hearing from you!**

   Which correction should be made to sentence 12?

   (1) change <u>I looks</u> to <u>I looked</u>
   (2) change <u>I looks</u> to <u>I looking</u>
   (3) change <u>I looks</u> to <u>I look</u>
   (4) change <u>from you!</u> to <u>from me!</u>
   (5) no correction is necessary

UNIT 4

Directions: Choose the <u>one best answer</u> to each question.

<u>Questions 10 through 13</u> refer to the following information.

(A)

(1) Civil cases and criminal cases has similarities and differences. (2) A civil case is a dispute between two or more people or corporations. (3) A criminal case is when a person or company is on trial for committing a crime.

(B)

(4) The person who brings the case to court is called the plaintiff. (5) In a civil case, the plaintiff asks the court to protect a right or recover money or property from the person or company accused. (6) In a criminal case, the plaintiff are the U.S. state that is pressing the charges, such as *New York v. Tom Doe.*

(C)

(7) The person or company that are accused becomes the defendant. (8) The defendant can choose to accept the plaintiff's claim, or he or she can present evidence to answer it.

---

10. Sentence 1: **Civil cases and criminal cases has similarities and differences.**

    Which correction should be made to sentence 1?

    (1) change <u>and</u> to <u>or</u>
    (2) change <u>has</u> to <u>have</u>
    (3) change <u>has</u> to <u>had</u>
    (4) remove <u>and</u>
    (5) no correction is necessary

11. Sentence 5: <u>**In a civil case, the plaintiff asks the court**</u> **to protect a right or recover money or property from the person or company accused.**

    Which is the best way to write the underlined portion of sentence 5? If the original is the best way, choose option (1).

    (1) The plaintiff asks the court
    (2) The plaintiff ask the court
    (3) The plaintiff was asked by the court
    (4) The plaintiff asked the court
    (5) The plaintiffs asks the court

12. Sentence 6: **In a criminal case, <u>the plaintiff are</u> the U.S. state that is pressing the charges, such as *New York v. Tom Doe.***

    Which is the best way to write the underlined portion of sentence 6? If the original is the best way, choose option (1).

    (1) the plaintiff are
    (2) the plaintiff be
    (3) the plaintiffs are
    (4) the plaintiff is
    (5) the plaintiffs is

13. Sentence 7: **The person or company that are accused becomes the defendant.**

    Which correction should be made to sentence 7?

    (1) change <u>or</u> to <u>and</u>
    (2) replace <u>person</u> with <u>persons</u>
    (3) change <u>are</u> to <u>is</u>
    (4) change <u>are</u> to <u>be</u>
    (5) no correction is necessary

Subject-Verb Separation
For use with student book pp. 86–87

① Review the Skill

Words and phrases sometimes separate the subject of a sentence from its verb. This is called **subject-verb separation**. A verb can appear before or after a subject in a sentence. However, despite these sentence variations, subjects and verbs must always agree: *My cousins, Mary and Steven, has extra tickets* (incorrect). *My cousins, Mary and Steven, have extra tickets* (correct). Check the glossary at the back of this book if you need help with unfamiliar terms.

② Refine the Skill

The words separating the subject and verb can add information to the sentence: *Picnics, when the weather is nice, are great.* Review the paragraphs and accompanying callouts. Then answer the question that follows.

TEST-TAKING TIPS

After you have finished writing, go back and check that you have used proper subject-verb agreement throughout your essay, especially in those sentences with interrupting phrases. Read the sentence to yourself, omitting the interrupting phrase.

A In sentence 2, the phrase *the ones in an apple orchard* separates the subject *Apples* from the verb *do*. Both the subject and verb are plural despite the interrupting phrase.

B In sentence 8, the verb *Have* appears before the subject *you*. This subject-verb order is helpful when you want to phrase questions.

(A)

(1) Have you ever gone apple picking? (2) Apples, found in apple orchards, do not begin to ripen until early fall. (3) Different kinds of apples ripen at different times. (4) Some of the first to ripen are McIntosh apples. (5) They have a sweet, but also a tart, taste. (6) On the other hand, Cortland apples are some of the last to ripen. (7) They tend to be crisp and juicy.

(B)

(8) Have you ever picked an apple before it was ripe? (9) Waiting until fall to pick apples is a good idea, even if they start appearing in the apple orchard in late summer. (10) Apples are tasty and enjoyable to eat. (11) Picking your very own apples out of an apple orchard is a great fall pastime.

(C)

(12) Apple season, which occurs during the fall, are a fun time of year. (13) You can enjoy picnics outside. (14) Set up a picnic beneath an apple tree, if the owner allows it, so that you can use the tree as shade and as a place to pick out your dessert.

1. Sentence 12: **Apple season, which occurs during the fall, are a fun time of year.**

   Which correction should be made to sentence 12?

   (1) change <u>season</u> to <u>seasons</u>
   (2) replace <u>fall</u> with <u>fallen</u>
   (3) change <u>are</u> to <u>is</u>
   (4) replace <u>time</u> with <u>times</u>
   (5) no correction is necessary

Directions: Choose the one best answer to each question.

Questions 2 through 5 refer to the following information.

(A)

(1) A jury trial involves many people directly or indirectly. (2) You, as a juror, is to listen to the evidence that the prosecution and the defense present. (3) The judge, with his many responsibilities, conduct the trial and rules on questions of law raised by the attorneys. (4) At the end of the trial, he reviews the applicable laws with the jury.

(B)

(5) Attorneys in the case, unless hired by the defendant, are appointed by the court. (6) The lawyers advise the participants on the law and represent them during the trial.

(C)

(7) Under oath, witnesses give their testimony to the court. (8) They tell the court what they saw at the time of the case. (9) They may also tell the court what facts they know about the case. (10) Attorneys, together with the judge, is the only court officials who can address questions to witnesses.

---

2. Sentence 2: **You, as a juror, is to listen to the evidence that the prosecution and the defense present.**

   Which is the best way to write the underlined portion of sentence 2? If the original is the best way, choose option (1).

   (1) You, as a juror, is to listen to the evidence
   (2) You, as a juror, are to listen to the evidence
   (3) You, as a juror, have listened to evidence
   (4) You, as a juror, has to listen to the evidence
   (5) You, as a juror, had to listen to the evidence

3. Sentence 3: **The judge, with his many responsibilities, conduct the trial and rules on questions of law raised by the attorneys.**

   Which is the best way to write the underlined portion of sentence 3? If the original is the best way, choose option (1).

   (1) The judge, with his many responsibilities, conduct the trial
   (2) The judge, with his many responsibilities, has conducted the trial
   (3) The judge, with his many responsibilities, have conducts the trial
   (4) The judge, with his many responsibilities, conducts the trial
   (5) The judge, with his many responsibilities, conducted the trial

4. Sentence 5: **Attorneys in the case, unless hired by the defendant, are appointed by the court.**

   Which correction should be made to sentence 5?

   (1) change Attorneys to Attorney
   (2) replace appointed with appoints
   (3) remove the commas
   (4) change are to is
   (5) no correction is necessary

5. Sentence 10: **Attorneys, together with the judge, is the only court officials who can address questions to witnesses.**

   Which correction should be made to sentence 10?

   (1) change Attorneys to Attorney
   (2) replace is with are
   (3) change is to has
   (4) change can to could
   (5) no correction is necessary

UNIT 4

Directions: Choose the <u>one best answer</u> to each question.

Questions 6 through 9 refer to the following information.

(A)

(1) If you have hardwood floors, these simple dos and don'ts will help you take care of them. (2) Use a damp cloth to blot spills and spots as soon as they happen. (3) Tough spot, including oil stains, paint stains, or cigarette burns, should be treated with nail polish remover. (4) Always avoid allowing spilled liquids to stay on your floors.

(B)

(5) The hardwood floors in many homes gets dirty easily. (6) Sweep, dust, or vacuum the floor regularly to keep dirt from building up on your floors. (7) Don't use steel wool or scouring pads on your floors. (8) Don't wash the floors with soap or any harsh cleaners. (9) Your floors, as well as your warranty, are fragile.

(C)

(10) We hope these dos and don'ts will help you care for your floors. (11) These tips for your hardwood floors, as well as other floor surfaces, be valuable for the lifetime of your floors!

---

6. Sentence 3: **Tough spot, including oil stains, paint stains, or cigarette burns, should be treated with nail polish remover.**

   Which is the best way to write the underlined portion of sentence 3? If the original is the best way, choose option (1).

   (1) Tough spot, including oil stains, paint stains, or cigarette burns, should be treated
   (2) A tough spot, including oil stains, paint stains, or cigarette burns, are treated
   (3) Tough spots, including oil stains, paint stains, or cigarette burns, is treated
   (4) Tough spots, including oil stains and paint stains and cigarette burns, was treated
   (5) Tough spots, including oil stains, paint stains, or cigarette burns, should be treated

7. Sentence 5: **The <u>hardwood floors in many homes gets</u> dirty easily.**

   Which is the best way to write the underlined portion of sentence 5? If the original is the best way, choose option (1).

   (1) hardwood floors in many homes gets
   (2) hardwood floor in many homes has gotten
   (3) hardwood floors in many homes got
   (4) hardwood floors in many homes get
   (5) hardwood flooring in many homes are getting

8. Sentence 9: **Your floors, as well as your warranty, are fragile.**

   Which correction should be made to sentence 9?

   (1) replace <u>are</u> with <u>is</u>
   (2) change <u>your</u> to <u>my</u>
   (3) change <u>your</u> to <u>our</u>
   (4) replace <u>are</u> with <u>be</u>
   (5) no correction is necessary

9. Sentence 11: **These tips for your hardwood floors, as well as other floor surfaces, <u>be valuable for the lifetime of your floors</u>!**

   Which is the best way to write the underlined portion of sentence 11? If the original is the best way, choose option (1).

   (1) be valuable for the lifetime of your floors
   (2) was valuable for the lifetime of your floor
   (3) is valuable for the lifetime of your floors
   (4) be valuable for the lifetime of your floor
   (5) are valuable for the lifetime of your floors

Lesson 10 | Subject-Verb Separation

Directions: Choose the <u>one best answer</u> to each question.

<u>Questions 10 through 13</u> refer to the following letter.

To Whom It May Concern,

(A)

(1) I would like to tell you about what happened at my school yesterday. (2) Several students, including me, was suspended for wearing t-shirts with sayings that protested a political candidate. (3) The principal said that the shirts broke the school's dress code. (4) I think that you can dress neatly and appropriately for school in a way that still allow freedom of speech. (5) Aren't schools supposed to be a place where different ideas are exchanged?

(B)

(6) I believe that students and parents, not the principal, should decides what students can wear to school. (7) Not allowing us to freely express our opinions, even if they are unpopular, hurts everyone.

Sincerely,

Katie Baker

---

10. Sentence 2: **<u>Several students, including me, was suspended for wearing t-shirts</u> with sayings that protested a political candidate.**

Which is the best way to write the underlined portion of sentence 2? If the original is the best way, choose option (1).

(1) Several students, including me, was suspended for wearing t-shirts
(2) Several students, including me, am suspended for wearing t-shirts
(3) Several students, including me, were suspended for wearing t-shirts
(4) Several students, including me, is suspended for wearing t-shirts
(5) Several students, including me, are suspended for wearing t-shirts

11. Sentence 4: **I think that you can dress neatly and appropriately for school in a way that still allow freedom of speech.**

Which correction should be made to sentence 4?

(1) change <u>think</u> to <u>thinks</u>
(2) replace <u>allow</u> with <u>allows</u>
(3) replace <u>way</u> with <u>ways</u>
(4) change <u>way that</u> to <u>way that is</u>
(5) no correction is necessary

12. Sentence 6: **I believe that students and parents, not the principal, should decides what students can wear to school.**

Which correction should be made to sentence 6?

(1) change <u>parents</u> to <u>parent</u>
(2) remove <u>not the principal,</u>
(3) replace <u>students</u> with <u>a student</u>
(4) change <u>should decides</u> to <u>should decide</u>
(5) no correction is necessary

13. Sentence 7: **Not allowing us to freely express our opinions, even if they are unpopular, hurts everyone.**

Which correction should be made to sentence 7?

(1) change <u>express</u> to <u>expresses</u>
(2) change <u>are</u> to <u>were</u>
(3) replace <u>hurts</u> with <u>hurt</u>
(4) replace <u>opinions</u> with <u>opinion</u>
(5) no correction is necessary

Capitalization

For use with student book pp. 96–97

① Review the Skill

As you learned in Unit 4, **capitalization** is used to identify proper nouns (*Joe*), and position titles (*Dr. Smith*). Capitalization is also used for proper adjectives (*United States government*), holidays (*Christmas*), days of the week (*Wednesday*), months of the year (*May*), beginnings of sentences (*The bank is open*), beginnings of quotations (*"Open a checking account," he said.*), published books (*The Firm*), and the word *I*.

② Refine the Skill

The table (right) provides general rules in determining whether to capitalize words. Certain proper nouns, including the names of people and places, require capitalization. Common nouns do not. Review the table, paragraph, and accompanying callouts. Then answer the question that follows.

☑ TEST-TAKING TIPS

Read the paragraph carefully and slowly. Then identify any words that should be capitalized. Determining the capitalization errors as you read will help save time when you answer the questions.

A Notice that each sentence begins with a capital letter. This is important because it helps organize the text and tells the reader where a new sentence begins.

B *Postage* should not be capitalized because it does not meet any of the criteria for capitalization.

(C)

(11) <u>There</u> are several obvious advantages to online banking. (12) For one thing, you'll save the money you're spending on <u>Postage</u>. (14) You will also save any money you're spending on late fees because many Online Banking Services provide you with real-time alerts.

COMMON NOUNS	PROPER NOUNS
the principal	Principal Smith
to eastern Liverpool	East Liverpool
the ocean	Pacific Ocean
a literature class	American Literature class
winter	December

1. Sentence 14: **You will also save any money you're spending on late fees because many Online Banking Services provide you with real-time alerts.**

   Which correction should be made to sentence 14?

   (1) replace <u>many Online Banking Services provide</u> with <u>many online banking services provide</u>
   (2) insert a comma after <u>You</u>
   (3) replace <u>real-time alerts</u> with <u>Real-Time Alerts</u>
   (4) change <u>late fees</u> to <u>Late Fees</u>
   (5) no correction is necessary

Directions: Choose the <u>one best answer</u> to each question.

<u>Questions 2 through 4</u> refer to the following information.

Fall Projects

(A)

(1) When the leaves begin to change colors in the fall, you'll suddenly notice that the Squirrels that have been frolicking in the yard all summer have given up their games for work. (2) They scurry to collect the acorns that have begun falling from nearby oak trees. (3) These creatures know that winter is coming, and it's time to prepare. (4) You would be wise to take this cue from nature and follow suit.

(B)

(5) While you may not need a supply of acorns to get through the winter, you will certainly need heat. (6) It's cost-effective to generate heat and keep it inside your home. (7) To this end, fall is a good time to think about weatherstripping and insulation. (8) You can use weatherstripping to seal doors and windows. (9) Consider adding insulation to your home in attics and basements.

(C)

(10) Knowing that winter brings precipitation in the form of rain or snow, it's a good idea to inspect your gutters, roof, and chimney. (11) Make sure the gutters are clear. (12) Repair any missing or broken shingles. (13) Invite a Chimney Sweep to inspect and clean your chimney.

---

2. Sentence 1: **When the leaves begin to change colors in the fall, you'll suddenly notice that the Squirrels that have been frolicking in the yard all summer have given up their games for work.**

Which correction should be made to sentence 1?

(1) change <u>summer</u> to <u>Summer</u>
(2) replace <u>Squirrels</u> with <u>squirrels</u>
(3) change <u>frolicking</u> to <u>Frolicking</u>
(4) replace <u>games</u> with <u>Games</u>
(5) no correction is necessary

3. Sentence 2: **They scurry to collect the acorns that have begun falling from nearby oak trees.**

Which correction should be made to sentence 2?

(1) change <u>oak</u> to <u>Oak</u>
(2) insert a comma after <u>acorns</u>
(3) replace <u>acorns</u> with <u>Acorns</u>
(4) change <u>have begun</u> to <u>are</u>
(5) no correction is necessary

4. Sentence 13: **Invite a Chimney Sweep to inspect and clean your chimney.**

Which correction should be made to sentence 13?

(1) change <u>your chimney</u> to <u>your Chimney</u>
(2) change <u>Invite</u> to <u>invite</u>
(3) replace <u>inspect</u> with <u>Inspect</u>
(4) replace <u>Chimney Sweep</u> with <u>chimney sweep</u>
(5) no correction is necessary

County Hospital
Human Resources Department
855 Second Avenue
Hot Springs, AR 85196

To: All Employees
From: Lana Little
Subject: Workplace Technology Etiquette

(A)
(1) human resources director Lana Little requests that all employees please make sure to observe the following etiquette guidelines when using technology in the workplace.

(B)
(2) Effective february 20, set all cell phones to silent when entering the building. (3) Vibrations, as well as ring tones, disrupt others who are working around you. (4) In addition, do not use cell phones, headphones, or wireless earpieces in common areas, including restrooms. (5) Again, these habits disrupt others using these areas.

(C)
(6) Do not involve co-workers in Blogging or Social Networking, including visual as well as text entries. (7) By keeping your work life and your private life separate, you will avoid awkward situations at work that may damage people's reputations or careers.

(D)
(8) Finally, make sure to follow electronic communications with personal contact. (9) Remember, e-mail is no substitute for a warm smile or a firm handshake.

5. Sentence 1: **of human resources director Lana Little requests** that all employees please make sure to observe the following etiquette guidelines when using technology in the workplace.

Which is the best way to write the underlined portion of sentence 1? If the original is the best way, choose option (1).

(1) human resources director Lana Little requests
(2) human resources director lana little requests
(3) human resources Director Lana Little requests
(4) Human Resources director Lana Little requests
(5) Human Resources Director Lana Little requests

6. Sentence 2: **Effective february 20, set all cell phones to silent when entering the building.**

Which correction should be made to sentence 2?

(1) change february to February
(2) move the comma to follow Effective
(3) change Effective to effective
(4) change building to Building
(5) no correction is necessary

7. Sentence 6: **Do not involve co-workers in Blogging or Social Networking, including visual as well as text entries.**

Which correction should be made to sentence 6?

(1) change involve to involves
(2) replace Blogging or Social Networking with blogging or social networking
(3) change visual and text to Visual and Text
(4) change co-workers to Co-Workers
(5) no correction is necessary

UNIT 5

How to Read a Nutrition Label

Nutrition Facts
Serving Size 1 potato (148g/5.3oz)

Amount Per Serving

Calories 100   Calories from Fat 0

	% Daily Value*
Total Fat 0g	**0%**
Saturated Fat 0g	**0%**
Cholesterol 0mg	**0%**
Sodium 0mg	**0%**
Potassium 720mg	**21%**
Total Carbohydrate 26g	**9%**
Dietary Fiber 3g	**12%**
Sugars 3g	
Protein 4g	

Vitamin A 0%	•	Vitamin C 45%	
Calcium 2%	•	Iron 6%	
Thiamin 8%	•	Riboflavin 2%	
Niacin 8%	•	Vitamin B$_6$ 10%	
Folate 6%	•	Phosphorous 6%	
Zinc 2%	•	Magnesium 6%	

*Percent Daily Values are based on a 2,000 calorie diet.

Sample Nutrition Label

(A)
(1) The nutrition label on a food product is easy to find and read. (2) Yet, understanding the label can be challenging. (3) First, note the serving size at the top of the label. (4) All of the information that follows relates to the serving size. (5) For example if there are 100 calories in one serving, there are 200 calories in two servings, and so on.

(B)
(6) Next, compare the "good" ingredients to the "bad" ingredients. (7) The "bad" ingredients, such as Fat, Cholesterol, and Sodium, are listed first. (8) You want to limit your intake of these items. (9) The % daily value number will help you accomplish this goal. (10) Use this rule of thumb when interpreting % daily value numbers: 5% is low and 20% is high. (11) For example, 21% Potassium is a bad high number.

(C)
(12) The "good" ingredients, such as vitamins, calcium, and iron, are listed last. (13) You want to increase your intake of these items. (14) Again, the % daily value number will help you accomplish this goal. (15) For example, 45% vitamin c is a good high number.

8. Sentence 7: **The "bad" ingredients, such as Fat, Cholesterol, and Sodium, are listed first.**

Which correction should be made to sentence 7?

(1) replace "bad" with "Bad"
(2) change are to is
(3) replace Fat, Cholesterol, and Sodium with fat, cholesterol, and sodium
(4) change ingredients to Ingredients
(5) no correction is necessary

9. Sentence 11: **For example, 21% Potassium is a bad high number.**

Which correction should be made to sentence 11?

(1) replace high number with High Number
(2) change Potassium to potassium
(3) change bad to Bad
(4) remove the comma after example
(5) no correction is necessary

10. Sentence 15: **For example, 45% vitamin c is a good high number.**

Which correction should be made to sentence 15?

(1) remove the comma after example
(2) change good high number to Good High Number
(3) change vitamin c to vitamin C
(4) change example to Example
(5) no correction is necessary

P ossessives and Contractions

For use with student book pp. 98–99

① **Review the Skill**

You can show possession, or to whom or what something or someone belongs, by using an apostrophe. These apostrophes are called **possessives**. Examples of possessives include: *child's game*; *Fergus's shovel*; *women's club*; *coaches' meeting* (the apostrophe comes after the *s* when the subject is plural); *father-in-law's lawn mower*; and *Ray and Burnice's yard*. You also should use an apostrophe to replace missing letters when you form a **contraction**: *I'll* (I will), *it's* (it is), *shouldn't* (should not), or *they've* (they have). Creating contractions enables you to use fewer words when writing informally.

② **Refine the Skill**

To reinforce the rules for using an apostrophe, study these common public signs. Can you identify the apostrophe errors? Review the text and callouts. Then answer the question that follows.

☑ **TEST-TAKING TIPS**

Remember not to confuse possessive pronouns, such as *your*, *its*, and *their*, with contractions, such as *you're*, *it's*, and *they're*.

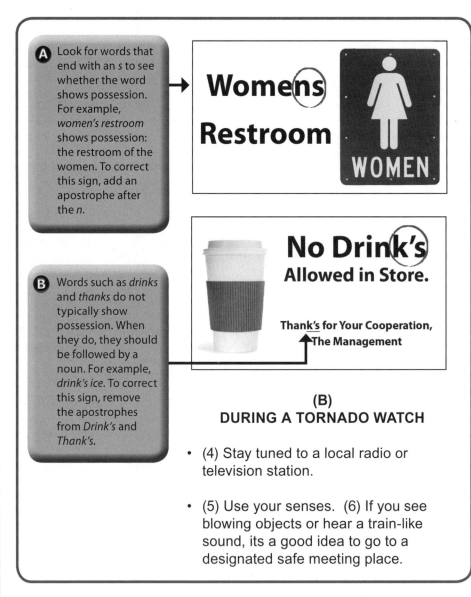

A Look for words that end with an *s* to see whether the word shows possession. For example, *women's restroom* shows possession: the restroom of the women. To correct this sign, add an apostrophe after the *n*.

B Words such as *drinks* and *thanks* do not typically show possession. When they do, they should be followed by a noun. For example, *drink's ice*. To correct this sign, remove the apostrophes from *Drink's* and *Thank's*.

(B) DURING A TORNADO WATCH

- (4) Stay tuned to a local radio or television station.

- (5) Use your senses. (6) If you see blowing objects or hear a train-like sound, its a good idea to go to a designated safe meeting place.

1. Sentence 6: **If you see blowing objects or hear a train-like sound, its a good idea to go to a designated safe meeting place.**

    Which correction should be made to sentence 6?

    (1) change <u>see</u> to <u>see's</u>
    (2) replace <u>objects</u> with <u>objects'</u>
    (3) change <u>you</u> to <u>you'll</u>
    (4) replace <u>its</u> with <u>it's</u>
    (5) no correction is necessary

UNIT 5

Directions: Choose the <u>one best answer</u> to each question.

Questions 2 through 4 refer to the following information.

Cancer Prevention

(A)

(1) Oral cancer affects about 1 out of every 98 people. (2) To prevent this common cancer, report persistent mouth sores to your doctor. (3) In addition, report color changes, pain, tenderness, or numbness in the mouth. (4) Limit or eliminate smoking and drinking alcohol. (5) Use sunscreen on your lips. (6) Finally, eat avocados. (7) Research suggests that chemicals in avocados' destroy oral cancer cells.

(B)

(8) Leukemia, another cancer, affects children and older adults. (9) Report the following symptoms to your doctor immediately: paleness, bruising, bleeding gums, tiredness, odd fevers, or bone or joint discomfort. (10) As a preventive measure, limit the number of CT scan's you undergo. (11) Excess radiation may trigger leukemia.

(C)

(12) Endometrial or uterine cancer affects about 1 out of every 40 women. (13) Most cases affect women older than 50. (14) Report the following symptoms to your doctor immediately: uncommon bleeding or pelvic pain. (15) Its also important to report one's family medical history to a physician. (16) To prevent endometrial cancer, maintain a healthy weight, exercise, and replace iron supplements with calcium supplements after age 50.

---

2. Sentence 7: **Research suggests that chemicals in avocados' destroy oral cancer cells.**

Which correction should be made to sentence 7?

(1) replace <u>cells</u> with <u>cell's</u>
(2) change <u>Research</u> to <u>research</u>
(3) replace <u>avocados'</u> with <u>avocados</u>
(4) change <u>destroy</u> to <u>destroys</u>
(5) no correction is necessary

3. Sentence 10: **As a preventive measure, limit the number of CT scan's you undergo.**

Which correction should be made to sentence 10?

(1) replace <u>scan's</u> with <u>scans</u>
(2) change <u>measure</u> to <u>measures'</u>
(3) replace <u>you</u> with <u>your</u>
(4) insert a semicolon after <u>measure</u>
(5) no correction is necessary

4. Sentence 15: **Its also important to report one's family medical history to a physician.**

Which correction should be made to sentence 15?

(1) replace <u>physician</u> with <u>physician's</u>
(2) change <u>one's</u> to <u>ones</u>
(3) replace <u>Its</u> with <u>It's</u>
(4) change <u>one's</u> to <u>ones'</u>
(5) no correction is necessary

> ## Job-Hunting Hints
>
> **(A)**
>
> (1) It once was fairly common for employees to work their entire careers at a single company. (2) However, today's employees often work for a number of businesses throughout their careers. (3) Although these employees are of different ages and backgrounds, they often compete for the same jobs. (4) Given the intensity of the competition for good jobs, it's important that one doesnot fall prey to common job-hunting mistakes.
>
> **(B)**
>
> (5) Remember that the purpose of a good résumé is to get an interview. (6) Make sure you're résumé includes contact information and references. (7) Additionally, make sure you can explain any gaps in your job history or frequent job changes. (8) Finally, use language that is varied but specific. (9) You want to find a happy medium between saying too much and saying too little about your background.
>
> **(C)**
>
> (10) Once you land the interview, remember that you are there to sell yourself. (11) Make sure that you are prepared for the interview. (12) You want to appear knowledgeable about the companys history, and you should ask intelligent and insightful questions. (13) Make sure that your responses to questions are positive and consistent. (14) Express your career goals, and indicate that flexibility is one of your most important characteristics.

5. Sentence 4: **Given the intensity of the competition for good jobs, it's important that one <u>doesnot</u> fall prey to common job-hunting mistakes.**

   Which is the best way to write the underlined portion of sentence 4? If the original is the best way, choose option (1).

   (1) doesnot
   (2) doesn't
   (3) doesnt'
   (4) doesnt
   (5) do'snt

6. Sentence 6: **Make sure you're résumé includes contact information and references.**

   Which correction should be made to sentence 6?

   (1) change <u>résumé</u> is to <u>résumés'</u>
   (2) change <u>references</u> to <u>reference's</u>
   (3) replace <u>you're</u> with <u>your</u>
   (4) replace <u>includes</u> with <u>include</u>
   (5) no correction is necessary

7. Sentence 12: **You want to appear knowledgeable about the <u>companys history</u>, and you should ask intelligent and insightful questions.**

   Which is the best way to write the underlined portion of sentence 12? If the original is the best way, choose option (1).

   (1) companys history
   (2) history's of the company
   (3) history of the companies
   (4) company's history
   (5) history of the company's

UNIT 5

Questions 8 through 10 refer to the following information.

> **Car Buying Tips**
>
> **(A)**
> (1) You're in the market for a new car, and you're wondering whether you should buy a new car or a used car. (2) Everyone has advice for you. (3) Your aunt says you should save money and buy a nice used car. (4) You weigh her opinion against your father's belief that buying a used car may cost you more money in the long run. (5) You find all of the advice to be overwhelming. (6) What's the best choice for you? (7) Here are some issues to consider.
>
> **(B)**
> (8) Buying a new car may be the best choice when interest rate's are low. (9) New cars also offer the latest technology, which results in better gas mileage and fuel savings, as well as state-of-the-art safety features such as air bags and tire-pressure gauges. (10) Also, new cars are under warranty, meaning that the maintenance costs for them are low. (11) These features make new cars dependable methods of everyday transportation.
>
> **(C)**
> (12) However, if you're on a tight budget, then buying a used car may offer the best value to you. (13) For less than half the price of the average new car, you can buy a used vehicle that may be larger and include more features. (14) However, buying a used car does not come without risks, which could include greater repair and maintenance costs. (15) Such costs probably won't be covered by a warranty.

8. Sentence 4: **You weigh her opinion against your father's belief that buying a used car may cost you more money in the long run.**

   What does the apostrophe in the underlined portion of this sentence indicate?

   (1) more than one person
   (2) possession of an opinion
   (3) a contraction
   (4) ownership of a car
   (5) a relationship between family members

9. Sentence 8: **Buying a new car may be the best choice when interest rate's are low.**

   Which correction should be made to sentence 8?

   (1) change rate's to rates
   (2) replace may with May
   (3) change interest to interests'
   (4) replace car with Car
   (5) no correction is necessary

10. Sentence 12: **However, if you're on a tight budget, then buying a used car may offer the best value to you.**

    Which correction should be made to sentence 12?

    (1) change you're to your
    (2) change you to your
    (3) replace offer with offers
    (4) change value to values
    (5) no correction is necessary

Homonyms

For use with student book pp. 100–101

① Review the Skill

There are two types of **homonyms**: **homophones** and **homographs**. Homophones are words that sound similar but have different spellings and different meanings, such as *buy* (purchase) and *bye* (farewell). In contrast, homographs are words that may or may not sound similar. They have the same spellings, but different meanings, such as *bill* (a record of money owed), *bill* (one dollar), and *bill* (beak). All homonyms share something in common: pronunciation or spelling. Check the glossary at the back of this book if you need help with unfamiliar terms.

② Refine the Skill

To practice using common homonyms, try creating riddles, like the ones provided. Review these riddles, the paragraph, and the accompanying callouts. Then answer the question that follows.

☑ TEST-TAKING TIPS

Use the surrounding text, or context of the sentence, to determine the correct homophone. The writer is discussing the habits of people. Which form—*click* or *clique*—is intended?

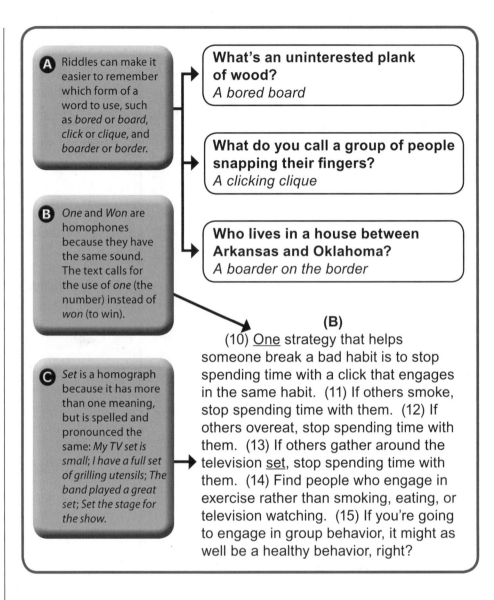

A Riddles can make it easier to remember which form of a word to use, such as *bored* or *board*, *click* or *clique*, and *boarder* or *border*.

What's an uninterested plank of wood?
A bored board

What do you call a group of people snapping their fingers?
A clicking clique

B *One* and *Won* are homophones because they have the same sound. The text calls for the use of *one* (the number) instead of *won* (to win).

Who lives in a house between Arkansas and Oklahoma?
A boarder on the border

(B)
(10) <u>One</u> strategy that helps someone break a bad habit is to stop spending time with a click that engages in the same habit. (11) If others smoke, stop spending time with them. (12) If others overeat, stop spending time with them. (13) If others gather around the television <u>set</u>, stop spending time with them. (14) Find people who engage in exercise rather than smoking, eating, or television watching. (15) If you're going to engage in group behavior, it might as well be a healthy behavior, right?

C *Set* is a homograph because it has more than one meaning, but is spelled and pronounced the same: *My TV set is small; I have a full set of grilling utensils; The band played a great set; Set the stage for the show.*

1. Sentence 10: **One strategy that helps someone break a bad habit is to stop spending time with a <u>click</u> that engages in the same habit.**

   In sentence 10, what does the writer *intend* the underlined word to mean?

   (1) to suddenly understand
   (2) a sound
   (3) a small group of people
   (4) to cluck the tongue on the roof of the mouth
   (5) to activate a computer icon

③ Master the Skill

Directions: Choose the one best answer to each question.

Questions 2 through 4 refer to the following information.

Who Says Nothing is Free?

(A)

(1) We live in a world of rising prices. (2) In such a world, it's difficult to believe that anyone achieves the feet of getting anything for free anymore. (3) However, there are a few businesses that use freebies as a marketing strategy. (4) Knowing who is giving away what may allow you to live the good life free of charge.

(B)

(5) One important tool in the search for free stuff is the Internet, of course. (6) With a good search engine, you can find a grate vacation home for free by linking up with a home exchange program. (7) In such an arrangement, you trade homes with another person for a period of time. (8) You also can find and download free movies and music on the Internet. (9) Additionally, there are a number of sites that offer free advice about the law, tax preparation, and money management.

(C)

(10) Another important area to explore in the search for free stuff is education. (11) That's right—people who are enrolled in coarses to become massage therapists, hair stylists, and manicurists need people on whom to practice their skills. (12) Now, there's a volunteer program that most of us would be willing to join.

---

2. Sentence 2: **In such a world, it's difficult to believe that anyone achieves the feet of getting anything for free anymore.**

Which correction should be made to sentence 2?

(1) change it's to its
(2) replace feet with feat
(3) change for to fore
(4) remove the comma after world
(5) no correction is necessary

3. Sentence 6: **With a good search engine, you can find a grate vacation home for free by linking up with a home exchange program.**

Which correction should be made to sentence 6?

(1) replace grate with great
(2) change for to four
(3) replace by with bye
(4) change by to buy
(5) no correction is necessary

4. Sentence 11: **That's right—people who are enrolled in coarses to become massage therapists, hair stylists, and manicurists need people on whom to practice their skills.**

Which correction should be made to sentence 11?

(1) change are to our
(2) replace right with rite
(3) replace coarses with courses
(4) replace their with there
(5) no correction is necessary

Questions 5 through 7 refer to the following information.

BOIL WATER ALERT
Rose Bud, Texas

(A)

(1) The Rose Bud City Counsel has issued a boil water advisory for the citizens of Rose Bud and the surrounding areas. (2) The advisory will be in affect until the Department of Environmental Protection has collected water samples and tested these samples at the state laboratory facility.

(B)

(3) This advisory has been issued due to high levels of several bacterias that have been identified in the city water supply. (4) In response to this situation, city officials have added chlorine to the water supply. (5) However, in the interest of safety, residents, particularly miners and the elderly, should continue to boil water until otherwise notified.

5. Sentence 1: **The Rose Bud City Counsel has issued a boil water advisory for the citizens of Rose Bud and the surrounding areas.**

    Which correction should be made to sentence 1?

    (1) replace Counsel with Council
    (2) change Rose Bud to rose bud
    (3) insert a comma after Bud
    (4) replace for with four
    (5) no correction is necessary

6. Sentence 2: **The advisory will be in affect until the Department of Environmental Protection has collected water samples and tested these samples at the state laboratory facility.**

    Which correction should be made to sentence 2?

    (1) change Department of Environmental Protection to department of environmental protection
    (2) replace affect with effect
    (3) change be to bee
    (4) remove at the state laboratory facility
    (5) no correction is necessary

7. Sentence 5: **However, in the interest of safety, residents, particularly miners and the elderly, should continue to boil water until otherwise notified.**

    Which correction should be made to sentence 5?

    (1) replace residents with residence
    (2) remove the comma after However
    (3) replace to with too
    (4) replace miners with minors
    (5) no correction is necessary

Lesson 3 | Homonyms

> ### Similarities and Differences Between Monkeys and Apes
>
> **(A)**
> (1) Monkeys and apes have physical characteristics that are both similar and different. (2) Monkeys have small builds, while apes have husky builds. (3) Monkeys have arms that are equal to or shorter than there legs, while apes have arms that exceed the length of their legs. (4) Monkeys have tales, while apes do not.
>
> **(B)**
> (5) Another difference between monkeys and apes is that sum monkeys have visible teeth, and sum apes, such as gorillas and chimpanzees, have the ability to use tools to solve problems. (6) However, monkeys are not completely different than apes; both are active during the day, and both lack a keen sense of smell. (7) Some similarities between monkeys and apes also include dry noses and fingernails.

8. Sentence 2: **Monkeys have small builds, while apes have <u>husky</u> builds.**

    In sentence 2, what does the underlined homograph mean?

    (1) a sled dog
    (2) a snow dog
    (3) something that is big and strong
    (4) something that is deep and hoarse
    (5) something that contains husks

9. Sentence 3: **Monkeys have arms that are equal to or shorter than there legs, while apes have arms that exceed the length of their legs.**

    Which correction should be made to sentence 3?

    (1) replace <u>are</u> with <u>our</u>
    (2) change <u>their</u> to <u>there</u>
    (3) replace <u>than</u> with <u>then</u>
    (4) change <u>there</u> to <u>their</u>
    (5) no correction is necessary

10. Sentence 4: **Monkeys have tales, while apes do not.**

    Which correction should be made to sentence 4?

    (1) replace <u>tales</u> with <u>tails</u>
    (2) change <u>do</u> to <u>dew</u>
    (3) replace <u>not</u> with <u>knot</u>
    (4) remove the comma after <u>tales</u>
    (5) no correction is necessary

11. Sentence 5: **Another difference between monkeys and apes is that sum monkeys have visible teeth, and sum apes, such as gorillas and chimpanzees, have the ability to use tools to solve problems.**

    Which correction should be made to sentence 5?

    (1) replace <u>chimpanzees</u> with <u>chimpanzees'</u>
    (2) change <u>gorillas</u> to <u>guerrillas</u>
    (3) replace <u>apes</u> with <u>ape's</u>
    (4) replace <u>sum</u> with <u>some</u>
    (5) no correction is necessary

Commonly Misspelled Words
For use with student book pp. 102–103

① Review the Skill

There are several hundred **commonly misspelled words** within the English language because they have spelling patterns that cannot be explained by traditional spelling rules. These rules include *i* before *e*, except after *c*, or when sounding like *a* as in *neighbor* and *weigh*; remove the *e* at the end of a word when adding a suffix that begins in a vowel, such as *-ed*, and *-ing*; and *x* is never immediately followed by an *s*, such as in *excited* and *boxes*.

② Refine the Skill

When you become aware of a word that you commonly misspell, take time to memorize the spelling and common spelling rules. A common way to memorize information is to use a method called *see it, say it, touch it, write it*. Review the paragraph and accompanying callouts. Then answer the question that follows.

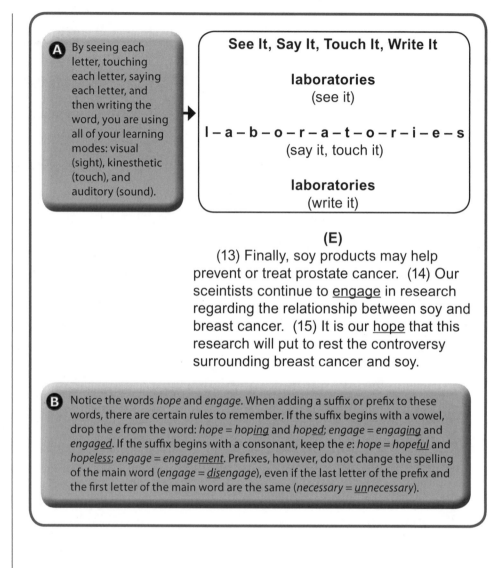

A By seeing each letter, touching each letter, saying each letter, and then writing the word, you are using all of your learning modes: visual (sight), kinesthetic (touch), and auditory (sound).

See It, Say It, Touch It, Write It

laboratories
(see it)

l – a – b – o – r – a – t – o – r – i – e – s
(say it, touch it)

laboratories
(write it)

(E)
(13) Finally, soy products may help prevent or treat prostate cancer. (14) Our sceintists continue to <u>engage</u> in research regarding the relationship between soy and breast cancer. (15) It is our <u>hope</u> that this research will put to rest the controversy surrounding breast cancer and soy.

B Notice the words *hope* and *engage*. When adding a suffix or prefix to these words, there are certain rules to remember. If the suffix begins with a vowel, drop the *e* from the word: *hope* = *hop<u>ing</u>* and *hop<u>ed</u>*; *engage* = *engag<u>ing</u>* and *engag<u>ed</u>*. If the suffix begins with a consonant, keep the *e*: *hope* = *hope<u>ful</u>* and *hope<u>less</u>*; *engage* = *engag<u>ement</u>*. Prefixes, however, do not change the spelling of the main word (*engage* = <u>*dis*engage</u>), even if the last letter of the prefix and the first letter of the main word are the same (*necessary* = <u>*un*necessary</u>).

✓ TEST-TAKING TIPS

Remember that there are exceptions to basic spelling rules, such as *i* before *e*. Anytime you encounter an exception to the rule, make a point to memorize it.

1. Sentence 14: **Our sceintists continue to engage in research regarding the relationship between breast cancer and soy.**

   Which correction should be made to sentence 14?

   (1) change <u>sceintists</u> to <u>scientists</u>
   (2) replace <u>Our</u> with <u>Are</u>
   (3) change <u>regarding</u> to <u>reguarding</u>
   (4) replace <u>engage</u> with <u>engaging</u>
   (5) no correction is necessary

UNIT 5

Directions: Choose the <u>one best answer</u> to each question.

<u>Questions 2 through 4</u> refer to the following letter.

Money Bank
200 North Street
Texarkana, AR 56513

Mr. Paul Wilford
1234 South Street
Texarkana, AR 56513

Dear Mr. Wilford,

(A)

(1) First, let me express my appreciation that you have chosen our bank to serve your financial needs upon your relocation to Texarkana. (2) We strive to provide our customers with quality services that satisfy every aspect of their financial portfolios, including saveings, bill payment, and education and retirement funds.

(B)

(3) In response to your inquiry regarding a checking account, the following items are necessary to open such an account: two forms of identification, including one with a picture; your social security number; and a $300 deposit. (4) Once you've gathered these items, one of our financial advisors will be happy to assist you in opening a checking account. (5) Please consider the option of opening a companion savings account as well. (6) The two accounts will garuntee that you have many options as you manage your monthly expenses.

(C)

(7) Please don't hesatate to contact me if you have other questions. (8) We look forward to serving you.

Sincerely,

Irma Bennet, Manager

---

2. Sentence 2: **We strive to provide our customers with quality services that satisfy every aspect of their financial portfolios, including savings, bill payment, and education and retirement funds.**

Which correction should be made to sentence 2?

(1) change <u>quality</u> to <u>quallity</u>
(2) change <u>every</u> to <u>evry</u>
(3) change <u>retirement</u> to <u>retirment</u>
(4) change <u>saveings</u> to <u>savings</u>
(5) no correction is necessary

3. Sentence 6: **The two accounts will garuntee that you have many options as you manage your monthly expenses.**

Which correction should be made to sentence 6?

(1) change <u>accounts</u> to <u>acounts</u>
(2) replace <u>garuntee</u> with <u>guarantee</u>
(3) change <u>manage</u> to <u>manege</u>
(4) replace <u>expenses</u> with <u>expences</u>
(5) no correction is necessary

4. Sentence 7: **Please don't hesatate to contact me if you have other questions.**

Which correction should be made to sentence 7?

(1) change <u>Please</u> to <u>Pleaze</u>
(2) replace <u>to</u> with <u>too</u>
(3) change <u>don't</u> to <u>dont</u>
(4) replace <u>hesatate</u> with <u>hesitate</u>
(5) no correction is necessary

UNIT 5

Questions 5 through 7 refer to the following information.

How to Hang a Picture

(A)

(1) Anytime you move into a new home, one job that inevitably follows is hanging pictures. (2) As simple as this job sounds, it can raise anxiety levels. (3) You don't want to put unnecessary holes in the new walls. (4) You don't want the pictures to hang too high or too low. (5) You don't want to be disatisfied with how the pictures are spaced on a wall. (6) Suddenly, a simple job has turned into a complex problem. (7) Perhaps these tips will reduce your anxiety and simplify matters for you.

(B)
Using Your Wall Space

- (8) Unframed works need to be surrounded by more wall space than framed works.

- (9) Related works can be grouped together, while unrelated works should be spaced apart.

- (10) An arrangement of related works should be grouped around a larger central piece.

- (11) Avoid hanging works in corners. (12) Lighting often is poor in corners, which can affect people's impressions of the pieces.

- (13) Hang the center of any piece at eye level.

---

5. Sentence 3: **You don't want to put unnecessary holes in the new walls.**

   Which correction should be made to sentence 3?

   (1) replace <u>to</u> with <u>too</u>
   (2) change <u>unnecessary</u> to <u>unecessary</u>
   (3) replace <u>holes</u> with <u>wholes</u>
   (4) replace <u>new</u> with <u>knew</u>
   (5) no correction is necessary

6. Sentence 5: **You don't want to be disatisfied with how the pictures are spaced on a wall.**

   Which correction should be made to sentence 5?

   (1) change <u>pictures</u> to <u>pitchers</u>
   (2) replace <u>wall</u> with <u>woll</u>
   (3) change <u>be</u> to <u>bee</u>
   (4) replace <u>disatisfied</u> with <u>dissatisfied</u>
   (5) no correction is necessary

7. Sentence 10: **An arrangment of related works should be grouped around a central piece.**

   Which correction should be made to sentence 10?

   (1) replace <u>related</u> with <u>reladed</u>
   (2) change <u>piece</u> to <u>peace</u>
   (3) replace <u>arrangment</u> with <u>arrangement</u>
   (4) change <u>central</u> to <u>centrel</u>
   (5) no correction is necessary

Join the Composting Craze

(A)

(1) Recycling and waste management are never as easy as when you leave them to nature. (2) When leaves, sticks, grass, fruits, and vegtables decompose, they feed the soil. (3) In turn, healthy soil produces more trees, grass, and produce. (4) When these organic materials are sent to landfills, they take up space and are unable to effectively do the job nature has assigned them. (5) One way to restore balance to this process is to accept the responsability of composting at home.

(B)

(6) To begin, you need a composting bin. (7) Such bins can be purchased or constructed from wood, wire, or garbage cans.

(C)

(8) To cause decomposition, you need substancial layers of four key ingredients: nitrogen, carbon, water, and air. (9) The following table describes those layers.

Nitrogen	(9) Think green: add grass, leaves, and produce.
Carbon	(10) Think brown: add dry leaves or sticks, hay, wood chips, or sawdust.
Water	(11) Think wet: use a hose to maintain moisture throughout the pile.
Air	(12) Think oxygen: use a pitch fork to ruffle the pile weekly.

8. Sentence 2: **When leaves, sticks, grass, fruits, and vegtables decompose, they feed the soil.**

   Which correction should be made to sentence 2?

   (1) change feed to fead
   (2) replace fruits with frutes
   (3) change vegtables to vegetables
   (4) replace decompose with decomposs
   (5) no correction is necessary

9. Sentence 5: **One way to restore balance to this process is to accept the responsability of composting at home.**

   Which correction should be made to sentence 5?

   (1) change accept to except
   (2) replace responsability with responsibility
   (3) change balance to balence
   (4) replace process with prossess
   (5) no correction is necessary

10. Sentence 8: **To cause decomposition, you need substancial layers of four key ingredients: nitrogen, carbon, water, and air.**

    Which correction should be made to sentence 8?

    (1) change nitrogen to nitrogin
    (2) replace ingredients with ingrediants
    (3) change substancial to substantial
    (4) replace carbon with carben
    (5) no correction is necessary

Commas

For use with student book pp. 104–105

① Review the Skill

Commas are used to form a series (*sweet, crisp, and juicy*), introductory phrases (*After that, we ate apples*), and interrupting phrases (*The apples, once ripe, were tasty*). They are also used in compound sentences (*I like apples, and I want one now*), complex sentences (*Although the apple was ripe, we didn't eat it*), and quotations (*"I want an apple," she said.*).

② Refine the Skill

Commas can also change the meaning of a sentence. For example, in the sentence *I'd like to thank my parents, John and Martha* it is clear that the writer's parents are named John and Martha. However, *I'd like to thank my parents, John, and Martha* indicates that the writer thanks John and Martha in addition to his or her parents. Review the paragraphs and accompanying callouts. Then answer the question that follows.

☑ TEST-TAKING TIPS

Writers sometimes use transitions, phrases, or clauses to introduce a sentence. Such introductory phrases are followed by commas: *After it rained, we picked oranges.*

(A)

(1) You've joined others in the grocery store, **Ⓐ** I'm sure, who were thumping watermelons or smelling cantaloupes in an effort to choose the best produce. (2) We love to eat watermelons and apples yet we've all experienced the disappointment of biting into a slice of watermelon or apple that wasn't sweet. (3) What's the secret to selecting produce that is **Ⓑ** ripe, sweet, crisp, or juicy? (4) Here are a few tips that may help.

(B)

(5) First, use your eyes. (6) Don't buy produce with bruises, mold, or holes on it. (7) Next, use your nose. (8) Don't buy any produce that doesn't smell good.

Ⓐ An interrupting phrase, such as *I'm sure* in sentence 1, provides extra information within a sentence. If this phrase was removed, the sentence would maintain its meaning: *You've joined others in the grocery store who were thumping watermelons or smelling cantaloupes in an effort to choose the best produce.*

Ⓑ The series in sentence 3 would not be clear if it were missing commas: *What's the secret to selecting produce that is ripe sweet crisp and juicy?* Adding commas allows for a natural pause and better understanding of the sentence.

1. Sentence 2: **We love to eat watermelons and apples yet we've all experienced the disappointment of biting into a slice of watermelon or apple that wasn't sweet.**

   Which correction should be made to sentence 2?

   (1) insert a comma after <u>We</u>
   (2) insert a comma after <u>apples</u>
   (3) insert a comma after <u>watermelon</u>
   (4) insert a comma after <u>yet</u>
   (5) no correction is necessary

③ Master the Skill

Directions: Choose the <u>one best answer</u> to each question.

<u>Questions 2 through 4</u> refer to the following information.

Herb Gardening

(A)

(1) You've been thinking about using an empty plot of ground in the backyard for a garden. (2) Yet you can't decide what to plant. (3) You might consider planting an herb garden. (4) Herbs are aromatic and they can be harvested for cooking. (5) You can grow herbs from seeds, or you can buy seedlings. (6) Consider planting a variety of herbs, such as rosemary sage basil dill mint thyme chives and parsley.

(B)

(7) Herbs will not grow in wet soil. (8) You need to ensure that your garden site has good drainage. (9) If not, you can remove 15 to 18 inches of top soil, and add broken rocks to the area. (10) Then, mix the top soil with compost before replacing it. (11) In general your herb garden should not need any additional fertilizer.

(C)

(12) Herb leaves may be harvested as soon as the plants are large enough to sustain growth. (13) You may use fresh leaves in cooking, or you may dry or freeze leaves for winter use. (14) You can dry leaves by hanging them upside down in a dark space for one to two weeks or baking them in the oven at a low heat for two to four hours.

---

2. Sentence 4: **Herbs are aromatic and they can be harvested for cooking.**

   Which correction should be made to sentence 4?

   (1) insert a comma after <u>and</u>
   (2) change <u>for</u> to <u>fore</u>
   (3) insert a comma after <u>aromatic</u>
   (4) insert a comma after <u>harvested</u>
   (5) no correction is necessary

3. Sentence 6: **Consider planting a variety of herbs, such as rosemary sage basil dill mint thyme chives and parsley.**

   Which correction should be made to sentence 6?

   (1) insert commas to create a series
   (2) remove <u>such as</u>
   (3) remove the comma after <u>herbs</u>
   (4) insert a comma after <u>and</u>
   (5) no correction is necessary

4. Sentence 11: **In general your herb garden should not need any additional fertilizer.**

   Which correction should be made to sentence 11?

   (1) change <u>your</u> to <u>you're</u>
   (2) insert a comma after <u>garden</u>
   (3) insert a comma after <u>your</u>
   (4) insert a comma after <u>general</u>
   (5) no correction is necessary

Dear Mr. Smith,

(A)

(1) I recently stayed in your hotel during an extended business trip. (2) I am writing to express my gratitude for a lovely experience. (3) As I'm sure you understand it is difficult to be away from one's home. (4) Yet your facility and your staff made this situation enjoyable for me.

(B)

(5) To begin, my room was well stocked with supplies, including soap, shampoo, and coffee. (6) My coffee station even included cream and sugar which is a rarity I can assure you. (7) I also had a large supply of fresh towels each day.

(C)

(8) The bed and shower were spacious, comfortable, and easy to use. (9) Additionally, the housekeeping staff did a thorough job of cleaning my room each day. (10) They were even gracious about coming back on the day that I decided to sleep late.

(D)

(11) Finally, the amenities at your hotel rounded out a wonderful stay. (12) I was able to swim, exercise, and eat while at the hotel. (13) It's worth noting that the food was not typical of hotel fare. (14) It was hot, tasty, and delicious.

(E)

(15) In closing, I can assure you that I will recommend your facility to my colleagues and I will be back for a return visit.

Sincerely,

Rita Jones

5. Sentence 3: **As I'm sure you understand it is difficult to be away from one's home.**

   Which correction should be made to sentence 3?

   (1) insert a comma after <u>understand</u>
   (2) insert a comma after <u>difficult</u>
   (3) change <u>one's</u> to <u>ones</u>
   (4) remove <u>from one's home</u>
   (5) no correction is necessary

6. Sentence 6: **My coffee station even included cream and <u>sugar which is a rarity I can assure you</u>.**

   Which is the best way to write the underlined portion of sentence 6? If the original is the best way, choose option (1).

   (1) sugar which is a rarity I can assure you
   (2) sugar, which is a rarity I can assure you
   (3) sugar, which is a rarity, I can assure you
   (4) sugar which is a rarity, I can assure you
   (5) sugar, which is a rarity, I, can assure you

7. Sentence 15: **In closing, I can assure you that I will recommend your facility to my colleagues and I will be back for a return visit.**

   Which correction should be made to sentence 15?

   (1) remove the comma after <u>closing</u>
   (2) insert a comma after <u>and</u>
   (3) insert a comma after <u>colleagues</u>
   (4) replace <u>In</u> with <u>Inn</u>
   (5) no correction is necessary

UNIT 5

Questions 8 through 10 refer to the following information.

Diabetes

(A)

(1) The body uses the hormone insulin to convert sugar starch, and other food sources into energy. (2) The body of a person with diabetes does not manufacture insulin or does not use insulin correctly. (3) Although the cause of diabetes remains unclear it appears that family history and health issues, such as obesity and inactivity, are contributing factors in the development of the disease.

(B)

(4) There are four types of diabetes. (5) A person with type 1 diabetes does not produce insulin. (6) A person with type 2 diabetes does not use insulin effectively. (7) A pregnant woman may develop gestational diabetes. (8) A person who has higher than normal levels of blood glucose is said to have pre-diabetes. (9) All types of diabetes can be diagnosed through a Fasting Plasma Glucose Test or an Oral Glucose Tolerance Test.

---

8. Sentence 1: **The body uses the hormone insulin to convert sugar starch, and other food sources into energy.**

   Which correction should be made to sentence 1?

   (1) remove the comma after <u>starch</u>
   (2) insert a comma after <u>body</u>
   (3) insert a comma after <u>sugar</u>
   (4) insert a comma after <u>insulin</u>
   (5) no correction is necessary

9. Sentence 3: **Although the cause of diabetes remains unclear it appears that family history and health issues, such as obesity and inactivity, are contributing factors in the development of the disease.**

   Which correction should be made to sentence 3?

   (1) remove the comma after <u>issues</u>
   (2) insert a comma after <u>unclear</u>
   (3) remove the comma after <u>inactivity</u>
   (4) insert a comma after <u>Although</u>
   (5) no correction is necessary

10. Sentence 9: **All types of diabetes can be diagnosed through a Fasting Plasma Glucose Test or an Oral Glucose Tolerance Test.**

    Which correction should be made to sentence 9?

    (1) insert a comma after <u>diagnosed</u>
    (2) replace <u>Fasting Plasma Glucose Test</u> with <u>fasting plasma glucose test</u>
    (3) change <u>Oral Glucose Tolerance Test</u> to <u>oral glucose tolerance test</u>
    (4) insert a comma after <u>Glucose Test</u>
    (5) no correction is necessary

Other Punctuation

For use with student book pp. 106–107

1 Review the Skill

Punctuation helps make written text easier to read. Colons introduce examples or lists: *The following are types of punctuation: commas, apostrophes, and question marks.* Quotation marks identify exact speech: *He asked "Did you eat?"* Hyphens create compound words (*high-end, well-known*) and are also used for some prefixes: *self-confidence, ex-girlfriend.* Parentheses separate text: *We ate at El Restaurante (on 4th and Pine Street).* Dashes are used if a sentence contains punctuation within an example or list: *All three books —Cinderella, Snow White, and Sleeping Beauty— are fairy tales.*

2 Refine the Skill

All punctuation can change the meaning of a sentence: *Let's eat, mommy* or *Let's eat mommy.*

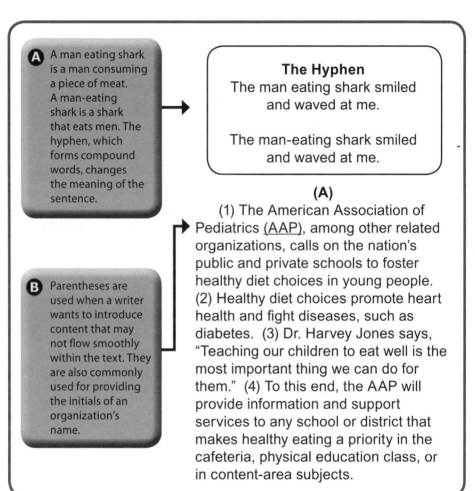

A A man eating shark is a man consuming a piece of meat. A man-eating shark is a shark that eats men. The hyphen, which forms compound words, changes the meaning of the sentence.

The Hyphen
The man eating shark smiled and waved at me.

The man-eating shark smiled and waved at me.

B Parentheses are used when a writer wants to introduce content that may not flow smoothly within the text. They are also commonly used for providing the initials of an organization's name.

(A)
(1) The American Association of Pediatrics (AAP), among other related organizations, calls on the nation's public and private schools to foster healthy diet choices in young people. (2) Healthy diet choices promote heart health and fight diseases, such as diabetes. (3) Dr. Harvey Jones says, "Teaching our children to eat well is the most important thing we can do for them." (4) To this end, the AAP will provide information and support services to any school or district that makes healthy eating a priority in the cafeteria, physical education class, or in content-area subjects.

TEST-TAKING TIPS

If you summarize someone's speech, you put it in your own words. Therefore, quotation marks are unnecessary. However, if you write someone's exact words, use quotation marks.

1. Sentence 3: **Dr. Harvey Jones says, "Teaching our children to eat well is the most important thing we can do for them."**

Which of the following statements best describes the underlined portion of sentence 3?

(1) an insightful comment from a patient
(2) a summary of the writer's opinion
(3) the exact words spoken by Dr. Jones
(4) a summary of the doctor's words
(5) the exact words of the writer

UNIT 5

③ Master the Skill

Directions: Choose the <u>one best answer</u> to each question.

<u>Questions 2 through 4</u> refer to the following information.

Putting Cash in Your Pocket

(A)

(1) Could you use some extra cash this month? (2) Of course you could. (3) There's always an unexpected expense or a desirable luxury item that arises among one's regular monthly bills car repairs, home repairs, or a weekend trip. (4) Consider the impact of an extra part-time job that could put $200 or more in your pocket each month. (5) Extra work means extra money, and extra money means financial freedom. (6) Here's a cheat sheet for well-paying part-time employment!

(B)

JOB	EMPLOYER
Administrative Assistant	Any office with customer-service needs
Auctioneer	Internet sites, such as eBay
Office or Restaurant Cleaner	Office buildings or restaurants
Weekend Helper	Catering, entertainment, photography, florist businesses, convention centers, sporting arenas
Freelance Writer or Editor	Newspapers, magazines, publishing companies
Delivery Person	Newspapers, pizza restaurants, correspondence companies, florists

---

2. Sentence 3: **There's always an unexpected expense or a desirable luxury item that arises among one's regular monthly bills car repairs, home repairs, or a weekend trip.**

    Which correction should be made to sentence 3?

    (1) insert a dash between <u>expense</u> and <u>or</u>
    (2) remove the comma after <u>car repairs</u>
    (3) insert a colon after <u>bills</u>
    (4) insert parentheses around <u>desirable luxury item</u>
    (5) no correction is necessary

3. Sentence 5: **Extra work means extra money, and extra money means financial freedom.**

    Which correction should be made to sentence 5?

    (1) replace the comma with a semicolon
    (2) remove the comma
    (3) replace the comma with a colon
    (4) add quotation marks before and after the sentence
    (5) no correction is necessary

4. Sentence 6: **Here's a cheat sheet for well-paying part-time employment!**

    Which correction should be made to sentence 6?

    (1) insert a colon after <u>sheet</u>
    (2) change <u>part-time</u> to <u>part time</u>
    (3) insert a hyphen between <u>cheat</u> and <u>sheet</u>
    (4) replace the exclamation point with a question mark
    (5) no correction is necessary

Saying What You Mean

(A)

(1) As one becomes more and more familiar with English usage and grammar, one truth eventually emerges. (2) It's difficult to say what one means. (3) There are so many ways to go wrong when constructing a sentence. (4) It's amazing that people are able to communicate at all nevertheless, they do. (5) Somewhere between garbled intentions and misunderstandings, people exchange information fairly successfully. (6) However, this doesn't mean that everyone shouldn't try to improve his or her communication skills, if even a little? (7) Try these basic tips to simply say what you mean.

(B)

(8) Say what you mean in the simplest language possible. (9) There are no bonus points in life for using the word *prose* when you mean *writing* or the word *tongue* when you mean *language*. (10) A thesaurus is a useful resource, but so is common sense. (11) Don't use a complex word when a simple word will accomplish the job.

(C)

(12) Don't be afraid to consult a dictionary. (13) It's a wonderful resource for verifying the meaning of a word before you use it. (14) This habit will help you communicate the correct meaning and save you from embarrassing situations. (15) After all, you don't want to be caught "complimenting someone on having a knick-knack for solving computer problems."

(D)

(16) Finally, make sure to use common sayings, or idioms, correctly. (17) Idiom errors are often overused, resulting in the spread of an error that seems correct. (18) For example, is the correct phrase *mute point* or *moot point*? (19) If you don't know, it's best to keep silent.

5. Sentence 4: **It's amazing that people are able to communicate at all nevertheless, they do.**

   Which correction should be made to sentence 4?

   (1) insert a semicolon after <u>at all</u>
   (2) remove the comma after <u>nevertheless</u>
   (3) change <u>It's</u> to <u>Its</u>
   (4) replace <u>nevertheless</u> with <u>never-the-less</u>
   (5) no correction is necessary

6. Sentence 6: **However, this doesn't mean that everyone shouldn't try to improve his or her communication skills, if even a little?**

   Which correction should be made to sentence 6?

   (1) replace the comma after <u>skills</u> with a colon
   (2) replace the comma after <u>However</u> with a dash
   (3) replace the question mark with a period
   (4) remove the comma after <u>However</u>
   (5) no correction is necessary

7. Sentence 15: **After all, you don't want to be caught "complimenting someone on having a knick-knack for solving computer problems."**

   Which correction should be made to sentence 15?

   (1) remove the comma after <u>After all</u>
   (2) remove <u>knick-knack</u>
   (3) insert a colon after <u>caught</u>
   (4) remove the quotation marks
   (5) no correction is necessary

Questions 8 through 10 refer to the following information.

Welcome to Hurricane Awareness Week!

(1) The purpose of this week is to help families respond to three important hurricane questions? (2) The answers to these questions may save lives during a hurricane.

- (3) Why is a hurricane dangerous?

- (4) How might a hurricane affect me?

- (5) What actions should I take in the event of a hurricane?

(6) To answer to these questions, participate in the following Hurricane Week activities:

Monday: (7) Study famous hurricanes; to learn about their causes and effects.

Tuesday: (8) Help weather experts track hurricanes: in the Atlantic, Caribbean, and Gulf of Mexico.

Wednesday: (9) Learn about hurricane hazards: storm surge, high winds, tornadoes, and flooding.

Thursday: (10) Create a family safety plan.

Friday: (11) Build a disaster kit.

---

8. Sentence 1: **The purpose of this week is to help families respond to three important hurricane questions?**

   Which correction should be made to sentence 1?

   (1) insert a comma after <u>week</u>
   (2) insert a hyphen between <u>hurricane</u> and <u>questions</u>
   (3) replace the question mark with a period
   (4) change <u>week</u> to <u>weak</u>
   (5) no correction is necessary

9. Sentence 7: **Study famous hurricanes; to learn about their causes and effects.**

   Which correction should be made to sentence 7?

   (1) change the semicolon to a colon
   (2) remove the semicolon
   (3) insert a comma after <u>causes</u>
   (4) replace <u>famous</u> with <u>well-known</u>
   (5) no correction is necessary

10. Sentence 8: **Help weather experts track hurricanes: in the Atlantic, Caribbean, and Gulf of Mexico.**

    Which correction should be made to sentence 8?

    (1) replace the colon with a semicolon
    (2) remove the colon
    (3) change <u>Atlantic</u> to <u>atlantic</u>
    (4) remove the comma after <u>Atlantic</u>
    (5) no correction is necessary

UNIT 5

Glossary

Adjective: A word that modifies or describes a noun or pronoun: *rd, fast, pretty, new, old*.

Adverb: Any word that modifies a verb, an adjective, or another adverb: *A deliciously ripe apple fell quickly from the tree*.

Analysis: Identification of a subject or subjects: *After further analysis, it has been proven that gravity pulls objects of different weights at the same rate*.

Antecedent: A subject that is replaced by a pronoun: *When Mary thought of George, she called him* (*Mary* and *George* are replaced by *she* and *him*).

Clause: A group of words that consists of a subject and a verb: *Mary jumps*.

Colon: A punctuation mark (:) used to separate clauses and to begin lists or examples.

Comma: A punctuation mark that is used within a sentence to represent a pause. Commas are also used to connect clauses, or phrases.

Compound subjects: When two or more subjects are joined by *and* or *or*: *Uncle Joe and Aunt Mary; the boy or girl*.

Conjunctive adverb: An adverb that generally shows cause and effect, sequence, contrast and comparison, and connects two clauses: *also, that is, so, therefore.* (It was snowing, so I was cold).

Coordinating conjunction: Words that combine two items of equal importance in regards to the rules of sentence structure: *for, and, nor, but, or, yet,* and *so*.

Dash: En dashes are used mostly to show ranges: He ran *10–15* yards. Em dashes are generally used to separate information within sentences: *This magazine—started by two college students—was founded in 1987*.

Dependent clause: A clause that is dependent on another clause, or group of words, and cannot stand alone: *That is why the bagels were cold*.

Facts: Information that can be proven true: *the sky is blue; people are mammals*.

First-person narrative: Text that is written from the *I* point of view: *I borrowed his car*.

Homophones and Homographs: Homophones are words that sound similar but have different spellings and different meanings: *acts* are deeds; an *ax* is a tool. Homographs are words that have the same spelling but different meanings: a *bat* is both a flying animal and a stick for hitting a ball.

Hyphen: Punctuation that is used to join two-word modifiers: *Her hair is reddish-blonde*.

Independent clause: A sentence or clause that can stand alone: *That is why the bagels were cold*.

Interrupting phrase: A group of words immediately preceded and followed by commas, and which interrupt a main clause: *Apple season, which starts in the fall, is a wonderful time for picnics*.

Introductory word/phrase: Words or phrases that introduce a main clause: *Finally, the movie was released; After the movie, we went to dinner*.

Object: Someone or something that receives or completes the subject's action: *Mary jumps rope*.

Parentheses: Punctuation that is used to isolate information relating to the main clause, but could be omitted: *The bridges (especially the long ones) are dangerous during the winter*.

Participles: A modification of verbs that indicates tense: *given; written; brought; taken*.

Phrase: A word or group of words that create a single idea or expression: *A dog is a man's best friend*.

Plural: A word or form of a word indicating more than one person or thing: *two cars; four books*.

Possessive: A word or form of a word that indicates ownership: *Mary's jump rope*.

Prefix: A small unit of letters added to the beginning of a word to change its meaning. For example, *un-, pre-,* and *dis-*: *unhappy, preexisting, dissatisfied*.

Pronunciation: The way a word is spoken.

Proper adjective: A proper noun, or a word that begins with a capital letter but does not necessarily begin a sentence, that describes another noun: *English books, Thanksgiving dinner*.

Punctuation: Marks that provide structure within written text, such as periods (.), commas (,), semicolons (;), quotation marks (" "), question marks (?), exclamation points (!), dashes (–), and hyphens (-).

Quotations: Exact speech which is preceded and immediately followed by quotation marks: _"Cortland apples are my favorite,"_ John said.

Scene: A single setting in which the action occurs. If the writer is telling a story about a new dog, one scene may be at the shelter where the dog is adopted and another at the house that will be the dog's new home. Each scene in the story needs its own paragraph.

Second-person narrative: Text that is written from the _you_ point of view: _You borrowed his car._

Semicolon: A punctuation mark (;) used between independent clauses without coordinating conjunctions, independent clauses linked by conjunctive adverbs, and items in a series that contains other punctuation.

Singular: A word or form of a word indicating one person or thing: _one car; a book._

Speaker: The narrator of the story or the character being quoted. For example, if you quoted a volunteer at the shelter saying "his favorite toy is a stuffed squirrel," then she would be the speaker. During the remainder of the essay, the writer is the speaker because the story is written from his or her perspective.

Statistics: Data that can be expressed in terms of quantity: _According to the Centers for Disease Control and Prevention, unmarried women are less likely to have health insurance._

Subject: The person or thing doing the action: _Mary jumps rope._

Subordinating conjunctions: A conjunction that introduces dependent clauses: _if, so that, because._

Suffix: An ending that is added to a word to change its tense or function. For example, _–ed_ and _–ing._

Syllable: A unit of measure in spoken language: _syl*la*ble_ has three syllables.

Theme: An idea or subject matter that is reflected throughout the essay.

Third-person narrative: Text that is written from the _he/she/it_ point of view: _She borrowed his car._

Verb: The action or state of being: _Mary jumps rope._

Vowel: The letters _a, e, i, o, u,_ and sometimes _y._

Answer Key

UNIT 1 ESSAY

LESSON 1, pp. 2–5

Refine, Fill in the mental map with your thesis statement and three supporting details: *My favorite food is sushi; It is healthy, quick, and artfully crafted.*

1. (4), This sentence states the topic of the essay; the writer's favorite food.

2. (5), This sentence introduces the three details that support the thesis: *pizza tastes great, pizza is easy to get, pizza is cheap.*

3. (3), This sentence states the topic of the essay.

4. (5), This statement is a detail that supports the thesis statement. The other answer options do not support the paragraph's thesis statement.

Prompt 1, The thesis statement should include a specific job you would like to have: *I have always wanted to be a herpetologist.*

Prompt 2, The thesis statement should include which of the provided traits you think is most important: *I have always believed that being organized is an important trait.*

Prompt 3, The thesis statement should include a specific work habit you think is valued: *It is important for an employee to be professional.*

Prompt 4, The thesis statement should include the reason why a friend should be loyal: *A true friend should be loyal because a friend is someone you can count on.*

LESSON 2, pp. 6–9

Refine, Fill in the reverse triangle that represents your introduction. The hook should be an anecdote, fact, or surprising detail about your favorite food: *Raw fish makes most people squirm, but not me.* The thesis statement should state your favorite food: *Sushi is my favorite food to eat.* The three supporting details must support why the food you have chosen is your favorite: *Sushi is healthy, quick, and artistic.*

1. (1), This sentence provides a surprising fact (hook) to introduce the essay. The other answer options include a thesis statement and supporting details, not a hook.

2. (5), This sentence states the topic of the essay. The thesis statement is provided with the prompt on this page.

3. (5), This sentence states the three details that support the thesis statement. The supporting details are provided with the prompt on this page.

Prompt 1, The introductory paragraph should include a hook, thesis statement, and three supporting details about your favorite food. *Raw fish makes most people squirm, but not me. Sushi is my favorite food to eat. Ever since I tasted sushi for the time, anytime a friend or relative would ask what I wanted to eat for dinner, my answer was always "sushi, please!" Sushi is healthy, quick, and an edible work of art.*

Prompt 2, The introductory paragraph should include a hook, thesis statement, and three supporting details about one of the traits you think is most important: *Imagine always knowing where to find your keys, or your favorite hat. Organization is important to all aspects of life, and I believe that being organized is an important trait for people to have. Organized people always know where to find their belongings, do well at their jobs, and tend to be prepared for any occasion.*

LESSON 3, pp. 10–13

Refine, Using the information you provided on page 7, fill in the information for the reverse triangle that represents your introduction. Next, fill in the information for the three boxes that represent each body paragraph. The transition should direct the reader from one paragraph to the next: *Another thing; When I was 12; Nowadays.* Each body paragraph should represent a supporting detail: *Sushi is healthy; Sushi is quick; Sushi is artistic.*

1. (4), This sentence states a transitioning phrase, "It was around this time," which shows time.

2. (5), Sentence 11 is a transitioning phrase and belongs at the beginning of the paragraph; therefore no correction is necessary.

3. (2), Sentence 25 contains a transitioning phrase, "When I earn my GED certificate," which shows time and introduces the topic of the writer's future. Therefore, sentence 25 should be moved to the beginning of paragraph D (a body paragraph).

Write, Using the information you provided on page 7, fill in the information for the reverse triangle that represents your introduction. Each body paragraph should be about one of the supporting details and begin with a transition. Possible transitions include *Another, The first time, Then,* and *After.*

LESSON 4, pp. 14–17

Refine, Using the information you provided on page 7, fill in the information for the reverse triangle that represents your introduction. Next, fill in the information for the three boxes that represents each body paragraph. Introduce your supporting detail: *Sushi is healthy.* Support the topic: *I like sushi because it is healthy.* Explain the details of the passage: *Sushi is healthy because the raw fish has nutrients and so do all the vegetables.* Explain why the passage supports your topic: *The nutrients in the sushi provide me with energy for my day. I feel good when I eat sushi.*

1. (4), The paragraphs are body paragraphs because each one is dedicated to explaining a supporting detail.

2. (2), Sentence 25 should be in paragraph C because it is part of the elaboration of the second supporting detail that Riley is protective. Sentence 13 belongs in paragraph D because it is part of the elaboration of the third supporting detail that Riley is a companion.

UNIT 1 (continued)

Write, Using the information you provided on page 7, fill in the information for the reverse triangle that represents your introduction. The body paragraph should represent the third supporting detail and include transitions and elaboration: *Just because sushi is quick to make doesn't mean it is thrown together. Rolls are hand-crafted by the sushi chefs, and each one is served on a fancy Oriental plate. Sushi is often accompanied by flowers, or vegetables cut to resemble flowers. The sushi chefs take pride in their creations, and I admire the work they do.*

LESSON 5, pp. 18–21

Prompt 1, Possible transitions include *In the meantime, First, Then*, and *Nowadays*. The restated thesis should be about one of your favorite places: *Whenever I need a mini-vacation, I like to go to the beach for a long weekend*. To end with an insightful thought means to leave the reader with something inspiring or which gives him or her insight into the part of your life you are writing about: *Ever since I started going to the beach to unwind, I have really learned a lot about myself and what it means to relax.*

Prompt 2, Possible transitions include *When I was young, Another, Also*, and *Finally*. The restated thesis should be about your favorite color: *That's when I realized my favorite color is red*. To end with a quote means to write word for word something you have heard from your family or friends or something that is a famous statement. *I guess that is why my mother has always said, "Red is the color of heroes."*

Prompt 3, Possible transitions include *After all, On the other hand, Therefore*, and *However*. The restated thesis should be about a person you would most like to meet: *It was then that I decided I would most like to meet LeBron James*. To end with a reference to a book, a movie, or popular culture, means to write something that relates to a well-known book or movie, or something from popular culture such as a sports team, a band, or a television show: *In my mind, LeBron James is the Iron Man of the NBA.*

1. (2), This sentence states the three details that support the thesis statement: *loving, protective, companion*.

2. (3), The third sentence of the conclusion contains a quote. Therefore, the writer chose to end the essay with a quote.

Write, Fill in the information for the triangle that represents the conclusion. Possible transitions include *In conclusion, Lastly, Finally*, and *Therefore*. The restated thesis should be about your favorite food: *Fortunately, my favorite food is sushi*. Possible endings include quotes, references to books, movies, and pop culture, and information that gives the reader insight into your life and what you have learned through the experiences you are writing about: *My friends don't have to ask me what I want for dinner anymore, because they know the answer will always be "sushi!"* Next, write the conclusion for the prompt about your favorite food. Include the information from the graphic organizer and combine it into a concluding paragraph. The conclusion must have transitions, a restated thesis statement, and the supporting details. It should also leave a lasting impression.

LESSON 6, pp. 22–25

Refine, Paragraph A is missing a hook: *Many teenagers today do not heed the advice of their parents. Instead, they are more likely to follow advice from a friend or an adult they trust*; Sentence 4 is missing one supporting detail. It should read: *It helped me make the right decision with my dog Scout, my Uncle Joe, and my future*; Paragraph B should be indented and should have a topic and example: *In the window was the cutest little beagle. His long floppy ears and sad brown eyes were pleading to go home with us*; Paragraph D should have elaboration: i.e. *I have been reading books about how to care for dogs. One of them was written by Dr. Eugene Smith, who wrote about how important his job was and how much he loved working with animals. That's when I knew what I wanted to do with the rest of my life*; Sentence 19 should read: *This summer, I am going to work for Scout's veterinarian, Dr. George*; Paragraph E should be indented and should have a transition: i.e. *Throughout this year, I have found Mrs. Morgan's advice to be very valuable*; Paragraph E should also have another supporting detail: *I have taken care of my dog and the neighborhood dogs.*

Write, Double-check your essay to ensure that it meets the criteria for the GED Language Arts/Writing Test. Rewrite any portions of your essay that do not meet the criteria of the GED Language Arts/Writing Test.

UNIT 2 ORGANIZATION

LESSON 1, pp. 26–29

1. (5), No correction is necessary because the text is correctly divided. Sentence 1 is in the correct place because it is part of the introduction.

2. (2), Sentence 3 should begin paragraph B because paragraph B shifts its focus to the first benefit of the health program (a supporting detail). Sentence 3 refers to this benefit.

3. (1), Sentence 5 should begin paragraph C because paragraph C shifts its focus to the second benefit of the health program (the second supporting detail). Sentence 5 refers this benefit.

4. (3), Sentence 7 should begin paragraph D because paragraph D shifts its focus to the required paperwork. Sentence 7 introduces the topic of the paperwork (the third supporting detail).

5. (4), Sentence 5 should begin paragraph B because paragraph B shifts its focus to the time it will take to make the barbecue sauce. Sentence 4 introduces this topic.

UNIT 2 (*continued*)

6. (1), Sentence 6 should begin paragraph C because paragraph C shifts its focus to the steps of the recipe. Sentence 6 introduces these steps.

7. (3), Sentence 11 should begin paragraph E because paragraph E is the conclusion and shifts focus to the time after the barbecue sauce has been made. Sentence 11 introduces this time period.

8. (4), Sentence 8 should begin paragraph B because paragraph B shifts focus to the time when the writer calls her mom. Sentence 8 introduces this time period.

9. (1), Sentence 10 should begin paragraph C because paragraph C shifts its focus to a time when the writer calls her mom to discuss why she has frustrations, angers, or failures. Sentence 10 refers to this period of time.

10. (2), Sentence 13 should begin paragraph D because it shifts focus to the writer's mother's ability to make people feel special. Sentence 13 refers to this idea.

LESSON 2, *pp. 30–33*

1. (1), This sentence is the topic sentence because it introduces the topic of five voting qualifications, which is what the paragraph is about.

2. (3), This sentence is the topic sentence of paragraph A because it introduces the topic of telephones in the workplace. Remember that the topic sentence generally appears as the first or second sentence in a paragraph.

3. (1), This sentence is the topic sentence of paragraph B because it introduces the topic of telephone use among family members. The other options do not stay on the topic of the telephone as an important communication device between family members.

4. (5), This sentence is the topic sentence of paragraph C because it introduces the topic of telephone use for emergency situations. The other options do not stay on the topic of the telephone as an important communication device for emergency situations.

5. (1), This sentence is the topic sentence of paragraph A because it introduces the topic of all departments reporting the successes of the school year. The other answer options focus on one department; therefore they are not correct answers.

6. (3), This sentence is the topic sentence of paragraph B because it introduces the topic of the parents providing feedback. Answer option (5) is not correct because it states that the parents are unhappy, which is not the case. The other answer options do not relate to the parents providing feedback; therefore they are not correct.

7. (4), This sentence is the topic sentence of paragraph C because it introduces the topic of Principal Chaney discussing discipline issues. The other answer options imply that discipline has been a problem, yet the paragraph is about Principal Chaney's satisfaction with decreased discipline issues.

8. (2), This sentence is the topic sentence of paragraph A because it introduces the topic of salary and middle class America. The title suggests that these jobs are in the middle class ("Middle of the Pack").

9. (5), This sentence is the topic sentence of paragraph B because it introduces the specific jobs that are discussed in the paragraph.

10. (4), This sentence is the topic sentence of paragraph C because it introduces the specific jobs that are discussed in the paragraph.

LESSON 3, *pp. 34–37*

1. (3), This sentence is the correct supporting detail because it is a fact. The paragraph already contains explanation, examples, and analysis. The other answer options also stray from the topic of time.

2. (2), This sentence is the correct supporting detail because it supports the topic that Park and Ride lots would be helpful to commuters by providing explanation. Saving money links to the details in sentence 7.

3. (1), This sentence is the correct supporting detail because it supports the topic that HOV lanes benefit commuters and the environment by providing an explanation.

4. (5), This sentence is the correct supporting detail because it supports the topic, which is about the inefficiency and expense of SUVs, by providing a fact.

5. (3), This sentence is the correct supporting detail because it supports the topic, which is about audience interaction, by providing examples of useful interaction techniques.

6. (1), This sentence is the correct supporting detail because it supports the topic, which is about memorable speeches, by providing examples of greetings or openers that would grab the audience.

7. (5), This sentence is the correct supporting detail because it supports the topic, which is about effective and prepared speeches, by providing examples of visuals.

8. (2), This sentence is the correct supporting detail because it supports the topic, which is about recording your spending, by providing explanation. Option 1 is not correct because many items are available at the grocery store, and it is difficult to track how much money you are spending on needs and how much money you are spending on wants.

9. (1), This sentence is the correct supporting detail because it supports the topic, which is about needs versus wants, by providing examples of bills that change or are not paid monthly.

10. (2), This sentence is the correct supporting detail because it supports the topic, which is about learning from your budget, by providing analysis. Option 3 is not correct because it introduces a new topic: debt.

UNIT 2 (*continued*)

LESSON 4, *pp. 38–41*

1. (3), "For instance" indicates an example, which provides a transition from sentence 5 to sentence 6. The other answer options indicate time or contrast. Therefore they cannot be correct.

2. (4), "In short" indicates a summary, which provides a transition from sentence 3 to sentence 4. The other answer options do not place the transitional word or phrase at the beginning of the sentence. Therefore they cannot be correct. The corrected sentence should read: *In short, follow these tips, and set your datebook by the telephone to start scheduling interviews.*

3. (2), "Consequently" indicates a cause, or consequence. Sentence 8 transitions from and explains the information in sentence 7. The other answer options indicate summary or examples. Therefore they cannot be the correct.

4. (2), "In summary" indicates summation of the previous sentences, while also providing a transition. The other answer options indicate examples or explanation. Therefore they cannot be correct.

5. (3), "For this reason" indicates explanation. The phrase provides a transition from sentence 3 to sentence 4. The corrected sentence should read: *For this reason, I am interested in beginning employment in an apprentice capacity as I finish my education.*

6. (4), "To illustrate" indicates an example is provided and transitions from sentence 6 to sentence 7.

7. (3), "Consequently" indicates a cause, or consequence. Sentence 10 transitions from and explains the information in sentence 7. The other answer options indicate time and comparison. Therefore they cannot be correct.

8. (1), "Finally" indicates time, which provides an accurate transition from sentence 5 to sentence 6. The other answer options do not place the transitional word or phrase at the beginning of the sentence. Therefore they cannot be correct. The corrected sentence should read: *Finally, practice answering relevant questions with a friend.*

9. (3), "Specifically" indicates an example, which provides a transition from sentence 7 to sentence 8. The other answer options do not indicate an example. Therefore they cannot be correct.

10. (5), The revised sentence contains transitions that indicate time. The other answer options do not indicate time; therefore they cannot be correct.

LESSON 5, *pp. 42–45*

1. (4), Sentence 14 should be moved to follow sentence 12 because it relates more closely to the idea of how to save water. Sentence 14 supports this topic by providing the *additional* example of not double washing the dishes.

2. (2), Sentence 2 should be moved to follow sentence 4 because sentence 2 explains how to wet the ground before getting rid of weeds. This should come after sentence 4, which is about why a wet ground is helpful.

3. (1), Sentence 9 should be removed because it does not support the topic of the paragraph. It relates more closely to purchasing tools than getting rid of weeds.

4. (4), Sentence 11 should be removed because it is not relevant to getting rid of weeds.

5. (1), Sentence 2 should be removed because it does not support the topic of community recycling.

6. (3), Sentence 6 should be moved to the end of paragraph B because it provides information that supports sentence 8. Sentence 8 introduces the idea that trees can be turned into mulch, and sentence 6 explains a benefit of the mulch.

7. (4), Sentence 9 should be moved to follow sentence 12 because it is about the results from the data mentioned in sentence 12.

8. (3), Sentence 3 should be removed because it does not support the topic of saving energy.

9. (2), Sentence 6 should be moved to follow sentence 9 because it is the answer to the question being asked in sentence 9.

10. (4), Sentence 17 should be removed because it is not about taking an energy tour; it is a tip.

UNIT 3 SENTENCE STRUCTURE

LESSON 1, *pp. 46–49*

1. (1), This sentence contains a subject (*the book club/Wednesday*), verb (*meet*), and complete idea (*the time the book club should meet*). Therefore, option 1 is the best answer. Options 2 and 3 are missing the verb (*meet*), and option 4 is missing a subject (*Wednesday*).

2. (2), Sentence 5 is not asking a question. Therefore, the sentence should end with a period: *Upright vacuums are good for large carpeted areas but clumsy on stairways.*

3. (1), Sentence 13 is missing the subject. Therefore, it is not a complete sentence. Adding the subject, *design*, makes it a complete sentence: *Design also affects whether the machine is manageable.*

4. (5), Sentence 15 contains a single idea and does not have any errors. Therefore, no correction is necessary.

5. (5), Sentence 3 is missing the subject (*the stars*); however, this subject is mentioned in sentence 2. By connecting the two sentences with a comma, one complete idea is formed: *However, you will remember that ancient sailors were able to navigate their ships according to the stars, suggesting an order behind the apparent chaos.*

UNIT 3 (continued)

6. (4), Sentence 11 should not begin with the phrase "Which is" and is missing a subject (*the North Star*). However, the subject is mentioned in the previous sentence. In order to make sentence 11 a complete sentence, it must be connected to sentence 10: *Here, you should locate the North Star, which is fairly bright.*

7. (3), Sentence 16 is missing the subject. Therefore, it is not a complete sentence. Adding the subject, *the North Star*, makes it a complete sentence: *Nonetheless, the North Star always aligns with two stars that make up the far edge of the Dipper's cup.*

8. (4), The subject of sentence 2 is "all correspondence." In this sentence, the subject does not have an action. Therefore, it is not a complete sentence. Adding the action, *requires a letter of transmittal*, makes sentence 2 complete: *All correspondence, whether delivered electronically or via hard copy, requires a letter of transmittal.*

9. (2), Sentence 5 is missing the verb. Therefore, it is not a complete sentence. Adding the verb, or action, *be signed*, makes it a complete sentence: *Each letter of transmittal must also be signed by the appropriate supervisor.*

10. (5), Sentence 7 contains a single idea and does not have any errors. Therefore, no correction is necessary.

LESSON 2, *pp. 50–53*

1. (1), Sentence 10 is a fragment because it does not express a complete idea. By connecting sentences 9 and 10 with a comma, one complete sentence is formed: *Some cold medicines may also help manage symptoms, such as a runny nose and cough.*

2. (3), Answer option 3 is a sentence fragment because it lacks a subject (*the mosquito*).

3. (3), Sentence 12 is a fragment because it is missing a subject (*you*) and does not express a complete idea. By connecting sentences 12 and 13 with a comma, one complete sentence is formed: *To double your efforts, you can also place potted lemongrass or geraniums near doorways and windows to keep mosquitoes from entering your home.*

4. (2), Sentence 15 is a fragment because it is missing a subject (*herbs*) and does not express a complete idea. By connecting sentences 15 and 16 with a comma, one complete sentence is formed: *In addition to repelling mosquitoes, these herbs create a fragrant garden.*

5. (1), Answer option 1 is a fragment because it lacks a complete idea. The sentence has a subject (*you*) and an action (*looking to impress*), but it is not a complete sentence. It begins with the word "If," which means that there is one idea and then another. For example, *If you are hungry, you should eat.* The clause *If you are hungry* is a dependent clause, and the clause *you should eat* is an independent clause. Therefore, this sentence needs another clause in order to be a complete sentence.

6. (3), This sentence is a fragment because it does not express a complete idea. By adding a comma to the end, this dependent clause can attach to an independent clause to form a complete sentence. For example, *To prepare for the trick, take a rectangular sheet of paper and fold it into an "S" shape without creasing the paper.*

7. (2), Sentence 19 is a fragment because it lacks a complete idea. The sentence has a subject (*you*) and an action (*lift your hands*), but it is not a complete idea. It begins with the word "When," which means that there is one idea and then another. For example, *When you look at the sun, your eyes will hurt.* The clause *When you look at the sun* is a dependent clause, and the clause *your eyes will hurt* is an independent clause. Therefore, this clause needs another clause in order to be a complete sentence. By connecting sentences 19 and 20 with a comma, one complete sentence is formed: *When you lift your hands, there will be two quarters under the left hand and no quarters under the right hand.*

8. (2), Sentence 4 is a fragment because it lacks a subject (*replacement sets*). By connecting sentences 3 and 4 with a comma, one complete sentence is formed: *The generator sets are replacement sets, which are being installed to serve additional loading that has been or is being connected to the system.*

9. (1), Answer option 1 is a fragment because it lacks a subject (*replacement foundations*).

10. (5), Answer option 5 is not a fragment because it has a subject (*replacement foundation*), a verb (*being installed*), and a complete idea (*Two replacement foundations are being installed*). If you read a sentence and you have to ask yourself, who are what is doing the action, then it is missing the subject. If you read a sentence and you have to ask yourself what the subject is doing, then it is missing a verb, or action.

LESSON 3, *pp. 54–57*

1. (3), The word "you" is the subject of the verb "need."

2. (2), Sentence 2 is a simple sentence because it contains a single idea.

3. (2), This sentence is a simple sentence because it contains one subject, one verb, and a single idea.

4. (1), The word "file" is the verb because it is the action being performed within the simple sentence.

5. (1), This is a simple sentence because it contains one verb, one subject, and a single idea.

6. (4), This is not a simple sentence because it contains more than one subject (*pills*; *capsules*; *liquids*) and verb (*mash, pull, mix*).

7. (5), The word "convenience" is the subject of the verb "is."

8. (1), The word "it" is the subject of the verb "involves."

9. (4), The word "are" is the verb because it is the subject's condition.

10. (2), This is a simple sentence because it contains one verb, one subject, and a single idea.

LESSON 4, *pp. 58–61*

1. (3), The word "yet" is a coordinating conjunction that indicates contrast and is used to create compound sentences. The two clauses in sentence 24 show contrast because man holds the wisdom, but he does not use it. Words such as *but*, *however*, and *yet* show contrast between clauses. Words such as *similarly* and *and* show similarities between clauses. The conjunctive adverb *finally* indicates time: *I have been waiting for my car for hours; finally, the mechanic called.*

2. (4), The punctuation mark (;) is a semicolon and is used to form compound sentences. The writer has chosen to use a semicolon because the two clauses are similar, or related ideas. In this case, words such as *similarly* and *and* are not necessary.

3. (1), The word "or" is a coordinating conjunction.

4. (5), This is a compound sentence because two independent clauses are connected by the coordinating conjunction "or." Answer option 5 is the only sentence that has two independent clauses.

5. (2), The word "and" is a coordinating conjunction that is used to form compound sentences by connecting two independent clauses.

6. (4), Answer option 4 is the correct answer because it is the only option with a semicolon before the conjunctive adverb (*consequently*). Semicolons and conjunctive adverbs are used to create compound sentences by connecting two independent clauses. Also, a comma should always come after a conjunctive adverb or coordinating conjunction when used in a compound sentence.

7. (3), The word "but" is a coordinating conjunction that shows contrast. It is used to form compound sentences by connecting these two contrasting independent clauses.

8. (1), Semicolons are used to create compound sentences by connecting two independent clauses. Sentence 3 has two independent clauses that should be connected. A semicolon can be used to connect related clauses: *Candidates hire advisors to help them capture the votes of women; they also hire advisors to help them capture the votes of particular religious or cultural groups.* In this case, words such as *however* and *but* are not necessary. Options 3 and 4 cannot be correct because *however* and *but* show contrast.

9. (3), Sentence 5 has two independent clauses. Semicolons and conjunctive adverbs are used to create compound sentences by connecting two related independent clauses.

10. (5), The word "and" is a coordinating conjunction that is used to form compound sentences by connecting two independent clauses. A comma should come after a coordinating conjunction when used in a compound sentence.

LESSON 5, *pp. 62–65*

1. (4), "When" is the subordinating conjunction because it begins the dependent clause: *When you have your supplies.* Clauses that begin with subordinating conjunctions must be attached to an independent clause.

2. (5), This is a complex sentence because the first clause in the sentence is a dependent clause that begins with a subordinating conjunction (*While*).

3. (1), This is the dependent clause because it cannot stand alone as a complete sentence, and it begins with a subordinating conjunction (*Before*). Option 3 is not the dependent clause because it is part of the independent clause in this sentence.

4. (4), Sentence 13 is a dependent clause and needs to be attached to an independent clause, such as sentence 14. Because the sentences are not both independent clauses, they cannot be combined with a semicolon. Therefore, they must be combined with a comma.

5. (1), This is an independent clause because it can stand alone as a complete sentence. Option 2 is a dependent clause, not an independent clause, because it begins with the subordinating conjunction "as." Option 3 is not an independent clause because it is missing a subject: who is looking at the trees? Option 4 is not an independent clause because it is missing the subject and the verb: what happens in the fall and who or what does it happen to? Option 5 is not an independent clause because it is missing the subject: *the leaves.*

6. (4), Answer option 4 is a complex sentence because it contains both a dependent and independent clause. The dependent clause begins with the subordinating conjunction "Since." The other answer options are simple sentences. It is important to remember that simple sentences can begin with a transitional word, such as *consequently.*

7. (4), Sentence 7 is a dependent clause and needs to be connected to an independent clause, such as sentence 8. Because the sentences are not both independent clauses, they cannot be connected with a semicolon. Therefore, they must be connected with a comma: *Because the days grow shorter in the fall, there is less sunlight.*

8. (3), This is a dependent clause because it cannot stand alone. Another clue that this is a dependent clause is that it begins with the subordinating conjunction "so." Options 1, 2, and 5 are independent clauses that can stand alone. Option 4 is a sentence fragment.

9. (2), "When" is a subordinating conjunction because it begins a dependent clause. "remove the jar from the water bath and take off the lid" can stand alone. "When the alcohol in the jar shows a dark color" cannot stand alone.

UNIT 3 (continued)

10. (5), This is a complex sentence because it contains a dependent clause and an independent clause that are connected with a comma. Options 1, 3, and 4 are simple sentences. It is important to remember that simple sentences can begin with a transitional word, such as *first* or *meanwhile*. Option 2 is a compound sentence because it has a conjunction that connects two independent clauses: *and*.

LESSON 6, pp. 66–69

1. (3), These sentences are combined concisely by eliminating repetitive words, such as "meeting location" from sentence 14. Using the conjunction "and" creates one complete compound sentence. Answer options 2 and 4 do not combine the sentences. Options 1 and 5 do combine the sentences; however they change the meaning of the original sentences.

2. (1), These sentences are combined concisely by eliminating repetitive or unnecessary words, such as "bulk" and "so on" from sentences 6 and 7. Using the conjunction "and" creates one complete compound sentence. This is the only answer option that combines the two sentences without leaving information out or changing the meaning of the sentence.

3. (3), These sentences are combined by adding a comma to create a series. Option 3 successfully combines the sentences without removing the necessary details.

4. (1), The subordinating conjunction "When" turns sentence 2 into a dependent clause. The new sentence would read: *When you are required to speak in front of a group at work or at church, consider adding a pictograph to your presentation.*

5. (3), Sentences 7, 8, and 9 could be combined into one sentence by eliminating the repetitive words and creating a series with commas: *You might list favorite fast foods, music types, and sports.*

6. (4), These sentences are combined by adding the subordinating conjunction "If" to the beginning of sentence 15 and connecting the clauses with a comma. This creates one complex sentence instead of two consecutive simple sentences, and does not change the sentence's meaning.

7. (1), These sentences are combined using the coordinating conjunction "and." This creates one complete compound sentence instead of two consecutive simple sentences.

8. (3), In addition to your family being impressed with your efforts, you will also feel good about the gesture. Therefore, "and" is the best answer option.

9. (2), These sentences are combined by adding the subordinating conjunction "When" to the beginning of sentence 7 and connecting the clauses with a comma. This creates one complex sentence instead of two consecutive simple sentences, and does not change the meaning of the original sentences.

10. (1), These sentences are combined using the coordinating conjunction "and." This creates one complete compound sentence instead of two consecutive simple sentences, and does not change the meaning of the original sentences.

LESSON 7, pp. 70–73

1. (3), This is the most effective revision of sentence 7 because the comma splice has been corrected using a period. The two independent clauses have become two complete sentences without changing the meaning of the original sentence.

2. (1), The period corrects the run-on sentence by forming two complete sentences: *Heart disease occurs as the result of fatty plaque deposits in the arteries that deliver blood to the heart. These plaque deposits cause the arteries to become narrow and hard.* Options 2 and 3 are not correct because in order to connect two independent clauses with a coordinating conjunction, such as *but* or *and*, a comma would also have to be inserted. Option 4 is not correct because two independent clauses cannot be combined with only a comma; they must also have a conjunction. A semicolon would be needed to combine two independent clauses if a conjunction (*and, but, or*) is not used.

3. (3), Option 3 is correct because the two independent clauses are correctly connected with a semicolon. Option 2 is not correct because a comma should not follow the word "these" (a comma splice). Option 4 is not correct because you should not use a semicolon with a conjunction (*and*). Remember that semicolons connect two independent clauses, and conjunctions cannot begin an independent clause. Option 5 is not correct because it creates a comma splice. The two independent clauses cannot be connected with only a comma. If a comma connects two clauses, then it must come before a conjunction (*and, but, or*).

4. (2), The period corrects the comma splice by forming two independent clauses, or complete sentences: *You should also avoid saturated fat. This so-called "bad" fat is found in some meats and dairy products.* Option 1 is not correct because adding the transition "Although" changes the meaning of the sentence and does not correct the comma splice. Option 3 is not correct because moving the comma does not correct a comma splice. Option 4 is not correct because the semicolon should be placed before "this," not after it, and only if you were using the method of inserting a semicolon to correct the comma splice.

5. (1), Two independent clauses are incorrectly connected by a comma. This is a comma splice.

6. (3), The coordinating conjunction "but" corrects the comma splice by forming one complete compound sentence. While the construction of option 2 and option 5 could be correct, the transitional phrases "For instance" and "for example" are not. Option 4 is not correct because, as a general rule, you should not begin a sentence with a coordinating conjunction, such as *and*.

UNIT 3 (*continued*)

7. (5), The two independent clauses are correctly separated by a comma; therefore no correction is necessary.

8. (1), The coordinating conjunction "and" corrects the comma splice by forming a complete compound sentence: *You've located a new place to live, and you've found a new job.* Option 2 would create a run-on sentence. Option 3 does not fix the comma splice. Option 4 is not the best revision because it creates two consecutive simple sentences.

9. (3), The coordinating conjunction "but" corrects the comma splice by forming a complete compound sentence.

10. (3), The period corrects the run-on sentence by forming two complete sentences: *Use clear or brown packing tape in a dispenser rather than masking tape to seal the boxes. Packing tape adheres better than masking tape, particularly if the boxes will get hot or cold during the move.* This is the only answer option that corrects the run-on sentence.

LESSON 8, *pp. 74–77*

1. (2), The word "colorful" is the misplaced modifier because it is not correctly placed within the sentence. Option 2 is correct because the writer intends the subject to be "decorations." Therefore, the modifier (*colorful*) should come before the intended subject in the sentence. Option 1 modifies the incorrect subject (*entertainment*). Options 3, 4, and 5 are not written with proper sentence structure.

2. (5), The word "often" is the misplaced modifier because it is not correctly placed within the sentence. The sentence should be rewritten: *One aspect of many vacations that is often overlooked during the budgeting phase is transportation.*

3. (1), The word "lively" is the misplaced modifier because it is not correctly placed within the sentence. The "parade" is "lively," not the "exhibit." The modified word should come last so there isn't confusion.

4. (1), The word "steaming" is the misplaced modifier because it is not correctly placed within the sentence. The "hot dogs" are "steaming" (not the "cart" or the "city"). The sentence should be written: *In a large city, you can find steaming hot dogs at a street vendor's cart.*

5. (5), The word "nearly" should modify the number of young people, not the adjective "affecting." The sentence states that this problem affects young people only, however young people are not the only ones affected. Instead, it should state that the problem affects almost all young people. The corrected sentence should read: *Every talk show and evening news program in America bombards viewers with facts and statistics about the obesity problem affecting nearly all young people.*

6. (4), The word "only" should modify the snacks, not the children. The sentence currently states that children are the only ones allowed to bring healthy snacks; instead it should state that only healthy snacks will be allowed. For example, *Teachers send home notes saying that children may bring only "healthy snacks and bottles of water" to school.*

7. (3), The misplaced phrase is "with the skewers" because you want to caution the children about safety with skewers; you do not want to use the skewers to caution the children. The corrected sentence should read: *Make sure to caution children about responsible and safe behavior with the skewers.*

8. (4), The supplier should have insurance, not Arkansas.

9. (2), The misplaced modifier is (*above-mentioned*). Option 2 is the best revision of sentence 6 because the modifier has been placed before its subject (*criteria*). The other answer options do not correctly revise this sentence without changing its meaning.

10. (5), Option 5 is correct because the word "current" should modify the conditions and recommendations. Option 1 is not correct because the modifier is not placed directly before or after its intended subject (*conditions/recommendations*). Option 2 is not correct because the sentence has been broken up into two sentences, and the second sentence is a fragment. It also changes the original meaning of the sentence. Option 3 is not correct because "required" is not the intended modifier, and it changes the meaning of the original sentence. Option 4 is not correct because the modifier is misplaced.

LESSON 9, *pp. 78–81*

1. (3), In sentence 4, the modifying phrase "To ensure success" is incorrectly placed, creating a dangling modifier (no subject to modify). The intended subject is "employees" because "employees" are the recipients of the wellness programs.

2. (3), The intended subject is "you" because "you" work on the family budget.

3. (2), "strategies" is the *actual* subject in the sentence because it immediately follows the modifying phrase "To reduce the financial pain of the check-out line," implying that the "strategies" reduce financial pain. However, the intended subject is "you" because the strategies help *you.*

4. (4), In sentence 10, the modifying phrase "Following through on rebate offers" is incorrectly modifying the word "companies." The intended subject is "you"; therefore answer option 4 is the best revision of sentence 10 because the subject is correctly modified within a complete sentence. In this case, the writer chose to create a dependent clause with the subordinating conjunction "When."

5. (4), The missing subject is "retailers" because "the encouragement" is provided by the retailers. Answer option 4 is the only option that includes the subject.

UNIT 3 (continued)

6. (5), Option 5 is correct because it is the only sentence that has the correct subject without changing the meaning of the original sentence. The intended subject is *store designers* because they design the stores to have frequent stops. These stops make it difficult for shoppers to get around.

7. (2), In sentence 12, the modifying phrase "Helping customers shop" is incorrectly modifying the word "stickers." The missing subject is "employees." Therefore answer option 2 is the best revision of sentence 12 because the subject is correctly modified within a complete sentence. Answer option 2 is the only option that includes the subject (*employees*).

8. (2), Sentence 5 is missing the subject of what suggests that chores are defined according to gender. The intended subject is "your answers." Therefore, answer option 2 is the best revision of the underlined portion of this sentence because the subject is correctly modified within a complete sentence. While all of the answer options include the subject (*answers to the questions*), the other answer options lose focus or change the meaning of the original sentence.

9. (1), Sentence 13 is missing the subject of who forms the conclusions. The intended subject is "I." Therefore, answer option 1 includes the groups of words that would most effectively revise sentence 13. This is the only answer option with the subject.

10. (3), Sentence 16 is missing the subject of who performs the studies. The intended subject is "men and women." Therefore, answer option 3 is the best revision of sentence 16 because the subject is correctly modified within a complete sentence. Answer option 3 is the only option that includes the subject. Option 1 would be correct if the subject was in the previous sentence, but it is not.

LESSON 10, *pp. 82–85*

1. (1), The words "bargaining," "negotiating," and "compromising" maintain parallel structure because they all end with *–ing*. The conjunction "and" indicates the need for parallel structure within the compound sentence.

2. (3), This part of sentence 10 lacks parallel structure because the two verbs are not in the same verb form (they don't have the same ending). Changing the verb forms to *happier* and *healthier* or *happy* and *healthy* would maintain parallel structure.

3. (2), The words "peaches" and "bananas" maintain parallel structure because they are both plural, whole objects: *Do you want apples, peaches, or bananas for lunch next week?* Changing "apple slices" to "apples" maintains parallel structure because "apple slices" means part of a whole, rather than a whole object, such as the apples.

4. (2), The word "plunging" maintains parallel structure with "dipping" because they both end with *–ing*. The other answer options do not maintain parallel structure because they have the word "to." Remember that *to* only comes before a verb that has not been changed: *to plunge*; *plunging*; *to dip*; *dipping*.

5. (5), The phrases "it's nice" and "it's nicer" maintain parallel structure because they both begin with "it's."

6. (3), Answer option 3 is correct because "you can spend one dollar" and "you can spend the other" are parallel forms. Because the verbs "can" and "spend" are both unchanged, they are parallel in structure.

7. (2), "Sturdy desk," "office chair," and "filing cabinet" maintain parallel structure because they are singular objects in a list and are not accompanied by verbs.

8. (2), "When to buy used" and "when to buy new" maintain parallel structure because they are both *to+verb* forms.

9. (4), The phrases "buy used" and "do not buy used" maintain parallel structure because both phrases have the same verb form: buy.

10. (4), The phrases "it's good" and "it's not good" maintain parallel structure because both phrases begin with "it's." Therefore, answer option 4 is the best revision of sentence 9.

UNIT 4 USAGE

LESSON 1, *pp. 86–89*

1. (3), "North Dakota" and "Eiffel Tower" are both proper nouns that must be capitalized because they represent a specific place. Therefore, answer option 3 is correct.

2. (4), "EZ Pay" is a proper noun that must be capitalized. The other words in the underlined portion do not need to be capitalized because they are not proper nouns.

3. (3), The word "from" is not a noun, but it is often put in the place of "form" (a noun) due to the similar spelling: *To sign up, call us today or return the attached form in the prepaid envelope.*

4. (5), This sentence does not contain any errors. Therefore, no correction is necessary.

5. (4), The word "information" is a noun because it is a thing.

6. (5), This sentence does not contain any errors. Therefore, no correction is necessary.

7. (2), "Judge" is not a proper noun because it is not the specific name of someone or something. While *judge* is a title, it would only be capitalized if it came before the judge's name: *Judge Smith*. When used alone, *judge* is always lowercase.

8. (4), The word "directs" is a verb and should be replaced with the noun "directions" to best correct this sentence.

9. (4), The words "A" and "Crime" are not proper nouns and do not begin a sentence. Therefore, they should be replaced with "a" and "crime."

10. (3), The word "don" is a proper noun. Therefore, it should be replaced with "Don." In this case, "Coffee" should be capitalized because it is part of the program's title.

UNIT 4 (*continued*)

11. (4), The noun "companies" indicates more than one, but the paragraph is about one company. Therefore, it should be replaced with "company." The noun "plan" indicates that there is only one plan, but the phrase "a few" comes before "plan." This means that "plan" should be replaced with "plans" (plural).

12. (2), "Scientists" is the best noun to be inserted into sentence 3 because sentence 2 references the scientists. This provides unity and coherence between sentences.

13. (1), This sentence does not contain any errors in capitalization or sentence structure. Therefore, the original is the best answer option.

LESSON 2, pp. 90–93

1. (2), The object pronoun "her" replaces the noun "grandmother" to reduce the number of times *grandmother* appears in the text. The first-person pronoun "I" should not be changed because the writer is telling the story in the first-person point of view (from his own point of view).

2. (3), The possessive pronoun "your" is used incorrectly in sentence 2 because there is not a possession that is shown. In this case "your" should change to the second-person pronoun "you" and "the system" should be replaced with the object pronoun "it."

3. (5), The phrase "the alerts" is repetitive. Therefore, it should be replaced with the pronoun "they" to reduce the number of times it appears in the text. The possessive pronoun "your" should not be changed because the "cell phone" is your possession (it belongs to you).

4. (2), The word "our" should not be changed because the speaker of this letter is the *college president and staff*. The plural object pronoun "us" should replace "the State College President and her staff" to eliminate unnecessary words or bulky sentences.

5. (5), This sentence does not contain any noun or pronoun errors. Therefore, no correction is necessary.

6. (1), Because the writer of the letter is writing from his own point of view (first-person), he should be using *I*, rather than using his name (third-person). Therefore, the proper noun "Ron Allenson" should be replaced with the subject pronoun "I." For example: *On June 10, I will be presenting a talk on how you can buy your first house.*

7. (3), Because the writer of the letter is writing from his own point of view (first-person), he should be using the *I* point of view, rather than using his name (third-person). Therefore, the proper noun "Ron Allenson" should be replaced with the subject pronoun "I" and the possessive pronoun "my."

8. (4), Because the writer of the letter is writing from his own point of view (first-person), he should be using the *I* point of view, rather than using his name (third-person). Therefore, the proper noun "Ron Allenson" should be replaced with the object pronoun "me" and the subject pronoun "I."

9. (2), Because the writer of the letter is writing from his own point of view (first-person), he should be using the *I* point of view, rather than using his name (third-person). Therefore, the proper noun "Ron Allenson" should be replaced with the object pronoun "me." For example: *Also, if you know anyone else who might be interested in attending, please let me know and pass this invitation along.*

10. (3), The subject of sentence 4 is the reader. This means that the summons is written in second-person (from the *you* point of view). Therefore, the plural subject pronoun "they" is used incorrectly and should be replaced by the singular subject pronoun "you."

11. (2), The subject of sentence 5 is the reader. This means that the summons is written in second-person (from the *you* point of view). Therefore, the plural possessive pronoun "their" is used incorrectly and should be replaced by the singular possessive pronoun "your." For example: *You will be mailed a reminder notice about 10 days before your scheduled date to appear.*

12. (1), Sentence 7 does not contain any noun or pronoun errors. Therefore, the original is the best way to write the underlined portion of this sentence.

13. (1), The writer of the Summons for Jury Duty is writing the letter in second-person (the *you* point of view). Therefore, the possessive pronoun "your," which refers to the reader rather than the writer, should replace "the person's." For example: *You may also postpone your juror service, if necessary.*

LESSON 3, pp. 94–97

1. (1), The subject of sentence 11 is the woman's daughter. Therefore, the plural subject pronoun "they" should be replaced with the singular subject "she," which best agrees with the object pronoun "her." For example: *She will bring her friends.*

2. (5), Sentence 2 is missing the pronoun that represents possession of the monthly bills. It also misuses the possessive pronoun "his" in reference to the computer. Therefore, "the" and "his" should be replaced with "your."

3. (5), In sentence 5, the plural subject pronoun "We" does not agree with the plural noun "customers" from sentence 4 because the letter is written in second-person, not first-person. Option 1 is not correct because while "you" are a customer, the letter refers to more than one customer (*they*). Therefore, "we" should be replaced with "they." For example: *They are hard to find these days.*

4. (2), The first use of the pronoun "it" in sentence 6 is used incorrectly because the antecedent needs to appear before the pronoun. In this case "EZ Pay" (the antecedent) should appear in the beginning of the sentence, and then the pronoun "it" should appear later in order to avoid repetition.

UNIT 4 (*continued*)

5. (3), In sentence 7, the antecedent is the singular noun "form." Therefore, the plural pronoun "them" should be replaced with the singular pronoun "it." For example: *We hope you will review the enclosed form and send it back as soon as possible.*

6. (3), In sentence 4, the antecedent is the plural noun "rooms." Therefore, the singular pronoun "it" should be replaced by the plural pronoun "they." For example: *They are newly decorated, too!*

7. (5), In sentence 6, the pronoun "They" agrees with the antecedent "points" from sentence 5. Therefore, no correction is necessary.

8. (4), In sentence 10, the antecedent is "you." Therefore, the pronoun "his" should be replaced with the possessive pronoun "your" because it best agrees with "you."

9. (1), In sentence 13, the antecedent is the plural noun "points." Therefore, the singular pronoun "it" should be replaced with the plural pronoun "they." For example: *Stay five more nights to earn more points, and they will add up to another free night!*

10. (2), In sentence 1, the antecedent is "Mrs. Shaver." Therefore, the pronoun in sentence 2 that would best agree is "she." Option 3 (*they*) is not correct because the sentence is referring only to Mrs. Shaver (one person).

11. (4), In sentence 3, the antecedent is "brother." Therefore, the pronoun that best agrees is "he" rather than "they."

12. (3), In sentence 4, the antecedent is the singular pronoun "him." Therefore, the singular pronoun "he" best agrees with "him" rather than the plural pronoun "they." For example: *However, if a student like him does not want to sing professionally, he may only need to rehearse once or twice a week.*

13. (3), In sentence 5, the antecedent is the singular male pronoun "he." Therefore, the singular male pronouns "he" and "his" should replace the plural pronouns "they" and "their."

LESSON 4, pp. 98–101

1. (2), The collective noun "group" takes the singular verb "perches" because the group of cats are acting as a single unit: *Some of the group perches on windowsills in the living room to watch for birds outside.*

2. (3), The collective noun "State College" takes the singular verb "plans" because the college is a single entity acting as a whole: *As part of a statewide effort to inform different audiences about major, safety-related news, State College plans to create a new Emergency Notification System.*

3. (1), The collective noun "Staff" takes the plural verb "choose" because the college's *staff* has members that act independently: *Department heads will be notified if staff choose not to receive the alerts.*

4. (2), The collective noun "student body" takes the singular verb "prefers" because the *student body* is acting as a single unit: *If the student body prefers to receive alerts as text messages, please e-mail the registrar's office.*

5. (1), Sentence 5 does not contain any errors. Therefore, the original is the best way to write the underlined portion.

6. (4), The collective noun "government" takes the singular verb "works" because it acts as a single unit: *Serving on a jury allows you to see how the justice system works, and allows you to gain a better understanding of how government works in general.*

7. (2), A jury is made up of more than one person. Therefore, *jury* is a collective noun. In sentence 4, "a jury of one's peer" should be replaced with "a jury of one's peers" because *peer* means one and *peers* means more than one: *The Constitution guarantees people the right to a trial by a jury of one's peers.*

8. (5), The noun "juries" is incorrect because there is only one "jury" in the passage. *Jury* is a collective noun because it is a group made up of more than one person and acts as a single unit. Because the jury acts as a single unit, the following verb should be "makes" (a singular verb).

9. (3), *Cans* is a noun not a verb. The collective noun "jury" should take the verb "can" in sentence 12 because *can* is both singular and plural: *After deliberations begin in the jury room, only the jury can discuss the case until the verdict is agreed upon.*

10. (4), The collective noun "team" takes the singular verb "is" rather than the plural verb "are" because the "team" acts as a single unit.

11. (1), Sentence 7 does not contain any errors. Therefore, the underlined portion is best written in its original form. The "team" is a singular unit that takes the singular verb "feels."

12. (3), In sentence 8, "team" should take the singular verb "has" because the team acts as a single unit: *If we want the Thunder to win the championship this season, then the team has to be shown our support.* Note that the word "the" is a helpful clue that the noun is singular.

13. (5), The noun "players" represents the individual members of the Thunder team (*team* is a collective noun). In sentence 9, "players" takes the plural verbs "put" and "ignore" because it is a plural noun.

LESSON 5, pp. 102–105

1. (3), Sentence 2 indicates future tense because it has the helping verb "will." Therefore, the past tense verb "opened" should be replaced with "open." For example: *Well, get ready, because the biggest action movie of all time will open in theaters on May 20th!*

2. (3), Sentence 2 indicates present tense. Therefore, "will kill" should be replaced with the present tense form "kills." For example: *The rise in water temperature kills many nutrients that fish eat for food.*

UNIT 4 (continued)

3. (2), Sentence 4 indicates present tense. Therefore, "formed" should be changed to the present tense "form." For example: *As the warmest water moves east, clouds and thunderstorms form over the Pacific.*

4. (5), Sentence 5 does not contain any errors. Therefore, no correction is necessary.

5. (5), Sentence 7 indicates present tense. Therefore, "will affect" should be replaced with the singular present tense "affects."

6. (4), Sentence 2 indicates future tense. Therefore, the present tense form "are listen" should be replaced with the future tense form "will listen."

7. (2), Sentence 4 indicates present tense. Therefore, the past tense verb form "reviewed" should be replaced with the present tense verb form "reviews." For example: *At the end of the trial, he reviews the applicable laws with the jury.* While "At the end of the trial" suggests future tense, this sentence is present tense because participants are being walked through the process in the present tense. If you were teaching someone to drive, for example, you might say *first we fasten our seatbelts* (present), *then you start the car* (present), *finally you check the mirrors* (present).

8. (2), Sentence 5 indicates future tense. Therefore, the helping verb "will" should be inserted after the noun "case" and before the verb "bring." For example: *The participants in the case will bring their own attorneys or their attorneys will be appointed by the court.*

9. (1), Sentence 9 does not contain any simple verb tense errors. Therefore, the underlined portion is best written in its original form.

10. (2), Sentence 1 indicates present tense. Therefore, the past tense verb form "checked" should be replaced with the present tense verb form "check." For example: *It is important to check the oil in your car often.*

11. (3), Sentence 6 indicates present tense. Therefore, the past tense verb form "located" should be replaced with the present tense verb form "locate." For example: *After you locate the dipstick, pull it out of the part of the engine that stores the oil.*

12. (1), Sentence 8 indicates present tense. Therefore, the past tense verb form "Made" should be replaced with the present tense verb form "Make." For example: *Make sure that you push it all the way into the engine.*

13. (4), Sentence 10 indicates present tense. Therefore, the past tense verb form "was" should be replaced with the present tense verb form "is" and the past tense verb form "needed" should be replaced with the present tense verb form "need." For example: *If the oil on it is below the line marked "full," you need to add a small amount of oil to your car.*

LESSON 6, *pp. 106–109*

1. (4), Sentence 7 indicates present and past tense. The viewer watches the movie in the present, but the movie was created in the past. Therefore, the past tense verb form "watched" should be replaced with the present tense verb form "watch," and the verb "create" should be replaced with the past tense verb form "created." For example: *May 20th will be the first day to watch the greatest action movie ever created.*

2. (5), Sentence 1 does not contain any regular verb tense errors. Therefore, no correction is necessary.

3. (3), The underlined portion of sentence 2 indicates past tense. The word "interesting" is not a verb; it is a modifier (*That movie was interesting*). Therefore, the modifier (adjective) "interesting" should be replaced with the past tense verb "interested."

4. (5), The underlined portion of sentence 4 indicates present tense. Therefore, the past tense verb "responded" should be replaced with the present tense verb "respond."

5. (3), The underlined portion of sentence 6 indicates present tense. Therefore, the verb "attend" should be replaced with the present tense verb form "attending."

6. (3), Sentence 2 indicates past tense. Therefore, the best revision of the sentence is answer option 3 because "start" is replaced with the past tense verb form "was started" and "changing" is replaced with the past tense verb form "changed."

7. (2), Sentence 3 indicates past tense. Therefore, the verb "link" should be replaced with its past tense verb form "linked." For example: *Electrical companies built power lines across the United States, and telephones linked homes and businesses.*

8. (4), Sentence 6 indicates past tense. Therefore, the helping verb "will" and the original verb "seem" should be replaced with the past tense verb form "seemed."

9. (1), Sentence 9 does not contain any regular verb tense errors. Therefore, the underlined portion is best written in its original form.

10. (2), The underlined portion of sentence 3 indicates past tense. Therefore, the original verb "tease" should be replaced with its past tense verb form "teased."

11. (3), When the word *to* comes before a verb, the verb should always be in its original form (*to dance, to sing, to run*). Therefore, "thinked" should be replaced with "think": *It's nice because they don't have to think about what they are going to wear.*

12. (3), Sentence 6 contains a *to+verb* form. Therefore, "to checking" should be replaced with the original verb form "to check." Remember that *to* comes before a verb that has not been changed.

13. (5), Sentence 8 does not contain any regular verb tense errors. Therefore, no correction is necessary.

UNIT 4 (*continued*)

LESSON 7, *pp. 110–113*

1. (5), Sentence 6 is past perfect tense because the writer is describing one event that happened before another event. For example, first the cats ran outside, and then they came inside. Therefore, answer option 5 is the best revision of the sentence because the helping verb "had" comes before the first action "run."

2. (2), Sentence 1 is present perfect tense because the writer is describing an action that started in the past and continues in the present. For example, the company learned lessons in the past and continues to learn lessons in the present. Therefore, "will have" should be replaced with the present perfect helping verb "has": *Our manufacturing company has learned many lessons during its first 80 years.*

3. (5), Sentence 3 is past perfect tense because the writer is describing one event that happened before another event. For example, first the power lines were built, and then telephones linked homes and businesses. Therefore, answer option 5 is the best revision of the underlined portion because "will have" is replaced by the past perfect tense helping verb "had."

4. (1), Sentence 7 is present perfect tense because the writer is describing an event that started in the past and continues in the present. For example, the products were made in the past and continue to be made in the present. Therefore, "has work" should be replaced with the present perfect tense helping verb "have" and the past tense verb "worked": *Even though our founders did not know it at the time, that failure opened the door to many other products that have worked much better.*

5. (4), Sentence 10 is future perfect tense because the writer is describing an event that he or she hopes will happen. For example, the company hopes that millions of toys will be used from now to an undetermined time in the future. Therefore, answer option 4 is the best revision of the underlined portion because the future perfect helping verbs "will have been" are now in the sentence.

6. (3), Sentence 1 is present perfect tense because the writer is describing an event that began in the past and continues in the present. For example, the newspaper made a discovery in the past that holds true in the present. Therefore, answer option 3 is the best revision of the underlined portion because the present perfect tense helping verb "has" is paired with the past tense verb "discovered."

7. (4), Sentence 4 is present perfect tense because the writer is describing an event that began in the past and continues in the present. For example, the survey was conducted in the past and the results hold true in the present. Therefore, the helping verb "has" should be inserted before the verb "shown": *A recently-conducted survey has shown that walkers and hikers in these areas outnumber ATV riders by more than 2 to 1.*

8. (5), Answer option 5 is the best sentence to insert before sentence 6 (in paragraph C) because it stays on topic: walkers and hikers do not want ATVs in state parks. It also has the helping verb "have," which matches the rest of the paragraph (present perfect tense). Option 1 is not correct because paragraph C is not about what the ATV can and cannot do. Option 2 is not correct because paragraph C is not about people liking the ATV. Remember that this editorial is an argument against ATVs in state parks. Option 3 is not correct because paragraph C is about ATV riders going other places to ride, specifically the southern part of the state. While it is true that ATVs are used in rural areas, option 4 is not the best answer because it is not focused on the point of the editorial.

9. (3), Sentence 7 is present perfect tense because the writer is describing an event that began in the past and continues in the present. The acres of coal mines became a tourist attraction in the past, and continue to attract ATV riders in the present. Therefore, the future perfect tense helping verb "will" should be removed from the sentence: *For example, thousands of acres of old coal mines in the southern part of the state have become a tourist destination for ATV riders from other states.*

10. (1), Sentence 1 is present perfect tense because the writer is describing an event that begins in the past and continues in the present. For example, the jury agrees on a verdict in the past, and the verdict is carried out in the present. Therefore, the past perfect tense helping verb "had" should be replaced with the present perfect tense helping verb "has": *Many things happen after a jury has agreed on a verdict.*

11. (4), Sentence 4 is present perfect tense because the writer is describing an event that began in the past and continues in the present. For example, the jury makes a decision in the past, but does not tell the judge its decision until the present. Therefore, option 4 is the best revision of the underlined portion because the present perfect tense helping verbs "has" and "been" are inserted into the sentence before the verb "told."

12. (2), Sentence 6 is future perfect tense because the writer is describing a possible event that could happen. This means option 2 is the best revision of the underlined portion because the future perfect tense helping verbs, "will" and "have," are inserted into the sentence before the *to+verb* form "to go."

13. (4), Sentence 10 is present perfect tense because the writer is describing an event that began in the past and continues in the present. For example, the jury reaches a decision in the past and presents its decision in the present. Therefore, option 4 is the best revision of the underlined portion because the future perfect tense helping verb "will" is replaced by the present perfect tense helping verb "has." In this case, *reach* should also be replaced. You cannot insert the helping verb *has* before an unchanged verb (*to reach*, never *has reach/have reach*). Even though "reached" is a past tense verb, it is correct in sentence 10 because of the helping verb "has."

UNIT 4 (continued)

LESSON 8, pp. 114–117

1. (1), Sentence 5 is past tense because the writer is describing an event/action that already happened. Therefore, the irregular verb "become" should be replaced with its past tense form "became": *My daughter attended your school and became so stressed that she withdrew.*

2. (2), Option 2 is the best revision of the underlined portion because the irregular verb "grow" is replaced by its past tense form "grew."

3. (3), Sentence 8 is past tense because the writer is describing something that already happened. Therefore, the irregular verb "do" should be replaced with its past tense form "did": *This was sad because it did not take into account how the team felt.* "Felt" is the past tense form of the verb *feel*, and is correctly used in this sentence. Option 2 is not correct because "does" is a present tense condition, and this sentence is about something that already happened.

4. (3), Option 3 is the best revision of the underlined portion because the irregular verb "know" is replaced with its past tense form "knew," and the irregular verb "give" is replaced with its past tense form "gave."

5. (5), This sentence does not contain any errors. Therefore, no correction is necessary.

6. (1), Sentence 2 is present perfect tense because the writer is describing an event/action that began in the past (jurors were selected) and continues to happen (jurors listen to testimony and reach a verdict). Therefore, the irregular verb "chose" (the past tense form of *choose*) should be replaced with its past particle "have been chosen." The helping verb "have" means the verb should be in its past participle form: *Jurors have been chosen to judge how reliable the witnesses are and must decide how valuable the testimony of each witness is.*

7. (4), Sentence 3 is present tense because the writer is describing something that is happening in the present. The irregular verb "give" is an exception to the past/present tense rule because in this present tense sentence, the irregular verb "give" should be replaced with its past participle form "given." This is because the present tense verb "is" is used as the helping verb.

8. (3), Sentence 6 is present tense because the writer is describing an event/action that is happening in the present, but it is also mentioning something that happened in the past (what the witnesses already saw). Therefore, option 3 is the best revision of the underlined portion because the irregular verb "see" is replaced with its past tense form "saw." The verb "say" should stay in its present tense form.

9. (1), Sentence 7 is written in the wrong tense. Therefore, option 1 is the best choice because the helping verb "will" is replaced by the helping verb "has," and the irregular verb "teach" is replaced by its past participle "taught." The helping verb "has" means the new sentence is written in present perfect tense.

10. (4), Sentence 2 describes a past time period. Therefore, option 4 is the best revision of the underlined portion because the irregular verbs "eat," "drink," and "fall" are replaced by their past tense verb forms "ate," "drank," and "fell."

11. (5), Sentence 3 does not contain any irregular verb errors. Therefore, no correction is necessary.

12. (2), Sentence 10 is written in present perfect tense because the writer is describing an action that happened in the past and continues to happen. Therefore, option 2 is the best revision of the underlined portion because the irregular verb "give" is replaced by its past participle "given." The helping verb "have" comes before the action and indicates present perfect tense.

13. (2), Sentence 12 is future tense (because of the verb "will") with a reference to a past action (the writer is expressing future feelings of a past action). Therefore, the irregular verb "do" should be replaced with its past tense verb form "did."

LESSON 9, pp. 118–121

1. (2), Sentence 3 contains a compound subject joined by "or," which means that the verb must agree with the subject closest to it. The singular subject "phone's recipient" must have a singular verb. Therefore, the plural verb "begin" should be replaced with its singular form "begins."

2. (3), The subject "riders" is plural. Therefore, the singular verb "is" should be replaced with its plural verb form "are" in order for the sentence to have proper subject-verb agreement: *The City Chronicle has discovered that riders of ATVs (All Terrain Vehicles) are supporting a new bill in the state legislature.* Option 4 is not correct because sentence 1 is present tense, and *were* is past tense.

3. (3), Sentence 4 contains a compound subject joined by "and." This means that the verb must agree with the plural subject. Therefore, the singular verb "outnumbers" should be replaced with its plural verb form "outnumber": *Walkers and hikers in these areas outnumber ATV riders by more than 2 to 1, according to a survey conducted last year.*

4. (5), Sentence 6 contains more than one error. The verb "riding" does not agree with the subject "people," and the verb "causes" does not agree with the subject "ATVs." Therefore, answer option 5 is the best revision of sentence 6 because the plural verb "ride" agrees with the plural subject "people," and the plural verb "cause" agrees with the plural subject "ATVs" in a complete sentence. The other answer options have errors.

5. (1), Sentence 7 does not contain any subject-verb agreement errors. Therefore, the original is the best way to write the underlined portion of the sentence.

UNIT 4 (*continued*)

6. (1), Sentence 2 does not contain any subject-verb agreement errors. Therefore, the original is the best way to write the underlined portion of the sentence.

7. (2), The subject "it" is singular. Therefore, the singular form "is" should replace the plural verb "were": *As an author, it is often hard for me to connect with individual readers.*

8. (4), Sentence 7 contains a compound subject joined by "and," which means that the verb must agree with the plural subject "News and information." Therefore, answer option 4 is the best revision of the underlined portion of the sentence because the plural verb "are" agrees with the plural subject. While option 5 does contain proper subject-verb agreement, it cannot be correct because we know that the author has written more than one book.

9. (3), Sentence 12 contains an exception to the rule because the subject "I" takes a plural verb (*I like/ They like; she likes/Tom likes*). Therefore, the singular verb "looks" should be replaced with the plural verb "look": *I look forward to hearing from you!*

10. (2), Sentence 1 contains a compound subject joined by "and," which means that the verb must agree with the plural subject "Civil cases and criminal cases." Therefore, the singular verb "has" should be replaced by the plural verb "have": *Civil cases and criminal cases have many important differences.*

11. (1), Sentence 4 does not contain any subject-verb agreement errors. Therefore, the original is the best way to write the underlined portion of the sentence.

12. (4), Answer option 4 is the best revision of the underlined portion of the sentence because there is only one plaintiff, and the subject (*plaintiff*) and verb (*is*) agree.

13. (3), Sentence 7 contains a compound subject joined by "or" which means that the verb must agree with the subject closest to it. Therefore, the plural verb form "are" should be replaced with the singular verb "is": *The person or company that is accused becomes the defendant.*

LESSON 10, *pp. 122–125*

1. (3), The phrase "apple season" is a singular subject. Therefore, the plural verb "are" should be replaced by the singular verb "is": *Apple season, which occurs during the fall, is a fun time of year.*

2. (2), *You* is an exception to the rule. In most cases *you* takes the plural verb form, such as *you go* or *you know.* In this case, the verb that best agrees is the plural verb "are." Therefore, answer option 2 is the best revision of the underlined portion of the sentence.

3. (4), "The judge" is a singular subject in a present tense paragraph. Therefore, the verb that best agrees is the singular verb "conducts." Answer option 4 is the best revision of the underlined portion of the sentence.

4. (5), Sentence 5 does not contain any errors. Therefore, no correction is necessary.

5. (2), The word "attorneys" is a plural subject. Therefore, the singular verb "is" should be replaced with the plural verb "are": *Attorneys, together with the judge, are the only court officials who can address questions to witnesses.*

6. (5), The singular noun "spot" should be replaced with the plural noun "spots" because the sentence provides examples of more than one type of spot. Answer option 5 is the best revision of the sentence because it contains the proper plural noun (*spots*), as well as proper subject-verb agreement (*spots should be*).

7. (4), The "hardwood floors" is a plural subject. Also keep in mind that this sentence is written in present tense. Therefore, the verb that best agrees is the plural verb "get." Option 4 is the best revision of the underlined portion of the sentence.

8. (5), Sentence 9 does not contain any errors. Therefore, no correction is necessary.

9. (5), Answer option 5 is the best revision of the underlined portion of sentence 11 because the subject "tips" is plural and agrees with the plural verb "are."

10. (3), The phrase "several students" is a plural subject. Therefore, the singular verb "was" should be replaced with the plural verb "were." Answer option 3 is the best revision of the underlined portion of the sentence because it contains proper subject-verb agreement.

11. (2), The singular subject of the sentence is the way to dress. Therefore, the plural verb "allow" should be replaced with the singular verb "allows": *I think that you can dress neatly, and appropriate for school, in a way that still allows freedom of expression.*

12. (4), Sentence 6 contains the compound subject "students and parents," which is plural. Therefore, the singular verb "decides" should be replaced with the plural verb "decide": *I believe that students and parents, not the principal, should decide what students can wear to school.*

13. (5), This sentence does not contain any subject-verb agreement errors. Therefore, no correction is necessary.

UNIT 5 MECHANICS

LESSON 1, *pp. 126–129*

1. (1), "Online Banking Services" is not a proper noun, nor does it begin a sentence. Therefore, it should not be capitalized: *You will also save any money you're spending on late fees because many online banking services provide you with real-time alerts.*

2. (2), The noun "Squirrels" is not a proper noun, nor does it begin a sentence. Therefore, it should not be capitalized: *When the leaves begin to change colors in the fall, you'll suddenly begin to notice that the squirrels that have been frolicking in the yard all summer have given up their games for work.*

3. (5), This sentence does not contain any capitalization errors. Therefore, no correction is necessary.

UNIT 5 (*continued*)

4. (4), The noun "Chimney Sweep" is not a proper noun, does not begin a sentence, and is not a formal title. Therefore, it should not be capitalized: *Invite a chimney sweep to inspect and clean your chimney.*

5. (5), Answer option 5 is the best revision of the underlined portion of sentence 1. When a professional title comes before a person's name, it should be capitalized: *President Obama; Dr. Crawford; Uncle Joe.*

6. (1), Months of the year are always capitalized. Therefore, "february" should be replaced with "February": *Effective February 20, set all cell phones to silent when entering the building.*

7. (2), The words "Blogging" and "Social Networking" are not proper nouns, nor do they begin the sentence. Therefore, they should not be capitalized: *Do not involve co-workers in blogging or social networking, including visual as well as text entries.*

8. (3), The nouns "Fat," "Cholesterol," and "Sodium," are not proper nouns, nor do they begin the sentence. Therefore, they should not be capitalized: *The "bad" ingredients, such as fat, cholesterol, and sodium, are listed first.*

9. (2), The noun "Potassium" is not a proper noun, nor does it begin the sentence. Therefore, it should not be capitalized: *For example, 21% potassium is a bad high number.*

10. (3), The noun "vitamin c" is not a proper noun. However, in the case of vitamins, such as vitamin A, vitamin B, vitamin C, and vitamin D, the actual vitamin letter always should be capitalized. Therefore, "vitamin c" should be replaced with "vitamin C": *For example, 45% vitamin C is a good high number.*

LESSON 2, *pp. 130–133*

1. (4), The possessive pronoun "its" does not belong in sentence 6 because the sentence does not intend to show possession. Therefore, "its" should be replaced with the contraction "it's": *If you see blowing objects or hear a train-like sound, it's a good idea to go to a designated safe meeting place.*

2. (3), The possessive noun "avocados'" does not belong in sentence 7 because the sentence does not intend to show possession. However, it does intend to indicate that there is more than one avocado. Therefore, the apostrophe should be removed and "avocados'" should be replaced with "avocados." The corrected sentence should read: *Research suggests that chemicals in avocados destroy oral cancer cells.*

3. (1), The possessive noun "scan's" does not belong in sentence 10 because the sentence does not intend to show possession. However, it does intend to indicate more than one scan. Therefore, the apostrophe should be removed: *As a preventative measure, limit the number of CT scans you undergo.*

4. (3), The possessive pronoun "its" does not belong in sentence 15 because the sentence does not intend to show possession. Therefore, "Its" should be replaced with the contraction "It's" (it is): *It's also important to report one's family medical history to a physician.*

5. (2), Answer option 2 (*doesn't*) is the correct way to contract the phrase *does not.*

6. (3), The contraction "you're" is short for *you are* and you wouldn't say *Make sure you are résumé.* Therefore, the possessive pronoun "your" should replace the contraction "you're." The corrected sentence should read: *Make sure your résumé is job-ready by providing contact information and references.*

7. (4), Answer option 4 is the best way to write the underlined portion of sentence 12 because sentence 12 refers to the history of the company. Therefore, "companys history" should be rewritten as "company's history" to show possession. The corrected sentence should read: *You want to appear knowledgeable about the company's history, and you should ask intelligent and insightful questions.*

8. (2), The apostrophe indicates possession of an opinion.

9. (1), The possessive noun "rate's" does not belong in sentence 8 because the sentence does not intend to show possession. However, it does intend to indicate more than one rate. Therefore, "rate's" should be replaced with "rates." The corrected sentence should read: *Buying a new car may be the best choice when interest rates are low.*

10. (5), This sentence does not contain any possession or contraction errors. Therefore, no correction is necessary.

LESSON 3, *pp. 134–137*

1. (3), Due to the context of sentence 10, the writer does not intend to say that you should stop spending time with a noise, understanding, or activation of a computer icon. However, the writer does intend to say that you should stop spending time with people (*clique*) who have bad habits.

2. (2), The word "feet" should be replaced with the word "feat" because *feet* are the things with which animals use to walk, and a *feat* is an achievement. The corrected sentence should read: *In such a world, it's difficult to believe that anyone achieves the feat of getting anything for free anymore.*

3. (1), The word "grate" should be replaced with the word "great" because *grate* means to make smaller or to irritate, and *great* means remarkable or magnificent. The corrected sentence should read: *With a good search engine, you can find a great vacation home for free by linking up with a home exchange program.*

UNIT 5 (*continued*)

4. (3), The word "coarses" should be replaced with the word "courses" because *coarse* refers to something rough in texture and cannot be made plural, while the word *course* refers to a class one takes in school or while training and can be made plural. The corrected sentence should read: *That's right—people who are enrolled in a course to become massage therapists, hair stylists, and manicurists need people on whom to practice their skills.*

5. (1), The word "Counsel" should be replaced with "Council" because *counsel* means to give advice, and a *council* is an administrative group or committee. The corrected sentence should read: *The Rose Bud City Council has issued a boil water advisory for the citizens of Rose Bud and the surrounding areas.*

6. (2), The word "affect" should be replaced with the word "effect" because *affect* means to influence something, and *effect* indicates a result or state of condition. The corrected sentence should read: *The advisory will be in effect until the Department of Environmental Protection has collected water samples and tested these samples at the state laboratory facility.*

7. (4), The word "miners" should be replaced with "minors" because a *miner* is a person who digs mines, and a *minor* refers to a person of a younger age (usually under 18). The corrected sentence should read: *However, in the interest of safety, residents, particularly minors and the elderly, should continue to boil water until otherwise notified.*

8. (3), The word *husky* has several meanings. However, in sentence 2, the writer means that the apes are big and strong.

9. (4), The word "there" should be replaced with the word "their" because *there* is an adverb that indicates a location, and *their* is a pronoun that indicates possession. Given the context of sentence 3, it is clear that the writer is referring to possession, not location. The corrected sentence should read: *Monkeys have arms that are equal to or shorter than their legs, while apes have arms that exceed the length of their legs.*

10. (1), The word "tales" should be replaced with the word "tails" because a *tale* is a story or narrative and a *tail* is something that some animals have, such as monkeys, cats, and dogs. The corrected sentence should read: *Monkeys have tails, while apes do not.*

11. (4), The word "sum" should be replaced with the word "some" because *sum* is the amount something equals or the act of summarizing, while *some* is an amount. The corrected sentence should read: *Another difference between monkeys and apes is that some monkeys have visible teeth, and some apes, such as gorillas and chimpanzees, have the ability to use tools to solve problems.*

LESSON 4, *pp. 138–141*

1. (1), The misspelled word in sentence 14 is "Sceintists" because it is one of the exceptions to the *i* before *e* except after *c* rule. The corrected sentence should read: *Our scientists continue to engage in research regarding the relationship between breast cancer and soy.*

2. (4), The misspelled word in sentence 2 is "saveings," which is spelled *savings*. Remember that when the suffix –*ing* is added to a word, you need to drop the *e*. The corrected sentence should read: *We strive to provide our customers with quality services that satisfy every aspect of their financial portfolios, including savings, bill payment, and education and retirement funds.*

3. (2), The misspelled word in sentence 6 is "garuntee," which is spelled *guarantee*. This is a commonly misspelled word that you may want to memorize. The corrected sentence should read: *The two accounts guarantee that you have many options as you manage your monthly expenses.*

4. (4), The misspelled word in sentence 7 is "hesatate," which is spelled *hesitate*. The corrected sentence should read: *Please don't hesitate to contact me if you have any other questions.*

5. (5), This sentence does not contain any spelling errors. Therefore, no correction is necessary.

6. (4), The misspelled word in sentence 5 is "disatisfied," which is spelled *dissatisfied*. Remember that when you add a prefix to a word, the spelling of the original word does not change. The corrected sentence should read: *You don't want to be dissatisfied with how the pictures are spaced on a wall.*

7. (3), The misspelled word in sentence 10 is "arrangment," which is spelled *arrangement*. Remember, when you add a suffix that begins with a consonant to a word that ends with an *e*, you do not remove the *e* before adding the suffix. The corrected sentence should read: *An arrangement of related works should be grouped around a central piece.*

8. (3), The misspelled word in sentence 2 is "vegtables," which is spelled *vegetables*. This is a commonly misspelled word that you may want to memorize. The corrected sentence should read: *When leaves, sticks, grass, fruits, and vegetables decompose, they feed the soil.*

9. (2), The misspelled word in sentence 5 is "responsability," which is spelled *responsibility*. This is a commonly misspelled word that you may want to memorize. The corrected sentence should read: *One way to restore balance to this process is to accept the responsibility of composting at home.*

10. (3), The misspelled word in sentence 8 is "substancial," which is spelled *substantial*. This is a commonly misspelled word that you may want to memorize. The corrected sentence should read: *To cause decomposition, you need substantial layers of four key ingredients: nitrogen, carbon, water, and air.*

UNIT 5 (*continued*)

LESSON 5, pp. 142–145

1. (2), The comma in sentence 2 should be placed after the word "apples" because "We love to eat watermelons and apples" is a dependent clause.

2. (3), A comma should be placed after the word "aromatic" because sentence 4 is a compound sentence containing two independent clauses. A comma should separate these clauses. The corrected sentence should read: *Herbs are aromatic, and they can be harvested for cooking.*

3. (1), Commas should be inserted after the words "rosemary," "sage," "basil," "dill," "mint," "thyme," and "chives" because these herbs are in a series. The corrected sentence should read: *Consider planting a variety of herbs, such as rosemary, sage, basil, dill, mint, thyme, chives, and parsley.*

4. (4), A comma should be inserted after "general" because "In general" is an introductory phrase (or transition). The corrected sentence should read: *In general, your herb garden should not need any additional fertilizer.*

5. (1), A comma should be inserted after "understand" because "As I'm sure you understand" is an introductory phrase. The corrected sentence should read: *As I'm sure you understand, it is difficult to be away from one's home.*

6. (2), Answer option 2 is the best revision of the underlined portion of the sentence because "which is a rarity I can assure you" is a dependent clause.

7. (3), A comma should be inserted after "colleagues" because sentence 15 is a compound sentence (it has two independent clauses). The corrected sentence should read: *In closing, I can assure you that I will recommend your facility to my colleagues, and I will be back for a return visit.*

8. (1), The comma should be removed from sentence 1 because it is not a compound or complex sentence. The corrected sentence should read: *The body uses the hormone insulin to convert sugar starch and other food sources into energy.*

9. (2), A comma should be inserted after the word "unclear" because "Although the cause of diabetes remains unclear" is a dependent clause.

10. (5), This sentence does not contain any spelling or comma errors. Therefore, no correction is necessary.

LESSON 6, pp. 146–150

1. (3), We can tell that the underlined portion of sentence 3 contains the exact words spoken by Dr. Jones because the speech begins and ends with quotation marks.

2. (3), A colon should be inserted after "bills" because it introduces a list of examples. The corrected sentence should read: *There's always an unexpected expense or a desirable luxury item that arises among one's regular monthly bills: car repairs, home repairs, or a weekend trip.*

3. (5), Sentence 5 is a compound sentence that correctly uses a comma, so no correction is necessary.

4. (3), A hyphen should be inserted between "cheat" and "sheet" because *cheat-sheet* is a compound word. The corrected sentence should read: *Here's a cheat-sheet for well-paying part-time employment.*

5. (1), A semicolon should be inserted after "at all" because sentence 4 contains two independent clauses that are not separated with a conjunction. The corrected sentence should read: *It's amazing that people are able to communicate at all; nevertheless, they do.*

6. (3), The question mark should be replaced with a period because sentence 6 is not a question. The corrected sentence should read: *However, this doesn't mean that everyone shouldn't try to improve his or her communication skills, if even a little.*

7. (4), The quotation marks should be removed from sentence 15 because the sentence does not contain direct speech. The corrected sentence should read: *After all, you don't want to be caught complimenting someone on having a knick-knack for solving computer problems.*

8. (3), The question mark should be replaced with a period because sentence 1 is a statement, not a question. The corrected sentence should read: *The purpose of this week is to help families respond to three important hurricane questions.*

9. (2), The semicolon should be removed from sentence 7 because the sentence does not contain two independent clauses. The corrected sentence should read: *Study famous hurricanes to learn about their causes and effects.*

10. (2), The colon should be removed from sentence 10 because the sentence does not introduce a list or examples. The corrected sentence should read: *Help weather experts track hurricanes in the Atlantic, Caribbean, and Gulf of Mexico.*

Index

Note: Page numbers in **boldface** indicate definitions or main discussions. Page numbers in *italic* indicate a visual representation. Pages ranges indicate examples and practice.

A

Adjectives, misplaced, 74–77
Adverbs, misplaced, 74–77
Antecedent, **94**, 94–95
Apostrophe, 130–133, 146

B

Body of essay, 10
    paragraphs of, 26–29
    elaboration of, 14–17
    supporting details, 10–13

C

Capitalization, **126**, 126–129
    of days of the week, 126
    of first word in quotations, 126
    of first word of sentences, 126, 128
    of holidays, 126
    of I, 126
    of months, 126, 128
    of proper adjectives, 126, 129
    of proper nouns, 86–89, 126–129
    of titles, 86, 126, 128
Checklists
    for body of essay, 13, 17
    for conclusion, 21
    for essay, 25
    for introduction, 9
    for review and revision, 24
    for thesis statement, 5
Clauses
    combining, 66–69
    in comma splices, 70–73
    in complex sentences, 62–65
    in compound sentences, 58–61
    as sentence fragments, 50–53
Coherence, **42**, 42–45
Collective nouns, **98**, 98–101
Colons, 146–149
Combining sentences, **66**, 66–69
Comma splice, **70**, 70–73
Commas, **142**, 142–145, 146–149
    between two clauses, 50–53
    change in sentence meaning, 142
    combining sentences with, 66–69
    in complex sentences, 62–65, 142–145

    in compound sentences, 58–61, 142–145
    following introductory word/phrase, 142–145
    in series, 66, 142–143
    setting off interrupting phrases, 142, 144–145
    setting off quotations, 142
Common nouns, 86–89
Commonly misspelled words, 138–141
Complete sentences, **46**, 46–49
Complex sentences, **62**, 62–65, 142
Compound sentences, **58**, 58–61, 142
Compound subject, **118**, 118–121
Compound words, 146–149
Conclusion, **18**, 18–21, 23–25
Conjunctions
    combining sentences with, 66–69
    conjunctive adverbs, 58–61
    coordinating, 58–61, 66–69, 70–73, 82–85
    correcting comma splice with, 70–73
    correcting run-on sentences with, 70–73
    sentence fragments and, 50–53
    subject-verb agreement and, 118–121
    subordinating, 62–65, 66–69, 70, 73
Conjunctive adverbs, 58–61
Contractions, **130**, 130–133
    its/it's, 130–131
    their/they're, 130
    your/you're, 130–132
Coordinating conjunctions
    combining sentences with, 66–69
    in compound sentences, 58–61
    correcting comma splice with, 70–73
    correcting run-on sentences, 70–73
    subject-verb agreement and, 118

D

Dangling modifiers, **78**, 78–81
Dashes, 146, 148
Dependent clause
    in complex sentences, 62–65
    as sentence fragments, 50–53

E

-ed, 106–109, 110–113, 114–116
Editing, viii
Elaboration, **14**, 14–17, 22–25
Ellipses, 26
-en, 114–116
End marks, 46–49
Essay, vii
    body, **10**, 10–13, 24–25
    conclusion, **18**, 18–21, 24–25
    elaboration, **14**, 14–17, 24–25
    hook, **6**, 6–9, 11, 13, 15, 17, 24–25
    introduction, **6**, 6–9, 24–25
    prompts, 3, 5, 7, 9, 11, 13, 15, 17,19–21, 25

    review and revise, **22**, 22–25
    supporting details, **2**, 2–5, 6–9, 10–13, 14–15, 17, 24–25, **34**, 34–37
    text division, 26–29
    thesis statement, **2**, 2–5, 6–9, 11, 13, 15, 17, 18–21, 24–25
    time management, 22
    topic sentence, **30**, 30–33
    transition, **10**, 10–13, 16–17, 18–21, 24–25, 38–41
    unity and coherence of, **42**, 42–45
    See also Organization; Paragraphs; Sentence structure
Exclamation point, 46–49, 146–149

F

Facts, 9, 34
Feminine pronouns, 90–93, 94–97
First-person pronouns, 90–93
Fragments, **50**, 50–53
Frontmatter
    About the GED Test, iv–v
        subject-area breakdown, iv
    About *GED Xcelerator*, vi
    About *GED Xcelerator Writing*, vii–ix
    Copyright/Acknowledgements, ii
    Study Skills, 1
    Table of Contents, iii
    Test-Taking Tips, x
    Title Page, i
Future perfect tense, **110**, 110–113
Future tense, 102–105

G

GED Tests,
    construction of, iv
    number of people taking/year, vi
    number of people who passed in 2007, vi
    preparation for, xi
    subjects tested/number of questions per subject, iv
    time limits for, iv
Gender
    pronoun agreement and, **94**, 94–97
    of pronouns, 90–93
Grammar, viii
    exceptions to rules, ix
Graphic organizers
    for combining sentences, *66*
    for essay writing, *3, 7–8, 11, 13, 15–17, 19–21*
    for supporting details, *34*
    for text division, *26*
    for topic sentences, *30*
    for transitions, *38*
    for unity and coherence, *42*
    to identify compound sentences, *58*
    to identify complex sentences, *62*

to identify dangling modifiers, *78*
to identify sentence fragments, *50*
to identify misplaced modifiers, *74*
to identify parallel structure, *82*
to identify parts of a sentence, *46*

H

Helping verbs, 102, 110–113, 114–117
Homographs, **134**, 134–137
Homonyms, **134**, 134–137
Homophones, **134**, 134–137
Hook, **6**, 6–9, 11, 13, 15, 17, 24–25
Hyphens, 146–149

I

I, 90–93, 126–129
-ied, 106–109
-ies, 106–109
Independent clause, 46–49, 62–65
     in run-on sentences, 70–73
-ing, 106–109
Interrupting phrase, 142, 144–145
Introduction, **6**, 6–9, 24–25
Introductory word/phrase, 142–145
Irregular verbs, **114**, 114–117

M

Masculine pronouns, 90–93, 94–97
Mechanics
     capitalization, **126**, 126–129
     commas, **142**, 142–145
     commonly misspelled words, **138**, 138–141
     contractions, **130**, 130–133
     homonyms, **134**, 134–137
     possessives, **130**, 130–133
     punctuation, **146**, 146–149
     See also Punctuation
Mental map, *3*, 14
Misplaced modifiers, **74**, 74–77
Modifiers
     combining with hyphen, 146–149
     dangling, **78**, 78–81
     misplaced, **74**, 74–77

N

Nouns, **86**, 86–89
     collective, **98**, 98–101
     common, 86–89
     as pronoun antecedents, 94–97
     pronouns agreement with, 94–97
     pronouns and, 90–97
     proper, 86–89, 126

O

Object pronouns, 90–93
Objects, 90–93
Organization
     supporting details, **34**, 34–37
     text division, **26**, 26–29
     topic sentences, **30**, 30–33
     transition, **38**, 38–41
     unity and coherence, **42**, 42–45
     See also Paragraphs

P

Paragraphs
     conclusion of, **18**, 18–21
     development of, 14–17
     introductory, **6**, 6–9
     supporting details, **10**, 10–13, **34**, 34–37
     text division into, **26**, 26–29
     topic sentences, **30**, 30–33
     transition in, **38**, 38–41
     unity and coherence, **42**, 42–45
     See also Organization
Parallel structure, **82**, 82–85
Parentheses, 146
Participles
     of irregular verbs, 114–117
Past participle
     of irregular verbs, 114–117
Past perfect tense, **110**, 110–113
Past tense, 102–105, 114–117
Perfect verb tense, **110**, 110–113
Period, 46–49, 146–149
Phrase
     interrupting, 142, 144–145
     introductory, 142–145
Plural words
     possessives, 130–133
     pronoun agreement, 94–97
     pronouns, 90–93, 94–97
     subject-verb agreement, 118–125
Possessives, **130**, 130–133
     pronouns, 90–93, 130–133
Prefix, 138, 146
Present perfect tense, **110**, 110–113
Present tense, 102–105
Prompts, vii, 3, 5, 7, 9, 11, 13, 15, 17, 19–21, 25. *See also* Topics
Pronoun agreement, **94**, 94–97
Pronouns, **90**, 90–93
     agreement with antecedent, **94**, 94–97
     contractions with, 130–133
     possessives, 130–133
     subject/object/possessive forms, 90
Proper adjectives, 126
Proper nouns, 86–89, 126
Punctuation, **146**, 146–149
     apostrophes, 130–133, 146
     colons, 146
     commas, 66–69, 70–73, **142**, 142–145, 146–149
     dashes, 146
     ellipses, 26
     end marks, 46–49, 146–149
     exclamation points, 46, 146
     hyphens, 146–149
     parentheses, 146
     periods, 46–49, 146–149
     question marks, 46–49, 146–149
     quotation marks, 142, 146, 148
     semicolons, 50–53, 58–61, 66–69, 70–73
     See also Mechanics

Q

Question marks, 46–49, 146–149
Quotation marks, 142, 146, 148
Quotations
     capitalization of, 126
     punctuation of, 142, 146

R

Regular verb tense, **106**, 106–109
Review, **22**, 22–25
Revise, **22**, 22–25
Run-on sentences, **70**, 70–73

S

s, 106
Second-person pronouns, 90
'See it, say it, touch it, write it' method, 138
Semicolon
     combining sentences with, 66–69
     in compound sentences, 58–61
     correcting run-on sentences, 70–73
     between two clauses, 50–53, 58–61, 66–69
Sentence fragments, **50**, 50–53
Sentence strips, 42
Sentence structure
     combining sentences, **66**, 66–69
     complete sentences, **46**, 46–49
     complex sentences, **62**, 62–65
     compound sentences, **58**, 58–61
     dangling modifiers, **78**, 78–81
     misplaced modifiers, **74**, 74–77
     parallel structure, **82**, 82–85
     run-on sentences, **70**, 70–73
     sentence fragments, **50**, 50–53
     simple sentences, **54**, 54–57
Series, 66
     commas in, 142–143
     parallel structure, 82–85
Simple sentences, **54**, 54–57
Simple verb tense, **102**, 102–105
Singular pronouns, 90–93, 94–97
Singular words
     possessives, 130–133
     pronoun agreement, 94–97
     pronouns, 90–93